WITHDRAWN

Duke Historical Publications

THE COLONIAL OFFICE
1868-1892

To Mary

Brian L. Blakeley

THE COLONIAL OFFICE
1868-1892

DUKE UNIVERSITY PRESS
Durham, N. C.
1972

PRINTED IN THE UNITED STATES OF
AMERICA BY HERITAGE PRINTERS

Contents

Contents

Introduction

The origins of the modern British Colonial Office are to be found in the early seventeenth century. Under a variety of titles—the Committee for Trade and Plantations, the Lords of Trade, the American Department, and the Board of Trade—the British government found it necessary throughout the next two centuries to have some established department or agency specializing in colonial questions. Regardless of its name, however, the basic function of this office remained the administration of the overseas dependencies with as little trouble and expense to the home government as possible. By bringing to this task "a code of rational routine work,"[1] the colonial officials institutionalized the work of their office. This process was slow and gradual. Changes in administrative technique or office organizaton were generally the result of some external pressure such as political considerations at home or changing responsibilities toward the colonies. The bureaucracy rarely, if ever, reformed itself.

The nineteenth century witnessed numerous far-reaching administrative changes which have led some authors to pose the question of a "revolution" in government. These changes, the most fundamental being the greater reliance on permanent as opposed to political officials, obviously occurred not only in the Colonial Office but in the entire English bureaucracy. Administrative studies of the Colonial Office during this period of "modernization" have tended to revolve around two dominant personalities—Sir James Stephen and Joseph Chamberlain. The attraction of each man to historians is relatively easy to understand. Stephen's fame, or infamy, to his contemporaries, his consciousness of the verdict of history and his resulting personal need to defend his actions both in official minutes and private writings,[2] and his unquestioned influence not only on the formation of

1. Daniel Lerner, "The Transformation of Institutions," *The Transfer of Institutions*, ed. William B. Hamilton (Durham, N.C., 1964), p. 3.
2. Exceptionally good insight into Stephen's personality and his relations with his political superiors is provided in T. Barron and K. J. Cable, "The Diary of James Stephen, 1846," *Historical Studies*, XIII (April, 1969), 503–519.

policy but on the structuring of the Colonial Office have justified the attention of numerous scholars. Administratively it is frequently asserted, and rightfully so, that Stephen exemplifies the growing influence of the permanent bureaucracy and that he was largely responsible for the ordering of the office and the introduction of administrative procedure that was both "more regular and more methodical."[3]

If Stephen created the "system," the man who has been frequently credited with attempting to use it for constructive ends, and therefore modernizing the Colonial Office, is Joseph Chamberlain. To contemporaries as well as to later writers Chamberlain was the man who took the office and roused it "to new life." Because of his political influence, his administrative ability, and above all his imperial vision, Chamberlain was supposed to have staffed the Colonial Office with exceptionally able men, remodeled and modernized the working conditions and routine of his office, and adopted an entirely new attitude toward relations between the Colonial Office and the empire. In short, he "superseded candles by electric light."[4]

The importance of Stephen and Chamberlain to the development of the Colonial Office is certainly not to be denied. Administratively, however, the development of the office was a gradual and continual process throughout the entire nineteenth century. Specifically, in the period after 1868 important changes were introduced at the Colonial Office. Not only did the secretariat resolve some of the administrative problems facing Stephen by opting for open competition, a rigid division of labor, and a delegation of authority, but by doing so they created the office through which Chamberlain attempted to implement his schemes of empire development. The secretariat also altered or reconstructed the Colonial Office's two most important subdepartments, the Crown Agents Department and the Colonial Land and Emigration Commission, and enabled them to survive as effective agencies into the twentieth century. Although lacking the notoriety and brillance of Stephen or the flamboyance and influence of Chamberlain, men such as Robert Herbert, Robert Meade, and the Earl of Kimberley were extremely important in creating an office capable of handling the new responsibilities thrust upon it.

3. John W. Cell, *British Colonial Administration in the Mid-Nineteenth Century: The Policy-Making Process* (New Haven, 1970), pp. 9–10.
4. For a summary of earlier views regarding Chamberlain at the Colonial Office together with a reassessment see Robert V. Kubicek, *The Administration of Imperialism: Joseph Chamberlain at the Colonial Office* (Durham, N.C., 1969), chap. ii.

Much of the impetus for administrative reform in the period after 1868 came, as earlier, not from the bureaucracy but from outside pressures—the demands of civil service reformers, new technology, a rapidly increasing volume of work, and changing relations between Britain and its colonies. The demands of civil service reformers had the most immediate and obvious impact on the Colonial Office. Sir Charles Trevelyan and Sir Stafford Northcote, arguing that the administrative efficiency of an office depended upon the intellectual ability of the clerks, suggested the introduction of open competition and a sharp division of labor between intellectual and mechanical clerks. These arguments were reinforced by the disasters in the Crimea, and in 1855 the Civil Service Commission, which had the power to disqualify incompetent applicants, was established. Partly because of the opposition of the senior civil servants, however, their two major reforms were introduced slowly and incompletely in the fifties and sixties.[5]

In 1870 the new Liberal chancellor of the exchequer, Robert Lowe, persuaded Granville, the colonial secretary, to introduce open competition as the usual method of recruitment. This reform was bitterly opposed by Sir Frederic Rogers, the permanent undersecretary, and most of the older clerks. These men remained more interested in the "moral qualities" of an applicant than in his intellect. Two years later, Robert Herbert, who succeeded Rogers, and the Earl of Kimberley decided to accept the administrative implications of open competition and to undertake a major reorganization of the office. Again following the Treasury's lead, they reduced the total number of administrative clerks and raised substantially the salaries of the clerks retained. This reorganization of 1872, as in the case of the introduction of open competition, was opposed by most of the older clerks. Herbert and Kimberley would have found it difficult to restructure their department without the active support of the Treasury. The results of the reorganization were very gratifying. During the seventies and eighties, the Colonial Office became, with the possible exception of the Treasury, the most popular department of the British civil service. Because of its high salaries and interesting work, most of the new clerks possessed first-class university degrees. The general improvement in the quality of the staff enabled Herbert and the colonial secretaries to

5. For a detailed discussion of recruitment before 1870 and division of labor in the civil service see Maurice Wright, *Treasury Control of the Civil Service, 1854–1874* (Oxford, 1969), chaps. iii, v.

meet the greatly increased volume of work in the seventies and eighties.

The rapid increase in the volume and complexity of work was another important factor contributing to rapid change in the organization and routine of the Colonial Office in the seventies. The only manner in which this additional work could be handled efficiently was for the colonial secretary and the secretariat to delegate more routine work to the new university-trained clerks. Herbert actively promoted this process in 1872 by permitting all classes of administrative clerks to minute papers. The clerks were also given the power to dispose of certain classes of routine business. The result was that Herbert and the secretary of state increasingly devoted their time to studying crisis questions, leaving the less important decisions to the assistant undersecretaries and the clerks. This increased devolution of responsibility enabled the Colonial Office to dispose of almost twice as many letters in 1890 as in 1870 with the same number of clerks. The counting of letters may not be the most accurate way of measuring the efficiency of a department, but it was the measure usually employed by the Treasury. Unlike Herbert and the colonial secretaries, the clerks tended to specialize in one colony or group of colonies or concentrate on one specific problem, such as finance, defense, or social reform. In this way the Colonial Office came to possess a considerable amount of detailed academic knowledge about the colonies and their problems. In the event of trouble there was usually someone in the office who could furnish Herbert and the secretary of state with the information on which to base a decision.

In addition to a general increase in the volume of work, the telegraph became an accepted method of communication during the seventies. It did much to change the atmosphere of the Colonial Office. No longer was it possible for the secretary of state to spend weeks considering important dispatches. He was increasingly called upon to make decisions quickly, often with only the barest information available. This placed the staff under continual strain. It also promoted the policy, implicit in the reorganization of 1872, of giving the administrative clerks more responsibility for the routine work of the office.

The growth in the business of the Colonial Office coincided with, and partially reflected, an increasing interest in the empire. The foundation of the Royal Colonial Institute in 1868 and Disraeli's Crystal

Palace speech of 1872, while not indicative of any fundamental change in policy, do at least show that imperial sentiment was becoming socially and politically acceptable. Parliament, if the number of questions asked is any indication, also took greater interest in colonial topics. Whereas earlier the value of the colonies had been considered largely in economic terms, sentiment and pride in the empire became increasingly important in the seventies. Numerous schemes for promoting closer union between Britain and the colonies were seriously discussed, leading to the foundation of the Imperial Federation League in 1884. Colonial statesmen began to take advantage of the improved communications to visit London in increasing numbers, consuming in the process a substantial amount of Herbert's and the colonial secretary's time. The larger colonies also began in the seventies to see the value of having permanent representatives in London. These "agents general" caused new problems, but they also provided a new, and frequently more intimate, link between the colonial governments and the Colonial Office. Within the office itself this change, gradual though it was, was reflected in the appointment of Herbert as permanent undersecretary in 1871. His appointment, as one of the clerks remarked, was the beginning of a "new era" of interest in the colonies.[6] Unlike Rogers, who expected the empire gradually to dissolve, or Sir Henry Taylor, who regarded the American colonies as "a sort of *damnosa haereditas*," Herbert and most of his colleagues were optimistic about the future of the empire they helped to administer.

Despite the increased efficiency of its staff and the improved methods of communication, the Colonial Office did not act as vigorously and decisively as might have been expected. There were several reasons for this, not the least being the personalities of Herbert and the other members of the secretariat. Although they were extremely able men, they were essentially pragmatic in their outlook. Herbert regarded his duty as the presentation of practical alternatives for the day-to-day problems of administering an empire. Theoretical considerations concerning the future of the empire seldom occupied his attention, nor did he believe that improved administrative efficiency somehow implied a greater role for his department in the affairs of the colonies. Certainly, the secretariat did not actively seek out new responsibilities. Herbert feared, for example, that the Imperial Federation League

6. Sir William Baille Hamilton, "Forty-four Years at the Colonial Office," *Nineteenth Century and After*, LXV (April, 1909), 601.

would "give themselves and others much trouble without finding a practical solution to the difficulty."[7] In addition, living and working in the cultured atmosphere of London, the secretariat undoubtedly found many of the problems facing the colonist on the frontier rather remote and unreal.

The failure of the Colonial Office to deal vigorously and imaginatively with the problems facing the empire cannot, however, be blamed solely upon the personalities and backgrounds of the members of the secretariat. The Colonial Office remained handicapped by the organization and personnel of the overseas colonial service. With the exception of the eastern cadetships, most of the positions at the disposal of the secretary of state were filled by patronage, and frequently men were chosen less because of their administrative ability than because of their political or personal claims on some member of the home government. The clerks in the Colonial Office, who had secured their positions by means of a competitive examination, naturally regarded themselves as the intellectual superiors of the men serving in the colonies. With few exceptions the Colonial Office regarded its servants in the colonies as ignorant, untrustworthy, quarrelsome, and indiscreet. When a really able man was needed for a difficult assignment the temptation was always great for Herbert to secure the services of a man from the outside, usually a military man. The officials in the colonies, on the other hand, frequently regarded their superiors in London as uninformed meddlers who should refrain from exercising close control over the colonies. Although tentative steps were taken to professionalize the colonial civil service and to give the clerks a better understanding of conditions in the colonies, the gap between the two services remained wide.

In assessing the influence and decisiveness of the Colonial Office in the seventies and eighties, it should also be remembered that it was only one department, and a minor one, of the British government. Although the secretaries of state were, with one or two exceptions, able men, their influence in the cabinet was never that great. Even Carnarvon, the most famous and imaginative of the colonial secretaries during this period, found it difficult to obtain cabinet support for his plans. He repeatedly complained that a colonial secretary was expected "to make bricks without straw or to live in a perpetual wrangle with

7. Herbert's minute of August 4, 1884, on Labillière to Derby, August 1, 1884, CO 323/359.

his colleagues."[8] Disraeli, Gladstone, and Salisbury still looked upon colonial debates in the cabinet or Parliament as burdens to be avoided if possible, and when a colonial topic did receive consideration it was usually because it affected Britain's foreign or defense policy. Thus the cabinet exhibited interest in New Guinea and the Newfoundland fisheries not because of their inherent interest but because these problems could lead to diplomatic disputes with Germany and France. There were numerous occasions when the Colonial Office might have acted more promptly and decisively except for the procrastination of the cabinet.

Only major policy decisions required the approval of the cabinet. Many minor questions, however, forced the Colonial Office to seek the cooperation and approval of other government departments. Colonial complaints about the indecision of the Colonial Office could frequently have been more accurately directed against the War Office, the Foreign Office, or the Treasury, each of which had a large, and frequently decisive, voice in the creation of policy. Important dispatches relating to foreign affairs, for example, were usually referred to the Foreign Office for comment. This consultation was often time consuming, and Salisbury complained that it took longer to exchange written replies with the Colonial Office than it did with the British ambassador in Berlin. He suggested that a hole be knocked in the wall separating the two departments in order to "expedite consultation."[9] A foreign power could, as in the case of Germany in New Guinea, take advantage of the poor communications between the Colonial Office and the Foreign Office. Similar problems arose between the Colonial Office and the War Office. The secretary of state for war naturally desired to keep his own estimates as low as possible by shifting much of the empire's defense burden onto the colonies and India. The Colonial Office, responsible for the annual estimates of many colonies, naturally attempted to tailor defense expenditures to a colony's needs and ability to pay.

When the interests of Great Britain and the colonies conflicted, the Colonial Office was frequently involved in a long and acrimonious dispute with another department. The Foreign Office often preferred to offend a colonial government rather than risk antagonizing France

8. Carnarvon's minute of March 22, 1876, on Bulwer to Carnarvon, December 31, 1875, CO 179/118.
9. Salisbury to Holland, copy, private, May 25, 1887, Salisbury Papers.

or Germany. In such cases the Colonial Office could do little. "I am sorry we can do no more for Australia [regarding New Guinea], but agree that the question of Egypt over-rides all others."[10] Some of the Colonial Office's clerks, especially the younger ones, believed that the office should represent the views of the colonists more strongly and go down fighting if necessary. In their opinion, the colonists should not feel that "the whole English Government is against them & that their immediate superiors who ought to be their protectors are no better than the rest."[11] Herbert and most of the members of the secretariat accepted, however, that the Colonial Office was a department of the British government and not the paid spokesman of the colonies. The Colonial Office should confine itself to presenting the views of the colonists in the discussions leading to "the collective decision of H. M. Govt."[12]

Finally, one of the major obstacles to the adoption of a more forceful colonial policy was the "paralyzing control" of the Treasury. This department had to approve even the most trivial expenditures from the public purse, and because the chancellor of the exchequer had to defend all new votes before a questioning House of Commons, he was not anxious to support new demands from other departments. Although Herbert and the secretariat recognized the importance of fiscal responsibility and Treasury control, they were frequently annoyed at the parsimony of "My Lords." The stringent financial control of the Treasury made it impossible to initiate any new developmental programs for the crown colonies. Other plans for improving administration by establishing new subdepartments were abandoned because of the virtual impossibility of obtaining Treasury approval. This ever present threat of Treasury disapproval was undoubtedly as important in shaping Colonial Office policy as formal Treasury intervention.

Although the personalities of Herbert and the other members of the secretariat, the heterogeneous character of the colonial civil service, and the obstruction of other government departments made it difficult for the Colonial Office to deal vigorously and decisively with the problems submitted to it, perhaps the resulting pragmatism and restraint were sources of strength rather than of weakness. Herbert and the other members of the secretariat were convinced that the

10. Derby to Granville, March 6, 1885, PRO 30/29/120.
11. Lucas' minute of January 29, 1891, on War Office to CO, January 1, 1891, CO 54/598.
12. Herbert's minute of February 3, 1891, *ibid.*

larger colonies would resist any attempts from London to strengthen the imperial connection. Thus instead of seeking to strengthen the position of the colonial governor, Herbert accepted the development of the agents general and increasingly used them as a channel of communication with the colonial governments. He saw nothing alarming in the fact that by 1875 the governor was merely "a gentleman whom the Colonists prefer to have nominated from home *to preside over their society.*"[13] Despite all of the colonial complaints about the indecisiveness of the Colonial Office, they would in all probability have objected more strongly to attempts to exercise vigorous control from Downing Street.

During the course of researching and writing this book, I have naturally incurred numerous obligations. I would first like to thank the various librarians and curators of the Duke University Library; the Public Record Office; the British Museum; Christ Church, Oxford; and the Institute of Historical Research. I would also like to express my appreciation to Professor Gerald S. Graham of King's College for his assistance while I was in London and to the Graduate School and the Commonwealth-Studies Center of Duke University for their financial support. I want especially to express my gratitude to Dr. William B. Hamilton for his helpful criticism, encouragement, and kindness during my studies at Duke. Finally, I would like to thank my wife Mary not only for her continued support but also for the long hours she devoted as research assistant and typist.

Brian L. Blakeley

Texas Tech University
June 1, 1971

13. Herbert's minute of June 8, 1875, on Stawell to Carnarvon, confidential, April 16, 1875, CO 309/113.

THE COLONIAL OFFICE
1868–1892

CHAPTER I

Background to Reorganization

EARL GRANVILLE became the colonial secretary in the new Liberal ministry of W. E. Gladstone on December 9, 1868. The routine and organization of his department were essentially the creation of Sir James Stephen, who had retired as permanent undersecretary in 1847. Stephen's two successors, Herman Merivale (1847–1860) and Sir Frederic Rogers (1860–1871), made certain minor alterations in the routine of the office, but they suggested no fundamental changes in its constitution. During their terms the Colonial Office naturally increased both in size and in cost, but the division of the clerks into four geographical departments and a chief clerk's department remained unchanged. In addition, despite the recommendations of the famous Northcote-Trevelyan Report, the duties and responsibilities of the clerks and undersecretaries remained basically the same as under Stephen. Only minor changes in the mode of circulating and disposing of the papers were made, and these changes were designed to meet specific problems or sudden increases in the work.

Major reform of the constitution and practice of the Colonial Office began in 1869. The impetus for this reform did not come from Rogers or his permanent staff but from Granville, who, in common with his colleagues in the cabinet, regarded the pursuit of economy and the elimination of inefficiency as one of his most important duties. The investigation that he ordered in 1869 proved what everyone, including Rogers, already knew; the manner in which the Colonial Office conducted its work was inefficient and wasteful. Granville attempted to improve the office through a departmental reorganization, but before the new system could be fairly tested, the cabinet decided to introduce recruitment by open competition. Robert Lowe, the chancellor of the exchequer, insisted that the ramifications of open competition should be faced, resulting in a further overhaul of the Colonial Office in 1872. This reorganizaton, combined with a rapid influx of new men into positions of responsibility, new means of communication, and a rapidly expanding volume of business, marked a major break with the past. The role of the Treasury in the 1872 reorganization also showed that the era of purely departmental reform was over. The Colonial Office increasingly became part of a consolidated British civil service and subject to the uniform regulations laid down for it. Before discussing these developments in detail, however, it is necessary to consider briefly the organization and faults of the old Colonial Office and some of the earlier proposals for reform.

Although the constitution of the Colonial Office changed little under Merivale and Rogers, it was in some respects in advance of its time. In the early nineteenth century the ministers of state were expected to perform personally most of the work of their departments, excluding the senior permanent officials from any important role in the formation of policy.[1] The Colonial Office was the first department in which the secretaries of state realized that their work was too voluminous and complex to handle without assistance. After considering reducing his work through the creation of special statutory boards, Lord Bathurst solved the problem by sensibly granting some of the permanent staff more responsibility.[2] This system took time to develop, but by the 1820's certain clerks and undersecretaries were occupied with duties that would more properly have fallen upon a "statesman" than on a "clerk."[3] It was no longer possible for a secretary of state to handle the work of the office alone. Lord Stanley, who distrusted Stephen and Sir Henry Taylor, attempted to do this in 1833–1834, but the work fell badly in arrears. When Stanley resigned Stephen and Taylor returned from the wilderness, and office practice reverted to what it had been.[4]

Despite Stephen's own concern at being personally responsible for

1. The permanent officials of the old American Department (1768–1782) had more important and responsible duties than their immediate successors. See Margaret Marion Spector, *The American Department of the British Government, 1768–1782* (New York, 1940), pp. 111–130.

2. D. M. Young, *The Colonial Office in the Early Nineteenth Century* (London, 1961), pp. 3–5. D. J. Murray argues that this change was largely due to the increased work arising as a result of the antislavery movement and the decision of the Colonial Office to secure improvements in the working conditions of the slaves. This new machinery not only made it possible for the Colonial Office to be more active in other areas of colonial administration, but it also placed it in the forefront of civil service development. *The West Indies and the Development of Colonial Government, 1801–1834* (Oxford, 1965), pp. 123–126.

3. Sir Henry Taylor, *Autobiography, 1800–1875* (2 vols.; London, 1885), I, 139.

4. Murray, *West Indies and Colonial Government*, pp. 212–214.

Colonial Office policies,[5] it became increasingly necessary for the secretary of state to rely upon the permanent staff for suggestions. In 1847 Earl Grey asked that all papers submitted to the political heads of the department be accompanied by recommendations from the senior permanent officials. He believed that these papers should "require no more than the initials of Mr. [Benjamin] Hawes and myself as assenting to what is suggested."[6] The recommendations of the senior permanent officials did not of course mean a devolution of responsibility, either in theory or in practice, for the decision actually taken. The secretary of state continued to see most of the dispatches and to have the decisive voice on all important questions.

The senior officials in the Colonial Office did, however, have a much greater role in the transaction of business and the formation of policy than their counterparts in the other important departments of state. As late as 1870 most dispatches arriving at the Foreign Office went directly to the permanent undersecretary. They were then submitted with little or no explanation to the secretary of state. Edmund Hammond complained that this procedure reduced his position as permanent undersecretary to "merely a channel" for communications.[7] The situation in the Home Office was somewhat different. There the permanent undersecretary was permitted and encouraged to offer suggestions, but Horatio Waddington, who occupied that position in the sixties, refused to extend this privilege to any of the other clerks. He regarded the minuting of papers as the prerogative of the permanent undersecretary.[8] Because of the long tradition of using senior clerks in an intellectual capacity, the Colonial Office's extension of this practice in the seventies and eighties can be seen not as a radical change of policy but as a rapid implementation of an old one. This is not true of other departments of state.

The daily routine of the Colonial Office in the mid-nineteenth century was described fully in testimony given before the 1849 Committee

5. Edward Hughes, "Sir James Stephen and the Anonymity of the Civil Servant," *Public Administration*, XXXVI (1958), 29–32.

6. John W. Cell, "The Colonial Office in the 1850's," *Historical Studies Australia and New Zealand*, XII (October, 1965), 48.

7. Sir John Craig, *A History of Red Tape* (London, 1955), p. 73. Lord Tenterden, who replaced Hammond as permanent undersecretary in 1873, continued in much the same manner. Tenterden's minute of February 24, 1874, FO 366/386.

8. "Second Report of the Royal Commission Appointed to Inquire into the Civil Establishments of the Different Offices of State at Home and Abroad," C. 5545, p. 28, *Parl. Paps. 1888*, XXVII.

of Inquiry into Public Offices.[9] All incoming letters were registered and then sent directly to the senior clerk of the appropriate department. With the assistance of the junior clerks under his control, the senior clerk collected all the relevant material on the subject, enabling him to summarize past action and perhaps to recommend a suitable reply. The letter and the minute of the senior clerk were then forwarded to the assistant undersecretary or the permanent undersecretary. After they had recorded their opinions the question was then submitted to the political heads of the Colonial Office for final decision. The papers were then returned to the senior clerk, who supervised the preparation of a draft reply embodying the decision of his superiors. Important drafts were frequently prepared by the undersecretaries. All draft dispatches required the approval of the permanent undersecretary or the secretary of state, and only then could the junior clerks or copyists prepare a fair copy for signature. Although modified in detail, the basic routine of the Colonial Office changed very little under Merivale and Rogers.[10]

This system, although producing neat and systematic records for the historian, suffered from obvious weaknesses which were recognized both by the Colonial Office staff and by civil service reformers. Despite the responsibility delegated to the senior clerks, too much work was still assigned to the senior officials. In the mid-fifties only about ten members of the Colonial Office establishment[11] were allowed any real role in the creation of policy. They included the two political heads of the office, the permanent undersecretary, the assistant undersecretary, the précis writer, the chief clerk, and the four senior clerks. The other sixty members of the office, including twenty-three first-class, second-class, and junior clerks, who might have been expected to play a more prominent role, were denied any truly responsible work.[12] The system also prevented the senior clerks from exercising any real initiative in making decisions. They could offer suggestions, that were usu-

9. "Reports of the Committees of Inquiry into Public Offices," No. 1715, pp. 79–82, *Parl. Paps. 1854*, XXVII.

10. W. P. N. Tyler, "Sir Frederic Rogers, Permanent Under-Secretary at the Colonial Office, 1860–1871" (doctoral dissertation, Duke University, 1962), p. 38.

11. The term "establishment" requires definition. The Colonial Office occasionally used it to refer to the body of upper-division clerks, or those men who after 1855 competed for their positions, CO to Treasury, March 8, 1872, CO 537/22. The more usual meaning, and that used by the Treasury, was the body of men "entitled to pensions under the Superannuation Acts." Under this definition the supplementary clerks and certain porters and housekeepers were included in the establishment. Treasury to CO, June 22, 1872, *ibid.*

12. Cell, *HSANZ*, XII, 55.

ally accepted in minor matters, but the final decision was still the responsibility of the secretary of state in actual fact. With few exceptions every letter received at the Colonial Office eventually found its way to the secretary of state's desk. Bound up tightly in questions of detail, he and the undersecretaries had little leisure to consider the larger questions of policy that could possibly have reduced the questions of detail submitted to them.[13]

The obvious solution to this problem, which became more serious as the volume of work increased, was to give more clerks a real role in the decision-making process by permitting them to minute papers and to make decisions on routine questions. This was the solution eventually adopted by the Colonial Office in the seventies and eighties. Until the reorganization of 1872, however, the position of the junior clerks was not an enviable one. Entering the Colonial Office while still a youth, the junior clerk was assigned only the most menial of tasks. Depending upon the health of his superiors, he could look forward to spending up to twenty years looking up papers, copying dispatches, and occasionally preparing simple drafts. During periods when business was slack, work was created for him. Sir William Baille Hamilton, who entered the Colonial Office as a junior clerk in 1864, later described this practice.

It was considered desirable, and no doubt rightly, that their time should be fully employed. With this laudable object in view, it was ordained that whenever more pressing affairs of State were for the moment in abeyance, we should devote ourselves to the less elevating occupation of copying letters and despatches, entering them in books—a singularly elaborate waste of time, as the actual draft of the letter or despatch would always be found attached to the document to which it related—and performing other mechanical and unattractive duties, that would very properly be regarded by a junior clerk of the present day with much the same feelings as would be experienced by a groom of the chambers who should be requested to clean the front doorstep or to assist the scullery maid in preparing the vegetables for dinner.[14]

This drudgery, combined with the natural restlessness of their age, led invariably to discontent among the junior clerks. Their frustration

13. The committees investigating public offices were well aware of this problem. One committee reported that the senior members of a department required time "to attend to general objects connected with their respective duties, which are often of more importance to the public interests than the everyday transactions of official routine." "Reports of Committees of Inquiry," No. 1715, p. 36, *Parl. Paps. 1854*, XXVII.

14. Hamilton, *Nineteenth Century and After*, p. 601.

was increased by the knowledge that seniority, not ability, was the usual criterion for promotion. Efficiency, even if detected, was seldom rewarded.

The Colonial Office not only failed to offer the junior clerks work commensurate with their abilities and aspirations but also failed to prepare them for the positions of responsibility and trust which they would eventually hold as senior clerks and perhaps as undersecretaries. The juniors were denied responsible work primarily because the older members of the office did not have sufficient confidence in them, but this was not the entire reason. Sir James Stephen realized that the Colonial Office was "a bad school for training up its younger Members,"[15] but many of his colleagues did not share this view. The senior clerks were naturally reluctant to condemn a system which had raised them to their thousand-pounds-a-year positions. Confident in their own ability and efficiency, they believed that their successors should undergo the same long apprenticeship. As late as 1870 William Robinson, the senior clerk of the general department, argued that it was unreasonable to expect any clerk to make decisions without first mastering the details of his department. This knowledge of detail could be acquired only "by assisting in copying and other mechanical work."[16] Robert G. W. Herbert, the assistant undersecretary in 1870, agreed that "plenty of copying" was essential if the juniors were to learn their work.[17] Other influential men, including Lord John Russell, argued that when a superior man was needed in a government office he should be recruited from outside the civil service.[18] This was a clear admission of the failure of the civil service to produce men of the necessary capacity for the higher positions.[19]

Stephen was keenly aware of the organizational weaknesses of the Colonial Office. He realized that the delegation of greater responsibil-

15. Stephen's memo of March 30, 1832, CO 537/22.
16. Robinson's memo of October 7, 1870, ibid.
17. Herbert's marginal comments on Robinson's memo of February 10, 1870, ibid. Sir Frederic Rogers disagreed. He "utterly abhorred" the idea of using copying as a means of educating an intelligent man, but in practice he did little to change the system. Roger's minute of February 12, 1870, on Robinson's memo of February 10, 1870, ibid.
18. Cell, HSANZ, XII, 52.
19. With the exception of T. F. Elliot, who was promoted from the ranks in 1847, the posts of assistant undersecretary and permanent undersecretary were filled from outside the Colonial Office until 1892. Sir F. R. Sandford, Sir Robert Herbert, Sir Henry Holland, Sir Robert Meade, W. R. Malcolm, Sir Julian Pauncefote, Sir John Bramston, and Sir Edward Wingfield were all drawn from other departments or from private occupations.

ity to the senior clerks,[20] naturally implied a change in the status of the younger clerks, who would eventually occupy these positions. It was not surprising therefore that the junior clerks "betook themselves to thought & composition on every possible opportunity; until the humbler labours of the desk & pen at length became irksome, as carrying with them some indication of inferiority to associates belonging to the same general rank, and bearing, in common with themselves, the name of clerks."[21] Although he was capable of analyzing the problem, Stephen was unsure of the solution. He believed that the separation of the mechanical work of the junior clerks from the intellectual work of the seniors was essential. This division might be maintained by establishing "a more firm & regular discipline," but it would never satisfy the juniors, "whose rank and habits of life altogether unfit them for the mechanical drudgery for which we have such constant demand."[22] Stephen therefore suggested the establishment of a new class of copyists to replace some of the junior clerks. He never considered, however, giving the remaining junior clerks more responsibile work. The weakness of the Colonial Office was a lack of copyists, and in Stephen's opinion, "One Man writing at 1d. per folio would do more work, and do it better, than twelve Young Gentlemen copying Papers in the interval between their morning Rides and their Afternoon Dinner Parties."[23]

Stephen's criticisms were expanded into a general indictment of the entire British civil service by the Northcote–Trevelyan Report of 1854. It charged that the civil service attracted only "the unambitious, and the indolent or incapable." There were two primary reasons for this. First, the appointment of civil servants by political ministers led to the admission of many unqualified persons. Sometimes this was the result of a personal or political claim upon the head of a department. Other ministers simply did not exercise enough care in the selection of their junior clerks. Nor did Northcote and Trevelyan believe that the probationary period and the examinations given in some depart-

20. For a discussion of this development see Young, *Colonial Office*, pp. 92–95.
21. Stephen's memo of March 30, 1832, CO 537/22.
22. *Ibid.* Although few of the junior clerks possessed university degrees at this time most of them had been to a public school and belonged to that portion of society to which, in Stephen's words, "a liberal education, and a cultivated address belong as a matter of course." *Ibid.* In general Stephen had a very low opinion of the industry, zeal, or knowledge of the clerks of the Colonial Office. "Papers on the Reorganization of the Civil Service," No. 1870, p. 75, *Parl. Paps. 1854–55*, XX.
23. Stephen's memo of March 30, 1832, CO 537/22.

ments guaranteed the elimination of incompetents from the civil service. Inefficient personnel were also a result of the way in which the government departments were organized. Because the young clerks spent years doing routine work, it was difficult to recruit able men or to inspire those already employed. Promotion by seniority and not by merit only made the system worse and led first to despair and ultimately to idleness.[24]

Northcote and Trevelyan proposed two important reforms. First, they suggested the establishment of a central board of examiners which would fill vacancies in the civil service by means of regularly scheduled competitive examinations. These examinations would exclude incompetents, but in order to attract really able candidates Northcote and Trevelyan believed that conditions of employment in the civil service would have to be improved. They stressed the necessity of employing men on work commensurate with their abilities, recommending the establishment of a class of supplementary clerks to relieve the superior clerks of their mechanical duties. They also argued that a division of labor would make it possible to judge the ability of each superior clerk and to introduce a meaningful system of promotion by merit.[25] Northcote and Trevelyan believed that once the clerks realized that their careers in the civil service depended "entirely on the industry and ability with which they discharged their duties," efficiency would quickly improve.[26]

The report received little support from civil servants outside the Treasury. Most senior officials felt compelled to defend themselves against the charges of "indolence" and "incompetence," and as a result they seldom considered impartially the recommendations of the report.[27] With the Aberdeen ministry split on the question of civil service reform, it appears that only the fiasco of the Crimean War saved a portion of the committee's recommendations.[28] Lord Palmerston, Aberdeen's successor, had little interest in civil service reform, but he

24. "Report on the Organization of the Permanent Civil Service," No. 1713, pp. 4-7, *Parl. Paps. 1854*, XXVII.

25. *Ibid.*, pp. 11-19. There were also proposals at this time to establish a central copying office. This would have greatly diminished the demand for manual labor in the other offices.

26. *Ibid.*, p. 9.

27. For the reaction of the civil service to the report see Emmeline W. Cohen, *The Growth of the British Civil Service, 1780-1939* (London, 1941), pp. 104-109, and "Papers on the Reorganization of the Civil Service," No. 1870, *Parl. Paps. 1854-55*, XX.

28. Asa Briggs, *Victorian People: A Reassessment of Persons and Themes, 1851-67* (Chicago, 1955), pp. 77-88. Aberdeen's ministry fell early in 1855 resisting an inquiry into the condition of the army in the Crimea.

felt that some action was politically desirable. The result was the Order in Council of May 21, 1855, establishing the Civil Service Commission, which was to insure that all nominees for the civil service were healthy and had sufficient knowledge and intelligence for their duties. The manner in which the departments filled their vacancies was, however, left to the discretion of the various ministers.[29] The Order in Council was a weak compromise. Not only was the Civil Service Commission powerless to frame uniform regulations designed to attract able men, but, equally important, nothing was said about the division of labor within the various offices. New clerks would henceforth possess a certain level of intelligence, but there was no guarantee that their abilities would be used to the best advantage. Sir Stafford Northcote declared in the House of Commons that excessive attention had been given the question of recruitment. This he argued was only one portion of the committee's recommendations.[30] This weakness was partially responsible for the relatively small impact which the Order in Council had upon the organization of the Colonial Office, and the civil service in general, in the sixties.

The Colonial Office, together with most of the other departments, combined patronage and competition in the selection of its clerks. The secretary of state nominated several candidates for each vacancy, and the new Civil Service Commission examined them, selecting the most able nominee. Sir Frederic Rogers, the permanent undersecretary from 1860 to 1871, warmly supported this new method of recruitment. By nominating candidates the Colonial Office obtained men who possessed the necessary "moral qualities." The examination insured that the clerks would also be competent.[31] Rogers was later an outspoken critic of unrestricted open competition.

Between 1857 and 1870 the number of nominees for each Colonial Office position ranged from a low of two to a high of nine; the mean was six.[32] The candidates were examined twice. The preliminary examination usually eliminated one or two of the weaker candidates. The final selection was made on the basis of a second examination

---

29. "Copy of an Order of Her Majesty in Council Regulating the Admission of Persons to the Civil Service of the Crown," No. 266, *Parl. Paps. 1854–55*, XLI.

30. Great Britain, 3 *Hansard's Parliamentary Debates*, CXXXVIII, 2082–2084, June 15, 1855.

31. Rogers' minute of February 17, 1870, on Treasury to CO, December 23, 1869, CO 323/297.

32. CO 537/19, *passim*. This volume contains the correspondence between the Civil Service Commission and the Colonial Office from 1858 to 1870. After 1870 this correspondence was included in the general (CO 323) file.

lasting several days. This examination stressed the classics (1,500 points), history and English composition (1,500 points), précis-writing (600 points), and mathematics (1,400 points). Proficiency in a modern foreign language was worth a maximum of only 500 points. Bookkeeping was allotted only 100 points.[33] Successful candidates usually scored well in the classics, précis-writing, and English composition. There were exceptions, however. E. B. Pennell scored nothing in the classics but redeemed himself by doing very well in French.[34] A. A. Pearson won primarily because of the 900 points he scored in mathematics.[35]

Although the examinations were not particularly rigorous, there does not appear to have been any attempt at political jobbery by Colonial Office officials.[36] It would have been difficult in any event because the Civil Service Commission did not hesitate to use its prerogative and refuse to certify unqualified candidates. G. W. B. De Robeck, the winner of the March, 1860, examination, was refused a position because of his failure in orthography.[37] Only after he again finished first in the examination was he appointed a probationary clerk.[38] In 1868 the Civil Service Commission twice refused to certify any of the candidates who presented themselves for examination.[39] Competition at the examinations was usually keen, and on several occasions only a few points separated the first two candidates. Edward Fairfield, one of the most able clerks who entered the Colonial Office in the sixties, competed twice before he received an appointment. On his first attempt he was narrowly defeated by William Baille Hamilton.[40]

Despite the dearth of biographical data,[41] it appears that the new

33. CSC to CO, April 7, 1859, CO 537/19.
34. *Ibid.*
35. CSC to CO, June 27, 1867, CO 537/19. The comments of Herman Merivale and the Duke of Newcastle on A. W. L. Hemming's examination results clearly show what subjects they regarded as important. Hemming did extremely well in modern history and English composition and moderately well in présis writing. The rest of his examination was a disaster. Although his cumulative score was not outstanding for a winner, Merivale believed that Hemming would prove a very successful appointment, and Newcastle hoped that he would live up to "so good an examination." CSC to CO, January 26, 1860, and minutes, *ibid.*
36. The financial secretary to the Treasury, Sir William Hayter, was reported to have kept two "Treasury Idiots" to run against the candidates he wished to appoint. Sir Algernon West, *Recollections, 1832 to 1886* (2 vols.; London, 1899), I, 70–71.
37. CSC to CO, March 28, 1860, CO 537/19.
38. CSC to CO, August 16, 1860, *ibid.*
39. CSC to CO, May 8, 1868, and CSC to CO, November 24, 1868, *ibid.*
40. CSC to CO, April 29, 1864, *ibid.*
41. For Edward Fairfield see Frederic Boase, ed., *Modern English Biography* (6 vols.; Truro, 1892–1921), V, 263. For Richard Ebden, John Hales, and G. W. B. De Robeck

"competitive" clerks were drawn from the same ranks of society as the patronage appointments. Fairfield's father was a major in the militia. Richard Ebden, F. R. Round, and John Hales were all sons of clergymen. De Robeck's father was a country gentleman, the third Baron of Leilip Castle, County Kildare. The new junior clerks were, however, better educated. Although they did not attend the very best public schools, Fairfield and Hamilton went to Harrow, Hales and A. A. Pearson went to Rugby, and Round attended Marlborough. Moreover, a university degree was no longer uncommon. Ebden, Hales, and De Robeck attended Cambridge, and Round was a graduate of Oxford (Balliol). Hamilton and Fairfield[42] were both called to the bar by the Inner Temple in 1872. In 1860 Herman Merivale stated that the new system of recruitment had eliminated incompetents from the civil service,[43] but a more positive statement seems justifiable. The new clerks proved to be both capable and energetic. Richard Ebden, chief clerk in 1879, F. R. Round, financial clerk in 1881, Earnest Blake, crown agent in 1881, and Edward Fairfield, assistant undersecretary in 1892, to mention only a few, were all notable successes at the Colonial Office.

Despite the introduction of limited competition, the prospects of the junior clerks in the Colonial Office improved only gradually. The result was that the Order in Council of May 21, 1855, tended to exaggerate an already difficult situation. The new junior clerks expected to be employed on intellectual work, and they were naturally disappointed when, instead of becoming statesmen, they were assigned only routine tasks.[44] In (Sir) George Barrow's African department they still received the letters from the registry, looked up previous correspondence, indexed dispatches, prepared the "more ordinary Drafts," and occasionally supervised the preparation of the arrears lists.[45] Their duties could be described most favorably as "a useful manipulation of

see J. A. Venn, ed., *Alumni Cantabrigienes*, Part II: *From 1852 to 1900* (6 vols.; Cambridge, 1940–1954), II, 194, 282, 379. For F. R. Round see Joseph Foster, ed., *Alumni Oxonienses, 1715–1886* (4 vols.; London, 1887–1888), III, 1227. The various editions of the *Colonial Office List* also provide some biographical information.

42. Fairfield to Sir Michael Hicks Beach, January 6, 1880, CO 323/347.

43. "Evidence before the Select Committee on Civil Service Appointments," No. 440, p. 310, *Parl. Paps. 1860*, IX.

44. Barrow's minute of February 20, 1869, CO 537/22. It is interesting to note that the new clerks invariably inserted in their biographical sketches in the *Colonial Office List* the fact that they had obtained their appointments after competitive examinations. They had no desire to be identified with the "patronage" appointees of earlier years.

45. *Ibid.*

books & papers in the way of search & otherwise partly in the drafting of Despatches and the framing of précis or Memoranda."[46]

The new clerks' pay remained low. Although they were somewhat older and had better educations, the assistant junior clerks (fourth class) still received an initial salary of only £100 rising by an annual increment of £10 to £150. The salary of the junior clerks (third class) advanced from £150 to £300 by increments of £15.[47] In a period of general prosperity, the financial position of new junior clerks was probably less favorable than in the fifties.[48] Their acquisition of financial independence was, however, somewhat accelerated by the employment of four juniors as private secretaries. These positions carried an additional salary of £150 a year.

Promotion, despite statements to the contrary,[49] continued to be based on seniority rather than merit. The retirement of several senior clerks who had entered the office in the twenties did, however, improve the position of the new junior clerks.[50] Richard Ebden, who entered the office in 1858, became an assistant clerk in only eight years. In 1874 he was promoted to principal (senior) clerk, and in 1879 he became chief clerk.[51] His advance was more rapid than those of his colleagues because he was the first of the new competitive clerks.[52] Nevertheless, the retirement of the older clerks gave all of the new juniors hope for rapid promotion and for more responsible work.

The introduction of limited competition did not result in any pronounced or immediate reform in the organization and routine of the Colonial Office, but certain minor changes naturally occurred. The most important of these changes, the assignment of less copying to the junior clerks, was characteristically unplanned and lacking in formality. Originally the assistant junior clerks had done most of the

46. CO to Treasury, March 28, 1870, CO 323/302. This letter requested a pay raise for the junior clerks and naturally placed their duties in the most favorable light.
47. Rogers' minute of April 19, 1869, *ibid*.
48. Colonial Office salaries were also lower than those of other departments. In 1870 the average annual income of established Colonial Office clerks was only £400, compared with £445 in the Home Office, £463 in the Foreign Office, and £565 in the Treasury. CO to Treasury, March 28, 1870, *ibid*.
49. Rogers' minute of July 5, 1866, CO 878/4, No. 5.
50. Promotion in the 1850's was unusually slow. Most of the higher positions were filled by men who had entered the office in the mid-1820's and who were not ready for retirement. Cell, *HSANZ*, XII, 51.
51. *Colonial Office List* (1891), p. 411.
52. For example, Edward Fairfield entered the office only eight years after Ebden, but, despite Fairfield's acknowledged ability, he waited fifteen years longer before becoming a principal clerk. *Colonial Office List* (1892), p. 383.

copying, and requisitions to the copying department were made only
in cases of extreme pressure.[53] In 1854, when the War Office and the
Colonial Office were separated, several copyists were brought into the
Colonial Office. Some people anticipated that the number of junior
clerks would be reduced, but the only apparent result was that the
juniors were relieved of much of their copying.[54] Not only were the
junior clerks partially relieved of their most stifling mechanical work,
but some of them received more responsible assignments. Edward
Fairfield assisted Sir Henry Taylor with the general prison, hospital,
asylum, and leprosy correspondence.[55] Although Fairfield was a very
junior member, he did not hesitate to disagree with his illustrious
superior.[56] A. W. Hemming, who developed into a very able dispatch
writer, was placed in charge of the preparation of circular dispatches
and the disposal of the replies. This had previously been part of the
chief clerk's duties.[57] The West Indian department furnishes a third
example of the devolution of responsibility. For reasons of health, Sir
Henry Taylor rarely attended the Colonial Office. Because of his absence, Richard Ebden, as Taylor admitted, "performed the most
laborious part of the business which it would otherwise have belonged
to me to do."[58] The junior clerks with responsible work were always
in the minority, however, and the duties they performed were assigned
to them as individuals and not as members of a particular class of
clerks.

The junior clerks also had limited opportunities for travel and work
in the colonies. Arthur Birch served as colonial secretary of British
Columbia and administered that colony from September, 1865, until
November, 1866. In 1871 he was appointed acting lieutenant governor

53. In the forties there were only four or five copyists assigned to the Colonial Office
costing between £400 and £500 a year. W. Robinson's memo of October 7, 1870, CO
537/22.
54. The cost of copying increased rapidly; in 1870 there were thirteen copyists costing
almost £3,000 a year. *Ibid.* Other offices had the same problem. The copying department
of the Board of Trade also grew rapidly because the junior clerks "threw [their] work
upon it & did nothing." The Board of Trade kept their juniors from idleness by dis-
missing many of its copyists. Herbert's minute of March 10, 1870, *ibid.*
55. Taylor's minute of February, 1869, *ibid.*
56. Henry L. Hall, *The Colonial Office: A History* (London, 1937), p. 144. When Taylor
retired in 1872 Fairfield assumed responsibility for these questions. He and Taylor de-
serve much of the credit for improving the sanitation and ventilation of these colonial
institutions.
57. Rogers' minute of April 1, 1868, CO 878/4, No. 43.
58. Taylor, *Autobiography*, II, 291. Ebden did the work with "admirable efficiency."
Ibid.

of Penang.[59] W. A. B. Hamilton went to Canada on a secret service mission in 1867.[60] The number of colonial assignments increased during the seventies and eighties. Robert Herbert, who succeeded Rogers in 1871, believed that such work improved the colonial service and also helped to recruit vigorous and able clerks who would enjoy an occasional respite from "the more homely routine of the ordinary Civil Service."[61]

Rogers' reluctance to give the junior and assistant clerks greater responsibility meant that the senior clerks and the undersecretaries were still overworked. This problem would have been even more serious if the volume of work had not remained relatively constant throughout the sixties.[62] The senior clerks, according to their own testimony,[63] frequently took work home in the evenings, although the six-hour working day and the wretched condition of the Colonial Office building undoubtedly contributed to this practice. The undersecretaries felt the greatest pressure of work. This was partially the result of Sir Frederic Rogers' appointment as permanent undersecretary in 1860. During the fifties, Rogers had handled the Colonial Office's legal work in addition to his duties at the Colonial Land and Emigration Commission. When he became undersecretary his legal work was also transferred to Downing Street. Because of this additional work, Rogers divided the supervision of the general work of the office with T. F. Elliot, the assistant undersecretary, each man being responsible for the work of two geographical departments. Rogers continued to deal with all legal questions, and Elliot supervised military and convict topics.[64] Rogers was still overworked, however,[65] and both Edward Cardwell and Lord Carnarvon believed that he should be given additional assistance.[66] Too much of his time was occupied with complex legal questions "to give the Secretary of State that full and considered

59. *Colonial Office List* (1873), p. 265.
60. *Colonial Office List* (1891), pp. 426–427.
61. Herbert's minute of July 23, 1870, on CSC to CO, July 9, 1870, CO 323/301.
62. The number of registered letters and dispatches rose from 13,349 in 1858 to only 14,327 in 1868. Chart prepared by W. A. Nunes, 1869, *ibid.*
63. George Barrow's minute of February 20, 1869; Charles Cox's minute of February 23, 1869; William Dealtry's minute of February 29, 1869; and Gordon Gairdner's minute of February 23, 1869, CO 537/22.
64. Rogers to Miss Katherine Rogers, May 4, 1860, in George Eden Marindin, ed., *Letters of Frederic Lord Blachford, Under-Secretary of State for the Colonies, 1860–1871* (London, 1896), p. 226.
65. Rogers to Carnarvon, November 26, 1866, Carnarvon Papers, PRO 30/6/154, f. 1714.
66. Rogers, "Notes of Autobiography," 1885, in Marindin, ed., *Letters of Blachford*, p. 264.

assistance which is indispensable for dealing with the various intricate
and comprehensive questions which form the most anxious part of
the business of the Office."[67]

There were two obvious solutions to the problem. Rogers could
either have been relieved of his legal work, or more of the general work
of the Colonial Office could have been delegated to other members of
the office. Rogers chose the first alternative because he did not believe
that the permanent undersecretary could be relieved "from a considerable amount of routine work."[68] The Treasury approved the
appointment of a new £1,200-a-year legal adviser on the understanding that the position of précis writer, which dated from 1799, would
be abolished as soon as possible.[69] Henry Holland, who was to have a
long and varied connection with the Colonial Office, was appointed
to the new post. Rogers' high regard for Holland's legal ability and
general intelligence,[70] enabled him to devote most of his time to
supervising the general work of the office. When Elliot retired in 1868,
Rogers discontinued the geographical division of work with the assistant undersecretary, making "a horizontal instead of a vertical sec-
tion of the business."[71] Rogers' decision to supervise all of the general
work naturally depressed the position of Sir Francis R. Sandford,
Elliot's successor. Although many people believed that the work of the
Colonial Office could be done more efficiently by two permanent heads,
there is no indication that Robert Herbert ever seriously considered
that step. It was not until 1925, when the Dominions Office was established with its own permanent undersecretary, that Rogers' decision
of 1868 was altered.

If Sir James Stephen had returned to the Colonial Office in 1868,
he would probably have felt at home. The atmosphere of the Colonial
Office was still relaxed and informal, more like a social club than a
government office. Office hours and leave regulations were still not
rigidly enforced; the day of the "fussy Orders in Council or inquisi-

67. CO to Treasury, December 17, 1866, CO 323/289.
68. Ibid.
69. Treasury to CO, January 4, 1867, CO 323/289. For a detailed discussion of the appointment of a legal adviser see B. A. Knox, "The Provision of Legal Advice, and the
Colonial Office Reorganization, 1866–7," Bulletin of the Institute of Historical Research,
XXXV (November, 1962), 178–197, and Wright, Treasury Control of the Civil Service,
pp. 146–147.
70. Rogers to Carnarvon, January 7, 1867, PRO 30/6/154, f. 1780. Rogers believed that
Holland's chief failing might be a want of "force." See also Rogers, "Notes of Autobiography," 1885, in Marindin, ed., Letters of Blachford, p. 264.
71. Rogers to Miss S. Rogers, December 20, 1868, in Marindin, ed., Letters of Blachford, p. 276.

torial Treasury Minutes" had not yet arrived.[72] The work of the office was still geared to "getting off the mails"; the telegraph, which reached North America in 1866, was too new to have any great influence on the conduct of business. Although the Order in Council of May 21, 1855, procured better clerks for the Colonial Office, the organization and duties of the staff had changed little. Authority and responsibility were still concentrated in the hands of a few senior members of the office with only a few tentative steps having been taken to relieve the pressure on the secretariat.[73]

There were several reasons for the absence of new administrative ideas at the Colonial Office in the sixties. Sir Frederic Rogers, who was trained under the old system, was not greatly interested in administrative reform. Although he "deplored" copying as a means of training intelligent juniors, he moved very slowly to improve their position. In addition, there was little pressure from outside the office. The volume of work remained nearly constant, and the appointment of Henry Holland in 1867 enabled the staff to handle its work in the traditional manner. Equally important, none of the colonial secretaries—the Duke of Newcastle, Edward Cardwell, the Earl of Carnarvon, or the Duke of Buckingham—showed any real interest in the reorganization of their office. In this they were simply reflecting the unwillingness of their governments to deal with the larger question of civil service reform.

The wretched condition of the Colonial Office building and the advanced age of the senior officials also supported and reflected to some extent the maintenance of the status quo. The old Colonial Office building in Downing Street had been condemned in 1837, and by the fifties it was totally inadequate for the needs of the staff. The fabric of the building had so deteriorated by 1868 that a safe could not be placed in the accounts department without endangering the structure.[74] Cracks in the ceilings let in rain and snow. Doors refused to close. Faulty chimneys made suffocation a danger. "Fetid and noxious" smells made work difficult.[75] And yet there was hope. The Foreign Office and India Office received new quarters in 1868, and the construction of a new Colonial Office and Home Office was begun. Al-

72. Hamilton, *Nineteenth Century and After*, p. 601.
73. In 1869 Rogers authorized the chief clerk to dispose of certain financial letters without consulting the undersecretaries. These letters included, however, only those involving no "questions of principle, or alterations of practice." J. S. Lewis' minute of March 2, 1869, CO 878/5, Vol. 4, No. 1.
74. Office of Works to CO, January 29, 1868, CO 323/297.
75. CO clerks to Rogers, 1868, CO 878/18.

though inevitable delays postponed occupation of this new building until 1876, the Colonial Office clerks could at least look forward to better working conditions.

The personnel of the office in the sixties were almost as antiquated as the building. The senior clerks, Arthur Blackwood, Henry Taylor, George Barrow, and Gordon Gairdner, had all served at least forty years. Together with Rogers, T. F. Elliot, who had entered the office in 1825, and William Strachey, the précis writer since 1848, they provided the Colonial Office with a staff of great experience and seniority. Their long service had, however, prevented the introduction of new men and ideas into the office. Blackwood's retirement in 1867 was the beginning of a rapid turnover in the supervisory personnel of the Colonial Office. By 1872 all of the men above had been replaced by officials who were relatively new to public service and who did not have the same respect for the traditions and practices of the office.[76] The new Colonial Office would not necessarily be a better department, but it would be different.

The reforms of 1870 and 1872 attempted to correct some of the obvious faults in the organization and routine of the Colonial Office. These problems were not, however, peculiar to the Colonial Office. In fact its constitution was, as mentioned earlier, in some ways in advance of its time. The Colonial Office as a department had a good reputation among people in public service. Henry Holland preferred the position of legal adviser to a similar post at the Board of Trade.[77] Lord Kimberley, the secretary of state from 1870 to 1874, and his outspoken colleague E. H. Knatchbull-Hugessen both thought highly of the efficiency of the Colonial Office. The office was "better manned" and "the work more efficiently performed" than in any other office in which they had served.[78] Robert Herbert, who served for a time at the Board of Trade, attested to the Colonial Office's high reputation among other civil servants. It had "a high character as being an office in which the work is well done, & the men work well together with a gentlemanly good feeling which is not the universal rule."[79]

76. Elliot retired in 1868, Gairdner and Strachey in 1870, Rogers in 1871, and Barrow and Taylor in 1872.
77. Holland to Carnarvon, January 3, 1867, PRO 30/6/142, ff. 1620–1621.
78. Knatchbull-Hugessen to Kimberley, June 19, 1872, and Kimberley to Herbert, June 20, 1872, CO 537/22. Kimberley had served at the Foreign Office and was Lord Privy Seal, 1868–1870. Knatchbull-Hugessen had served at the Treasury and Home Office.
79. Herbert's minute of July 23, 1870, on CSC to CO, July 9, 1870, CO 323/301.

CHAPTER II

The Formation of the New Colonial
Office, 1868-1872

THE FORMATION OF
William Gladstone's first ministry in 1868 and Granville's appointment as colonial secretary were of considerable importance to the history of the empire and the development of the British civil service. Sir
Frederic Rogers later recalled with great surprise what a short time
Granville had actually served at the Colonial Office; his eighteen-month
term occupied "so large and so bright a space" in Rogers' recollections.[1]
Together with Edward Cardwell, Granville insisted that Canada and
the other large self-governing colonies undertake military obligations
equal with the degree of political autonomy they enjoyed.[2] After considerable hesitation, Granville decided to extend responsible government to the Cape Colony.[3] He also supported administrative reform
and confederation in the British West Indies.[4] Less characteristically,
he permitted tentative steps to be taken toward consolidating and ex-
tending British holdings on the Gold Coast.[5]

Granville's policies reflected his belief that the settlement colonies
would mature politically and that this would result in a weakening of
their political ties with England. Granville did not regard this prospect
with alarm, believing that the best solution to Canadian problems
would be "that in the course of time and in the most friendly spirit
the Dominion should find itself strong enough to proclaim her independence."[6] This attitude, together with his strong free trade views,

1. Blachford to Granville, February 2, 1886, Granville Papers, PRO 30/29/213.
2. For Granville's role in the withdrawal of the British troops from Canada see C. P.
Stacey, *Canada and the British Army, 1846–1871: A Study in the Practice of Responsible
Government* (rev. ed.; Toronto, 1963), pp. 205–228.
3. Cornelius W. de Kiewiet, *British Colonial Policy and the South African Republics,
1848–1872* (London, 1929), pp. 276–279.
4. Bruce Hamilton, *Barbados and the Confederation Question, 1871–1885* (London,
1956), pp. xvi–xvii.
5. Douglas Coombs, *The Gold Coast, Britain and the Netherlands, 1850–1874* (London,
1963), pp. 63–77.
6. Granville to Russell, August 28, 1869, in Lord Edmond Fitzmaurice, *Life of Granville George Leveson Gower, Second Earl Granville, 1815–1891* (2nd ed.; 2 vols.; Lon-

naturally meant that he opposed the further annexation of territory, especially if it appeared likely to lead to native problems.[7]

Granville's term as colonial secretary was also important in the area of administrative reform. He instigated a thorough inquiry into the organization of his office and attempted to correct some of its more obvious weaknesses. He also approved a reorganization of the Order of St. Michael and St. George, improved the crown agents' department, and carried through a "small departmental good deed" by emancipating the crown colonies from "the financial dominion of the Treasury."[8] These departmental reforms resulted as much from his personality as from his interest in reform and economy.

Granville, who grew up in diplomatic society, impressed his contemporaries with his social grace, tact, and apparent lack of drive and ambition. Rogers regarded him as "the pleasantest and most satisfactory chief of those under whom [he] served." He had the ability to enjoy "the characteristic and amusing side of business."[9] This "courtliness of an earlier time"[10] gave Granville the reputation of being an idler, and Lord Kimberley, Granville's successor at the Colonial Office, believed that he was much too "nonchalant and yielding" for a minister.[11] There is little doubt that his official habits were lax. Arthur Godley, one of his private secretaries, observed that Granville worked on the principle that correspondence if ignored would eventually answer itself. Much of his time was spent "in conversation and

---

don, 1905), II, 22. These views coincided closely with Rogers'. He believed that the primary function of the Colonial Office should be "to secure that our connexion, while it lasts, shall be as profitable to both parties, and our separation, when it comes, as amicable as possible." Rogers, "Notes of Autobiography," 1885, in Marindin, ed., *Letters of Blachford*, pp. 299–300. For Rogers' general views see Tyler, "Sir Frederic Rogers," pp. 92–101.

7. For Granville's views on the extension of British control over the Gold Coast, the Malay States, and Fiji see Coombs, *The Gold Coast*, p. 60; C. D. Cowan, *Nineteenth Century Malaya: The Origins of British Control* (London, 1961), p. 153; J. D. Legge, *Britain in Fiji, 1858–1880* (London, 1958), p. 26; and Ethel Drus, "The Colonial Office and the Annexation of Fiji," *Transactions of the Royal Historical Society*, 4th series, XXXII (1950), 92–93.

8. Blachford to Granville, February 2, 1886, PRO 30/29/213.

9. Rogers, "Notes of Autobiography," 1885, in Marindin, ed., *Letters of Blachford*, p. 265. For a similar assessment see Arthur Godley (Lord Kilbracken), *Reminiscences of Lord Kilbracken* (London, 1931), p. 105.

10. West, *Recollections*, II, 18.

11. John, First Earl of Kimberley, *A Journal of Events during the Gladstone Ministry, 1868–1874*, ed. Ethel Drus (London, 1958), p. 32. "His great fault is that he lives from hand to mouth, & trusts too much to the chapter of accidents. He seems never to give himself the trouble to reason out any matter completely, & he is singularly ignorant of the details of the questions he has to deal with. This laziness makes him an indifferent departmental Minister. As leader in the House of Lords he is in his true element." *Ibid.*, p. 31.

occupations which had nothing at all to do with politics."[12] Granville, who was well aware of his reputation, seems to have taken a certain pride in it.[13]

The criticisms of Granville's official habits resulted partially from the traditional belief that a good administrator was personally concerned with the detailed workings of his office. Unlike his predecessor, the Duke of Buckingham, who possessed a "natural turn for detail,"[14] Granville was unable to conform to this ideal.[15] His secretary, (Sir) Robert Meade, explained that he preferred to trust his subordinates in minor matters "while holding all the threads in his hands."[16] Certainly Granville interfered very little in matters of detail, allowing Rogers to make most of the decisions from 1868 to 1870.[17] In Granville's defense, it should be remembered that he had heavy responsibilities as the Liberal leader in the House of Lords.[18] Gladstone also relied heavily on Granville's tact to keep peace among members of the cabinet[19] and to appease the Queen, with whom his own relations steadily deteriorated.[20] Granville simply found it impossible to devote his entire energy to colonial questions.

Despite Granville's administrative failings, or perhaps because of them, his secretaryship was very important in the development of the Colonial Office. He attempted to eliminate some of the office's archaic procedures by introducing administrative techniques learned at the Foreign Office. He was also responsible for appointing (Sir) Robert G. W. Herbert and (Sir) Robert H. Meade to the secretariat of the Colonial Office. Finally, Granville agreed to fill Colonial Office clerk-

12. Godley, *Reminiscences*, pp. 102–104.

13. *Ibid.*, p. 103. See also Granville to Gladstone, December 31, 1868, in Agatha Ramm, ed., *The Political Correspondence of Mr. Gladstone and Lord Granville, 1868–1876* (2 vols.; London, 1952), I, 6–7.

14. Rogers, "Notes of Autobiography," 1885, in Marindin, ed., *Letters of Blachford*, p. 264.

15. Kimberley believed that this resulted from inadequate training in "subordinate office work." Kimberley, *Journal*, p. 31.

16. Fitzmaurice, *Life of Granville*, II, 500. Rogers stated that Granville "trusted his subordinates in matters of detail," and acted vigorously "in what may be called ministerial as distinguished from departmental policy." "Notes of Autobiography," 1885, in Marindin, ed., *Letters of Blachford*, p. 264.

17. Tyler, "Sir Frederic Rogers," p. 67.

18. Little of Granville's voluminous correspondence with Gladstone concerned the colonies. Irish questions, education, and patronage predominated. Ramm, ed., *Political Correspondence, 1868–1876, passim.*

19. Donald Southgate, *The Passing of the Whigs, 1832–1886* (London, 1962), p. 343.

20. Agatha Ramm, ed., *The Political Correspondence of Mr. Gladstone and Lord Granville, 1876–1886* (2 vols.; Oxford, 1962), I, xxxv; Philip Guedalla, ed., *The Queen and Mr. Gladstone* (2 vols.; London, 1933), I, 45.

ships by open competition, enabling his successor, Lord Kimberley (1870–1874), to undertake further reforms.

The pressure on Granville's time led him to undertake immediate administrative changes. Following Foreign Office precedent, he authorized the undersecretaries to sign dispatches for him, arguing that his time was too valuable to be used signing dispatches "which merely convey acknowledgment, or transmit documents, or request formal information, or signify the acquiescence of the Secretary of State in arrangements of detail, on which it is not usual to interfere with the discretion of the Governor."[21] Lord Kimberley, on Herbert's recommendation, also adopted this practice.[22] This change relieved the colonial secretary of needless work and reduced the time each paper remained in circulation.

Granville also requested that minute papers be attached to all incoming letters and dispatches.[23] Although minute papers had been used earlier, the minutes were frequently written directly on the dispatch. The result was, as Henry Taylor observed, that some clerks "seem unconsciously to measure an available corner by the eye & fill it so exactly that there is no room left for a leading word of the minute that follows & connection is lost—some go backwards some forwards—some across, & when every hole and corner of the minuted despatch has been occupied, recourse is had to the back of enclosures."[24] Minute papers reduced eyestrain and prevented small letters and dispatches from being misplaced.[25]

Granville was also critical of the Colonial Office's slowness in answering its mail. Rogers investigated the problem and discovered that the office took an average of eleven to twelve days to answer domestic letters. He believed that half that time would be excessive in "a house of business."[26] Rogers placed most of the blame for the delay on the Colonial Office's traditional method of circulating papers. Too many letters of "the merest routine" were sent to the permanent undersecretary or the secretary of state three times: once for minuting, once in

21. Granville's circular dispatch of January 30, 1869, CO 878/5, Vol. 4, No. 41.
22. Kimberley's minute of August 26, 1870, on Granville's circular dispatch of January 30, 1869, CO 878/5, Vol. 4, No. 41.
23. Rogers' memorandum of December 10, 1868, CO 878/4, No. 66.
24. Taylor's minute of March 13, 1868, CO 878/4, No. 38A.
25. Hemming's minute of April 6, 1868, CO 878/4, No. 45.
26. Rogers' minute of March 14, 1870, CO 878/5, Vol. 4, No. 21A. Rogers stated that dispatches from colonial governors generally received a reply by the next outgoing mail.

the form of a draft, and once for signature. He therefore proposed certain shortcuts in the circulation of the papers. He urged that when there was little doubt regarding the correct answer to a letter that a draft reply, or even a fair copy of the reply, be sent to him in the first instance. In this way he hoped that many letters could be answered on the day of their arrival. Although these "anticipations" would occasionally miscarry and result in extra work, Rogers believed that they would result in a "general increase of promptitude."[27]

The geographical division of work between the permanent undersecretary and the assistant undersecretary was also discontinued. Granville desired "that the responsibility for the whole business of the office should rest with one person to whom the S[ecretary] of S[tate] should be entitled [to] look primarily for assistance without distinction of Colony."[28]

These changes in office routine were supplemented by formal changes in the organization of the office which required the consent of the Treasury. Shortly after his appointment as colonial secretary Granville asked Rogers and Sir Francis Sandford, who had replaced Elliot as assistant undersecretary in 1868, to investigate the efficiency and cost of the Colonial Office and to recommend changes in its constitution. Their report formed the basis of the reforms submitted to the Treasury.[29]

In initiating his investigation Rogers instructed the senior clerks to describe the duties of the clerks under their control, the amount and type of work transacted in their departments, and the rules governing leave, office hours, and occasional absences. He also invited them to suggest improvements in the organization of the office.[30] The replies were disappointing. Charles Cox, the senior clerk of the Eastern department, stated that his duties were too "various and complicated"

27. Rogers' minute of March 14, 1870, CO 878/5, Vol. 4, 21A. In his last years at the Colonial Office, Rogers frequently dictated draft replies to his private secretary or composed them himself. These drafts were sent with the minutes for the approval of the colonial secretary. Tyler, "Sir Frederic Rogers," p. 39.
28. Rogers' minute of December 21, 1868, CO 878/4, No. 68.
29. Sandford, probably because of his limited experience in the office, played a minor part in the investigation. He remained in the Colonial Office only two years, electing to return to the Education office in 1870 when the secretaryship of that department was offered to him. He held that post until 1884. Sir Leslie Stephen and Sir Sidney Lee, eds., *Dictionary of National Biography* (25 vols.; Oxford, 1917–1927), XVII, 760. Rogers regarded him as a steady worker and above all as "a good churchman." Rogers to Miss S. Rogers, December 20, 1868, in Marindin, ed., *Letters of Blachford*, p. 276.
30. Rogers' minute of February 18, 1869, CO 537/22.

to describe in writing. He had no suggestions to offer on improving the efficiency of the office.[31] His reply was typical.[32] For whatever reason, an irrational attachment to the old system, their age, or a sincere belief in the efficacy of the existing Colonial Office, the senior clerks showed no interest in a reorganization of the office. Only Gordon Gairdner, the chief clerk, favored any change. Gairdner, who was secretary and registrar of the Order of St. Michael and St. George, was also responsible for supervising the accounts work, preparing legal commissions and warrants, dealing with the general and honors correspondence, and supervising the work of the office servants, porters, and messengers. He urged that his department, consisting of himself, an accountant, one permanent clerk, and four copyists, be given additional help.[33] Rogers agreed that this department at least required reorganization.[34]

The replies of the senior clerks revealed other problems demanding attention. For example, there were no uniform regulations governing the duties of the different classes of clerks. The junior and assistant clerks in Henry Taylor's West Indian department had much more responsibility than those in George Barrow's African department. Short leaves of absence were granted at the discretion of the senior clerks, a practice defended as instilling in the clerks a desire "to do their duty."[35] There were no fixed office hours, although most clerks attended from 11:30 or 12:00 until 5:30 or 6:00.[36] Even with the short office hours Barrow admitted that he could not keep his clerks fully occupied when the work, which came in cycles, was at "low ebb."[37] Junior clerks rarely, if ever, took work home.

After studying these reports, Rogers and Sandford submitted their recommendations for improving the efficiency of the office to Granville. Possibly because of the indifference shown by the senior clerks to

31. Cox's minute of February 22, 1869, *ibid.*
32. Barrow's minute of February 20, 1869; Taylor's minute of February, 1869; Dealtry's minute of February 20, 1869, *ibid.*
33. Gairdner's minute of February 23, 1869, *ibid.*
34. Rogers' minute of February, 1869, *ibid.*
35. Cox's minute of February 22, 1869, *ibid.* This was in addition to the annual two-month holiday.
36. Cox's hours depended upon whether he was living in London or in the country, "coming earlier going earlier in one case—coming later going later in the other. *Ibid.* Such a practice made it very difficult to give proper supervision to his junior clerks. Taylor rarely attended the office.
37. Barrow's minute of February 20, 1869, *ibid.* Afternoon games of "fives" were regularly held in some unoccupied rooms on the upper floor of No. 11 Downing Street, the chancellor of the exchequer's house. Hamilton, *Nineteenth Century and After*, p. 602.

reform, their report suggested no change in the structure of the four geographical departments. Rogers did not feel justified in altering "a system already working so well." He argued that the junior clerks must continue to handle much of the office's mechanical work. This work was useful in training them in "methodical habits," familiarizing them with the past history of the colonies, and acquainting them with the "antecedents" of the colonial officials.[38]

Rogers did, however, recommend the creation of a new general department. This department would assume many of the chief clerk's duties, but it would also supervise the registry and the library. The only reduction in the new department's work came from the establishment of an independent accounts department, which the senior clerks could not effectively supervise. Because of the additional duties assigned to the new department, Rogers did not believe that the chief clerk, who was usually the oldest of the senior clerks, should necessarily supervise it. He therefore recommended that the position of chief clerk be "disjoined from any special duty" and be given, together with the secretaryship of the Order of St. Michael and St. George, to the most meritorious of the senior clerks. Upon becoming chief clerk a man should not be required to change departments.[39]

Rogers and Sandford also proposed certain changes in the secretariat of the office. William Strachey, the précis writer, had originally dealt with lengthy or complex questions requiring compression, but by 1869 his primary function was to give advice on the finances of Ceylon and Mauritius. These questions could be assigned to the geographical departments, and Rogers proposed that Strachey's post be abolished.[40] In reality the position was little more than a sinecure. William Hamilton described Strachey as follows:

Another official who held a highly-paid appointment, the nature of which nothing should induce me to reveal, but which had then become practically a sinecure, never appeared at the office at all during the daytime. But an occasional belated junior clerk, hurrying away at what would then be considered an outrageously late hour for departure, would come across a mysterious and secretive looking individual, stealing along a passage to a sequestered apartment where he was accustomed to perform such work as could be found for him during the watches of the night; and would be informed on enquiry that it was Mr. ——, the ——. I only once, I think,

38. Rogers' and Sandford's minute of April 19, 1869, enclosed in CO to Treasury, June 28, 1869, CO 323/302.
39. *Ibid.*
40. *Ibid.*

caught sight of him myself, and I never knew of anyone who referred to him as more than a chance acquaintance.[41]

Rogers also recommended that Henry Holland, the legal adviser, be made an assistant undersecretary. Holland advised on legal matters in the same way that Sandford advised on financial questions, and as an assistant undersecretary Holland would have equal power to sign letters and to give instructions. Promotions would also be easier. Under existing arrangements, if Holland were promoted to assistant undersecretary a new lawyer would have to replace him as legal adviser. If, however, the Colonial Office had two assistant undersecretaries only one of them would require legal experience.[42]

Rogers' final recommendation was a raise in the salaries of the junior clerks. The junior clerks were divided into two classes: the assistant juniors (fourth class) began at £100 and rose by annual increments of £10 to £150, and the juniors (third class) began at £160 and rose by increments of £15 to £300. Rogers suggested that part of the £1,995 saved by the abolition of the position of précis writer[43] and the creation of the new general department be used to establish a single class of junior clerks with salaries rising from £100 to £300 by increments of £15. The small increase in the initial annual increment would accelerate the acquisition of financial independence by the younger members of the office.[44]

Granville said little about the proposals submitted to him. He did, however, believe that they would improve the efficiency of the office, and he warmly approved of the reduction in expenditure "by an amount which in Mr. Gladstone's opinion [was] very creditable.[45] With this praise Rogers' recommendations were sent to the Treasury for approval.

The Treasury sent James Stansfeld, the financial secretary, to discuss the reorganization of the Colonial Office with Sir Francis Sandford in January, 1870. Stansfeld did not object to the new general de-

41. Hamilton, *Nineteenth Century and After*, p. 600. Strachey appears to have been unpopular with the senior clerks, partly because of his personality and partly because of the independent nature of his position. Cox's minute of December 19, 1871, CO 537/22.

42. Rogers' and Sandford's minute of April 19, 1869, enclosed in CO to Treasury, June 28, 1869, CO 323/302.

43. There was no savings here. When the office of legal adviser had been created in 1867, the Colonial Office had promised to abolish the post of précis writer as soon as possible. This type of argument helps to explain the watchfulness of the Treasury.

44. Rogers' and Sanford's minute of April 19, 1869, enclosed in CO to Treasury, June 28, 1869, CO 323/302.

45. Granville's minute of June 7, 1869, CO 323/302.

partment, which he regarded as a purely departmental affair. He did not favor, however, Holland's appointment as a second assistant undersecretary. In his opinion the duties of a legal adviser were inconsistent with those of an administrative officer. For financial reasons, Stansfeld also opposed giving the junior clerks an increased annual increment. Stansfeld actually spent most of his time trying to persuade Sandford of the desirability of employing more "mechanical clerks" and fewer well-educated junior clerks, a reform which applied to all government offices.[46]

Sandford, not being prepared to discuss departmental reorganization in such broad terms, requested that Stansfeld discuss the question with Granville before the Treasury's criticisms were embodied in an official letter. Sandford felt that the colonial secretary, who knew the requirements of his department, should determine how his office was staffed.[47] Granville agreed, taking the precaution of enlisting cabinet support for his impending clash with Robert Lowe, the chancellor of the exchequer. Granville argued that if the Treasury opposed a departmental reorganization but could advance no arguments for economy, then the chancellor of the exchequer had no right to appeal to the cabinet "other than the right apart from Departments, which all of us have to complain of any colleague who is in our judgment about to commit a foolish act."[48]

Granville's informal meeting with Stansfeld resulted in a compromise settlement. The only trouble was that Lowe did not support his subordinate's action, and the Treasury's official letter embodied Stansfeld's original criticisms of the Colonial Office's reorganization. Accompanied by a private note from Granville, the Colonial Office dashed off a spirited rejoinder. In a typical bit of histrionics, Granville expressed amazement at the Treasury's "queer" letter which reopened a settled question. He was also injured to think that Lowe would deal so shabbily with one of "the few members of the Cabinet

46. Sandford to Granville, January 10, 1870, PRO 30/29/75, ff. 107–108.
47. *Ibid.*, ff. 109–112. He also believed that the Treasury's plan to remodel the civil service on an "intellectual and mechanical basis" was unsound.
48. Granville to Clarendon, Bruce, and Cardwell, January 12, 1870, private, PRO 30/29/68, ff. 37–39. Henry Bruce (Home Office) and Lord Clarendon (Foreign Office), who were both under heavy pressure from Lowe because of their refusal to support open competition, were prepared to stand "shoulder to shoulder" with Granville. Cardwell (War Office) took a more restrained and constitutional stand and stressed the responsibilities of the Treasury in the field of finances. Bruce to Granville, private, January 13, 1870; Clarendon to Granville, private, January 15, 1870; and Cardwell to Granville, private, January 15, 1870, PRO 30/29/68, ff. 35–36.

who still struggle on."[49] Lowe, who was not "the least disposed to contend that the letters of the Treasury were models either of style or courtesy,"[50] agreed to reconsider the question,[51] and the two offending letters were eventually withdrawn.

In a new letter the Treasury approved all the changes except the increased annual increment for the junior clerks.[52] The Colonial Office again argued that if the financial prospects of the juniors were not improved it would be difficult to recruit able men.[53] The Treasury capitulated. Lowe was not convinced by the Colonial Office's arguments, however. He believed that superior men could be recruited only if the number of upper-division clerks did not exceed the demands of "really responsible work." The clerks could then be given higher salaries and better prospects for promotion.[54] The approved changes in the constitution of the Colonial Office were put into effect by an Order in Council of March 31, 1870.

Lowe's weak opposition to an administrative reform which he felt was incomplete was due to more than Granville's vigorous intervention. Officials in both the Treasury and the Colonial Office believed that further reform was essential. It was necessary to implement Granville's decision to introduce open competition into the Colonial Office. In addition, Rogers admitted privately that the cost of his department was excessive, and he promised to consider reducing the number of junior clerks.[55] The reorganization of 1870, although important, was only a partial solution.

The question of recruitment by open competition was first raised by the Treasury in December, 1869.[56] The higher permanent staff of the Colonial Office was solidly opposed to this reform.[57] Sandford argued that competitive clerks would demand to be freed from all

49. Granville to Lowe, copy, private, February 10, 1870, PRO 30/29/66. Granville's expression of surprise was feigned. Stansfeld, shortly after his meeting with Granville, had warned him that Lowe absolutely refused to give the Colonial Office a second assistant undersecretary. Stansfeld urged Granville to deal directly with Lowe on the subject. Stansfeld to Granville, private, January 21, 1870, PRO 30/29/75, f. 452.
50. Lowe to Granville, November 5, 1872, PRO 30/29/66.
51. Lowe to Granville, February 13, 1870, ibid.
52. Treasury to CO, February 28, 1870, CO 537/22.
53. CO to Treasury, March 28, 1870, ibid.
54. Treasury to CO, March 31, 1870, CO 323/302.
55. Rogers' minute of March 12, 1870, CO 537/22.
56. Treasury to CO, December 23, 1869, CO 323/297. The cabinet decided on December 7, 1869, to allow Lowe to raise the question of open competition formally. Gladstone Papers (Cabinet Minutes), Add. MS 44637, f. 115.
57. Granville to Lowe, January 19, 1871, PRO 30/29/66.

mechanical work, something which was obviously impossible.[58] Sir Frederic Rogers, despite his pretensions as a Gladstonian Liberal, was an even more outspoken critic. His primary concern was that open competition implied that a public office was "a prey to be scrambled for fairly" and not a "machine to be made the most of." He feared that the government, with its desire to remove class favoritism and to promote "fair play," would impair the efficiency of the bureaucracy.[59]

I think it probable that, if the efficiency of the office would be best se-cured by obtaining simply the most hardheaded, regular & industrious men at the smallest price, unrestricted competition wd. effect this. You might get—or at any rate have a chance of getting—the most active and clever of a class without connexion, who having no other opportunities of getting on in the world would sell their abilities cheap.

But I think that certain moral qualities—integrity & honourable *esprit de corps,* are as really valuable for our purpose as intellect & its appen-dages. . . . The C. O. is parallel not to a great system like that of India— or it may be of Rothschilds or Barings, where a clever untrustworthy man may be placed out of temptation or where he can do no harm, but like a Banking House of 40 or 50 persons under the same roof and sharing in different degrees the same confidence. I cannot easily imagine the head of such an establishment making the admission of his clerks dependent on the issue of an open competitive examination. . . . [60]

Rogers believed that social status in itself was valuable "as some guar-antee for certain moral qualities."[61]

Despite his membership in a government with a program "to abolish class privileges and unbar to all the doors of political, economic and cultural opportunity,"[62] Granville's first reaction was to agree with his permanent undersecretary. On further reflection, however, he felt that Rogers had exaggerated the dangers of open competition. He argued that a properly designed examination would exclude men of inferior position who might damage the esprit de corps of the de-partment. With the warm support of William Monsell, the parlia-mentary undersecretary,[63] Granville accepted recruitment by open

58. Sandford to Granville, January 10, 1870, PRO 30/29/75, f. 110.
59. Rogers' minute of February 17, 1870, on Treasury to CO, December 23, 1869, CO 323/297.
60. *Ibid.*
61. *Ibid.*
62. R. C. K. Ensor, *England, 1870–1914* (Oxford, 1936), p. 3.
63. Monsell to Granville, February 22, 1870, CO 323/297.

competition, promising also to consider the feasibility of employing more lower-class clerks and of initiating a real division of labor within the office.[64] In communicating this decision to the Treasury, Granville and Rogers reserved the power to prescribe an entrance examination that was a "fair test of the candidate having received the highest class of education given in this country and calculated to maintain the necessary character of the office." They also proposed that the new clerks take a second examination after their probationary periods to insure that they possessed the ability to discharge their duties efficiently.[65]

Granville's support of open competition was not as strong as his letter to Monsell might imply. Lowe was never certain of Granville's position,[66] and the impetus for this reform came almost entirely from the Treasury.[67] Although Granville accepted open competition at the Colonial Office, he later refused to introduce it at the Foreign Office. At that time he argued that Lord Clarendon, his predecessor, had already decided against open competition and that any attempt to alter this decision would have been "most distasteful" to the staff.[68]

Granville could easily have refused to introduce recruitment by open competition at the Colonial Office. When Henry Bruce and Clarendon objected to Lowe's proposals, their departments, the Home Office and the Foreign Office, were simply excepted from the provisions of the Order in Council of June 4, 1870.[69] Granville's decision not to follow their example was important to the future development of the Colonial Office. Unlike the Foreign Office, the Colonial Office never developed a separate tradition of service; it was placed in the mainstream of civil service reform. Unlike the Home Office, which did not adopt open competition until 1876, there was no delay in the implementation of the new system.

Before the ramifications of open competition could be faced, however, two new men entered the Colonial Office. Robert G. W. Herbert replaced Sir Francis Sandford as assistant undersecretary on February 1, 1870, and Lord Kimberley succeeded Granville as secretary of state

64. Granville to Monsell, February 21, 1870, *ibid.*
65. CO to Treasury, March 1, 1870, *ibid.*
66. Lowe to Gladstone, November 22, 1869, Add. MS 44301, ff. 106–107.
67. John Morley, *Life and Letters of W. E. Gladstone* (3 vols.; London, 1943), II, 314–315.
68. Granville to Lowe, January 19, 1871, PRO 30/29/66.
69. Cohen, *Growth of the British Civil Service*, p. 122; Wright, *Treasury Control of the Civil Service*, pp. 94–96.

on July 6, 1870. Granville retired to the more congenial surroundings of the Foreign Office on the death of Lord Clarendon. Both Herbert and Kimberley were to play important roles in the subsequent Colonial Office reorganization.

The membership of the secretariat furnishes an important element of continuity to the history of the Colonial Office in the seventies and eighties. Sir Robert Herbert, the permanent undersecretary from 1871 until 1892, served longer at that position than any of his predecessors or successors. Robert Meade, John Bramston, and Edward Wingfield, assistant undersecretaries, also played key roles in colonial administration during this period. They and their ideas and prejudices dominated the Colonial Office in much the same way that Merivale, Elliot, Taylor, and Rogers had done in the fifties and sixties. Their backgrounds and careers also make these men excellent representatives of the higher civil service of late Victorian England.

Robert G. W. Herbert was a bona fide member of the English aristocracy; his father was the younger son of the first Earl of Carnarvon. Herbert spent his childhood on his father's estate at Ickleton, Cambridgeshire, where he received his early education from private tutors.[70] In later life he retained close ties with the village of Ickleton. He spent considerable time at his country home there entertaining colonial visitors and indulging his interest in natural history. He also filled the usual positions of magistrate and deputy-lieutenant of the County of Cambridge.[71]

Herbert went to Eton in 1844 at the age of thirteen. There he met Lord Carnarvon, his first cousin and future chief at the Colonial Office, Lord Robert Cecil, and Sir Roundell Palmer. He also came into contact with such future civil servants as Algernon West (Board of Inland Revenue), Philip Currie (Foreign Office), and Reginald Welby (Treasury). "Algy" West later boasted, "My contemporaries and I captured the Civil Service by storm." Robert Lowe had a somewhat different explanation. "It was a case of Eton v. Education, and Eton always won."[72] In any event, Herbert's early school friendships help to explain both his rapid rise in the civil service and his ability to discharge his duties efficiently in later life.

From Eton Herbert proceeded to Balliol College, Oxford. Later one

70. *DNB*, XXIII (1901–1911), 253.
71. *Times* (London), May 8, 1905, p. 6c–d.
72. West, *Recollections*, I, 52–53.

of the principal recruiting grounds for the overseas colonial service, at this time Balliol trained numerous civil servants for the home government. During the course of his "victorious career at Oxford," Herbert won the Hertford, Ireland, and Eldon scholarships, the Latin verse prize, and obtained a first class in classical moderations. In 1854 he was elected a fellow of All Souls.[73] At Balliol, Herbert also became a close friend of John Bramston, who was later an assistant undersecretary at the Colonial Office. After leaving Balliol both men went to London where they were called to the bar at Inner Temple.

In common with many higher civil servants of the late nineteenth century, Herbert began his official career as a private secretary. He was Gladstone's private secretary for "a dismally short time" in 1855,[74] improving his political contacts and gaining a certain amount of experience. Herbert's first real opportunity came in 1859 when Sir George Bowen, the first governor of the new colony of Queensland, selected him as colonial secretary.[75] Bramston tagged along as Bowen's private secretary.

Herbert was an immediate success in Queensland. As colonial secretary, he supervised much of the administrative work while the electoral rolls were being prepared. At the first election he was returned unopposed to the legislative assembly, becoming, with Bowen's support, Queensland's first premier at the tender age of twenty-nine. Herbert held that position for almost six years, a record which few if any nineteenth-century Australian politicians equalled.

Herbert's real purpose in going to Queensland may have been to prepare himself for a position in the British civil service, perhaps the Colonial Office. His numerous minutes on various colonial topics forwarded to the Colonial Office, as well as the circumstances of his appointment, tend to support this view.[76] On the other hand, he invested

73. *DNB*, XXIII (1901–1911), 253. Herbert studied under Benjamin Jowett, and the two men appear to have been quite good friends. Evelyn Abbot and Lewis Campbell, *The Life and Letters of Benjamin Jowett* (2 vols.; London, 1897), II, 464. Herbert also developed a friendship with Max Müller, the Anglo-German orientalist, and was responsible for getting him elected to All Souls, the first foreigner to receive this honor. Georgina Max Müller, ed., *The Life and Letters of the Right Honourable Friedrich Max Müller* (2 vols.; London, 1902), I, 221–223.

74. Gladstone to Granville, January 4, 1870, PRO 30/29/57. Gladstone was chancellor of the exchequer in Aberdeen's ministry. He had a high regard for Herbert's ability. Gladstone to Newcastle, copy, August 13, 1859. Add. MS 44263, f. 96.

75. Bowen to Gladstone, August 10, 1859, Add. MS 44392, ff. 123–124.

76. Sir Frederic Rogers referred to Herbert as one of the promising new men in the colonial service. This, as he admitted, was hardly the way to refer to a responsible colonial minister. Rogers' minute of April 20, 1866, on Bowen to Cardwell, February 13, 1866, CO 234/15.

heavily in land in northern Queensland,[77] purchased two tropical islands,[78] and helped some young men from Ickleton to settle in the colony.[79] These activities are not those associated with a transient politician. On leaving Brisbane in 1866, Herbert wrote that he would "probably return to look after [his] sheep and cattle at no distant date."[80] If he had not received a civil service appointment, he might have settled permanently in Queensland.

One thing is clear, however. Herbert never looked upon himself as a typical responsible minister nor was he regarded as such by his colleagues in the legislative assembly or by the local press. He and Bowen believed that in the first years of responsible government it was essential for the governor and his ministers to work closely together.[81] They should endeavor to restrain the impulsive and irresponsible colonists and to establish high standards of legislation and administration which future ministries would feel compelled to follow.[82] As a result, Herbert's legislative program was basically a conservative one.

Although he supported and encouraged agriculture, much of Herbert's political support came from the powerful squatting interests in Queensland. These men appreciated Herbert's "sound" financial ideas and his interest in opening the "outback" areas of the colony. He also received the support of the majority of the politically moderate middle class, who were impressed with his honesty and ability. Herbert showed, however, little understanding or sympathy for the political and economic aspirations of the working classes. He and Bowen were too ready to equate their opposition with agitation.[83] As long as he possessed the support of "the more respectable and educated colonists,"[84] Herbert

77. G. C. Bolton, *A Thousand Miles Away: A History of North Queensland to 1920* (Brisbane, 1963), pp. 29, 37. Herbert was in partnership with the Commissioner for Crown Lands for the Districts of Kennedy and Carpentaria and operated more as a "sleeping partner." Dorothy Jones, *Cardwell Shire Story* (Brisbane, 1961), pp. 65, 81. For Bramston's financial activities see G. P. Taylor, "Business and Politics in Queensland 1859–1895," *New Zealand Journal of History*, I (April, 1967), 79–80.

78. Herbert's minute of October 4, 1873, on Bulwer to Kimberley, July 26, 1873, CO 144/40.

79. *DNB*, XXIII (1901–1911), 253.

80. Herbert to Carnarvon, August 20, 1866, PRO 30/6/146, f. 1522.

81. Herbert later stressed the value of a governor in teaching new ministers "the rudiments of government." Minute of January 9, 1873, on Barkly to Kimberley, December 2, 1872, CO 48/462.

82. R. B. Joyce, "Political Portraits: Bowen and Herbert," *passim*. I am very grateful to Professor Joyce of the University of Queensland for supplying me with a copy of this unpublished manuscript.

83. *Ibid.*, pp. 66–73.

84. Herbert to Carnarvon, August 20, 1866, PRO 30/6/146, f. 1520.

could do without "the drunken and unwashed,"[85] and by 1866 he had lost the support of the rapidly increasing working class.[86] One of Queensland's more provincial historians has described this process as follows:

The Governor [Bowen] *knew* men; Herbert did not. The Governor was emphatic, but knew the value of a strategic retreat; Herbert was equally emphatic, but thought it colossal impertinence that the other fellow did not retreat. He loved to ape the Governor, but entirely overlooked the fact that, while the Governor was a representative of the Crown, he was the representative of the people. . . . Subsequently he was more of a success as an official of the Colonial Office than as a Parliamentary leader. . . . We don't import Premiers today. We don't manufacture much, but we can turn them out with comparative ease, and naturally enough the local product is the best suited to our requirements.[87]

Despite Herbert's trouble in Queensland, there was no doubt within the Colonial Office that he had performed well and that the colony's great progress had been largely due to his ability.[88]

Herbert returned to England permanently in 1867.[89] Carnarvon immediately offered him the position of lieutenant governor of Natal,[90] but Herbert preferred the more homely position of assistant secretary of the Board of Trade's railway department.[91] Although he held that position for only two years, John Bright, the president of the Board of Trade, was very impressed with Herbert's work and disappointed when Granville requested permission to offer him the assistant undersecretaryship of the Colonial Office.[92] This offer was a substantial promotion because Granville told Bright privately that Herbert would in all probability succeed Rogers, who was about to

85. Herbert to Graham (Carnarvon's private secretary), February 20, 1867, PRO 30/6/146 f. 1528.
86. Joyce, "Political Portraits," pp. 72–73. Shortly before he left Queensland, Herbert narrowly missed a dunking in the river because of his opposition to a "greenback" plan. N. I. Graham, "Sir George Bowen's Governorship of Queensland: 1859–1867" (unpublished Master's thesis, University of London, 1962), pp. 192–194.
87. C. A. Bernays, *Queensland Politics during Sixty (1859–1919) Years* (Brisbane, 1919), pp. 9–10.
88. Minutes on Bowen to Cardwell, February 13, 1866, CO 234/15.
89. He served as Queensland's financial agent and emigration agent for a short time after his return. Bowen to Carnarvon, November 2, 1866, CO 234/16.
90. Carnarvon to Herbert, private and confidential, December 24, 1866, PRO 30/6/146, ff. 1517–1518.
91. Carnarvon also considered appointing Herbert, his first cousin, legal adviser to the Colonial Office in 1866. Rogers feared, however, that this would prove politically damaging, and Holland received the appointment instead. Knox, *Bulletin of the Institute of Historical Research*, pp. 190–191.
92. Bright to Granville, January 5, 1870, PRO 30/29/52.

retire.[93] Herbert's letter of acceptance suggests that Granville also intimated this likelihood to him. In any event, Herbert was pleased to serve in a department in which he had a "special interest."[94]

Herbert began his duties at the Colonial Office on February 1, 1870. Rogers divided the office's work between Herbert and Henry Holland, the assistant undersecretaries, on both geographical and topical lines. Holland became responsible for the work of the African and Mediterranean department and the North American and Australian department, and Herbert supervised the work of the West Indian and Eastern departments. Holland also dealt with legal questions, while Herbert handled financial matters and appointments. As permanent undersecretary, Rogers continued to supervise all of the office's work, paying particular attention to political, social, ecclesiastical, and military questions.[95] Rogers also gave Herbert, the heir apparent, primary responsibility for proposing new changes in the routine and structure of the office. This somewhat ambiguous relationship continued longer than had been anticipated because of Granville's transfer to the Foreign Office in July, 1870. Lord Kimberley, Granville's successor, persuaded Rogers to stay another year to facilitate the work of the office.[96]

Herbert's contemporaries were more impressed with his administrative skill, tact, and ability to manage men than with his statesmanship or vision.[97] His management of the office won praise from both his superiors and subordinates. M. E. Grant Duff regarded him as the "ideal colleague."[98] Sir Michael Hicks Beach, who was probably the most demanding colonial secretary under whom Herbert served, was very satisfied with his performance.[99] Kimberley expressed similar views; Herbert was "in every sense a gentleman, loyal and straightforward to the back bone." Kimberley believed, however, that Herbert's abilities were "more or less those of tact and the power of manag-

93. Granville to Bright, December 30, 1869, *ibid.*

94. Herbert to Granville, January 6, 1870, PRO 30/29/73, ff. 475-476. The *Times* thought it unfortunate that a man with so much administrative talent should be given a post "of much apparent authority, but no real power." January 8, 1870, p. 9e.

95. Rogers' minute of April 8, 1870, CO 878/5, Vol. 4, No. 24.

96. Kimberley's speech of May 26, 1892, on Herbert's retirement from the Colonial Office, Royal Colonial Institute, *Proceedings*, XXIII (1891-1892), 355.

97. For example see *ibid.*, p. 355; *Times* (London), May 8, 1905, p. 6c; *Spectator*, May 20, 1905, p. 746; *DNB*, XXIII (1901-1911), 253-254; and T. H. S. Escott, ed., *Pillars of the Empire: Sketches of Living Indian and Colonial Statesmen, Celebrities, and Officials* (London, 1879), pp. 115-121.

98. Mountstuart E. Grant Duff, *Notes from a Diary, 1873-1881* (2 vols.; London, 1898), II, 337. Grant Duff was parliamentary undersecretary in 1880-1881.

99. Minute of March 5, 1880, on Treasury to CO, October 27, 1879, CO 323/340.

ing men, than of supreme control where personal action and decision [were] required."[100] Herbert, who was "not as a rule an alarmist,"[101] projected the image of a man always in complete control of his official work. "The hill Difficulty" did not exist for him; he would deal with each of fifty crises in its proper turn "with calmness and entire success."[102]

Herbert's reputation for perfect control in times of pressure and crisis reflected both a strength and a weakness. Although he could calmly dissect each complex colonial question in its proper turn, Herbert had great difficulty in committing himself to any long-range policy. It is very difficult to determine exactly what he thought of the empire, a result not only of an absence of private reflections on this subject but also of his essentially pragmatic nature. He believed that his duty was to present the secretary of state with practical alternatives for the day-to-day problems of administering an empire and not to bother him with theories of empire. Herbert always pressed his point of view strongly, but he was perfectly willing to defer graciously to the wishes of his political superiors.[103] He was thus able to function effectively under a variety of personalities, from the weak-willed Derby to the domineering Hicks Beach.

Possibly because of his experience as Queensland's first premier, Herbert sympathized with colonial demands for a more forward policy of expansion, especially if he feared that British reluctance would damage the imperial connection. Within this general policy, however, he found room for practical reasons to oppose the annexation of Fiji while supporting the acquisition of New Guinea. He regarded Matabeleland but not Swaziland as essential to British interests in

100. Kimberley to Ripon, private, December 23, 1894, Ripon Papers, Add. MS 43526, ff. 259–260.
101. Stanley to Salisbury, December 17, 1885, Salisbury Papers (Christ Church College, Oxford).
102. Grant Duff, *Diary, 1873–1881*, II, 337.
103. Charles Wentworth Dilke was impressed by Herbert's ability and willingness to support any decision of the secretary of state. This made him the "perfect permanent official." Dilke cites how

> on one of these occasions Hicks Beach, who had been Colonial Secretary, gave notice to call attention to salaries of officers on the West Coast of Africa, and I at once sent over to the Colonial Office to tell Herbert that he had done so. Herbert immediately replied that the salaries were low, and the coast unhealthy, and that salaries could hardly be reduced; while on the other hand, when Sir Michael had been Secretary of State, he had not proposed to raise them; but that so soon as we could learn which it was that he intended—i.e. to lower or to raise—he would send me, "in either event, a perfect case."

Stephen Gwynn and Gertrude M. Tuckwell, *The Life of the Rt. Hon. Sir Charles W. Dilke* (2 vols.; London, 1918), I, 288–289.

South Africa. Certainly the Colonial Office did not accept added responsibility eagerly. Instead of viewing new colonies as opportunities to exhibit their administrative skills, Herbert and his colleagues tended to regard them simply as additional burdens. The Colonial Office accepted responsibility for the Straits Settlements (1867)[104] and that "damnosa heriditas,"[105] Cyprus, very reluctantly. When the transfer of Aden from the India Office to the Colonial Office was mooted in 1874, Herbert raised so many objections that the proposal was quickly dropped.[106]

Herbert and Robert Meade, his successor, were quick to criticize the plans and ideas of other men, but they often had difficulty in presenting constructive suggestions of their own. Although the empire meant a great deal to him, Herbert had no clear idea of what form it would take as more and more power passed into the hands of the colonists. He desired essentially a maintenance of the status quo. Certainly he was too pragmatic to embrace with enthusiasm any movement as controversial and sweeping as imperial federation. As one author has remarked, "it would have been alien to his nature to have become deeply involved in controversial issues of this magnitude.[107] The Colonial Office consequently remained hostile to any formal attempt to tighten the political bonds between Britain and its large colonies. In 1868 the Royal Colonial Institute was founded to promote popular understanding of the empire. The Colonial Office, which became suspicious of its activities, refused to assist the new organization by donating unneeded copies of parliamentary papers on colonial topics.[108] Later Herbert and Meade were both highly critical of the activities of the Imperial Federation League. To Herbert, federation was a topic on which there was a great deal to say but very little to be done. He feared that the league would "give themselves and others much trouble without finding a practical solution to the difficulty."[109] The Colonial Office was also frequently reluctant to support less ambitious projects. In 1884 the Prince of Wales requested that the office secure the cooperation of the crown colonies for an exhibition. Herbert's

104. Cowan, *Nineteenth-Century Malaya*, p. 26.
105. Kimberley to Ripon, private, October 4, 1880, Add. MS 43522, f. 257. See also minutes on Treasury to CO, September 14, 1880, CO 323/344.
106. Herbert's minute of August 14, 1874, on FO to CO, July 17, 1874, CO 323/319.
107. David M. L. Farr, *The Colonial Office and Canada, 1867–1887* (Toronto, 1955), p. 44.
108. Minutes on Royal Colonial Institute to CO, March 26, 1872, CO 323/310.
109. Herbert's minute of August 4, 1884, on Labillière to Derby, August 1, 1884, CO 323/359.

only concern was whether the project would cause much trouble for his staff.[110]

"Exceedingly brilliant and capable,"[111] Herbert nevertheless lacked some of Sir Frederic Rogers' warmth and faith in human nature. He did not subscribe to "the doctrine of human perfectibility," but as one of his contemporaries remarked, "if he does not think that everything is for the best in this best of all possible worlds, he perhaps considers that the world is as good as could reasonably be expected, and that matters are on the whole rather better than might have been feared."[112] Although Herbert was very tactful and pleasant, he was somewhat of a cynic,[113] and he tended to think the worst of people and their arguments. This was especially true of his opinion of missionaries, many of whom were "bad and mischievous men."[114] In fact, any critic of Colonial Office policy was in danger of being regarded, at least in private, as an irresponsible troublemaker. Part of the trouble was that few of the senior officials in the office had any real contact with the colonies during this period, and even Herbert, who spent six years in Queensland, showed little appreciation of the aspirations and problems of the "unwashed." Living and working in the cultured atmosphere of London, they must have found the problems facing the colonist rather remote and unreal.

Herbert's success in dealing with colonial secretaries like Carnarvon, Kimberley, Knutsford, and Granville was partially the result of the similarity of their backgrounds. They were all landowners; they all possessed the same type of education; and unlike some of his predecessors, especially Stephen, Herbert was an excellent conversationalist and was reported to be as effective in polite London society as he was in the committee room.[115] An inveterate club joiner, Herbert be-

110. Herbert's minute of March 21, 1884, on Prince of Wales to Derby, March 17, 1884, *ibid.*
111. Margaret Olivier, ed., *Sydney Olivier: Letters and Selected Writings* (London, 1948), p. 32.
112. Escott, *Pillars of the Empire*, p. 121.
113. Sir Algernon West, *Contemporary Portraits: Men of My Day in Public Life* (London, 1920), p. 93; and Escott, *Pillars of the Empire*, pp. 120–121.
114. Herbert's minute of November 6, 1879, on Archbishop of Canterbury to Hicks Beach, November 4, 1879, CO 179/132. For his general views on missionaries in the South Pacific see minutes of June 2, 1871, on O'Connel to Kimberley, March 20, 1871, and of June 26, 1871, on O'Connel to Kimberley, April 15, 1871, CO 234/26. One author has attributed the decline of missionary influence partly to Rogers' retirement in 1871. O. W. Parnaby, *Britain and the Labour Trade in the Southwest Pacific* (Durham, N.C., 1964), p. 79.
115. *Times* (London), May 8, 1905, p. 6c. Herbert was undoubtedly on better personal terms with the heads of other important departments than Stephen. Cell, *British Colonial Administration in the Mid-Nineteenth Century*, p. 12.

longed to the Saville, The Club, the Cosmopolitan, the Athenaeum, and Grillion's, where he was secretary.[116] As a member of these clubs Herbert had the opportunity of meeting socially with the important political statesmen of both parties. The social gap between the higher permanent officials and their parliamentary chiefs was easily bridged in the late nineteenth century.

His tact and pleasing personality also made Herbert a success with the Colonial Office's "special public,"[117] the visiting colonial statesmen and representatives of the various pressure groups. In fact, some people believed that his "good nature and amiability" was almost a handicap. Frequently he left an applicant with "a more favorable impression than he really intended to convey." This could lead to trouble later.[118] Robert Meade, his successor, put it more bluntly: Herbert's chief fault was "his inability to say no & his readiness to make every kind of promise without reflection.[119] Whatever his failings, however, Herbert was sufficiently popular with the colonists to be considered as governor of the Cape or Queensland after his retirement in 1892.[120] He chose to remain in England.

Herbert's relations with the permanent staff of the Colonial Office were also smooth and cordial. His years as premier of Queensland taught him the necessity of devolving responsibility and authority onto subordinate officials.[121] One of his first tasks as permanent undersecretary was to reorganize the Colonial Office on similar lines. It is doubtful whether Rogers could ever have functioned efficiently under the new system.[122] In what appears to have been a conscious effort to encourage initiative on the part of subordinate clerks, Herbert was careful to record his appreciation for a good draft or a thoughtful min-

116. Anonymous, *Saville Club: 1868–1923* (London, 1923), p. 100; R. Welby, ed., *Annals of The Club, 1764–1914* (London, 1914), p. 93; T. H. S. Escott, *King Edward and His Court* (London, 1908), pp. 130–131; Grillion's Club, *Grillion's Club: A Chronicle, 1812–1913* (London, 1914), p. 65; William S. Childe-Pemberton, *Life of C. B. Adderley, 1st Lord Norton, 1814–1905* (London, 1909), pp. 301–302.

117. This term is used in H. E. Dale, *The Higher Civil Service of Great Britain* (London, 1941), p. 181.

118. Kimberley to Ripon, private, December 19, 1894. Add. MS 43526, f. 259.

119. Meade to Ripon, December 19, 1894, Add. MS 43558, f. 24. A. W. L. Hemming, a clerk at the Colonial Office, agreed. *Spectator*, May 20, 1905, p. 746.

120. Meade believed that such an appointment would be greeted with "general applause." Meade to Ripon, December 19, 1894, Add. MS 43558, f. 29. See also Meade to Ripon, September 12, 1893, Add. MS 43557, f. 7, and Rosebery to Ripon, December 22, 1894, Add. MS 43516, f. 189.

121. Joyce, "Political Portraits," pp. 7–8.

122. Already in 1870 Rogers believed that the Colonial Office was "getting into a way of having the same matter considered by too many persons." Minute of October 27, 1870, CO 878/5, Vol. 4, No. 47.

ute. He never disregarded advice simply because it was given by a junior clerk, and he frequently went to considerable trouble to answer a subordinate's criticisms.[123] He did not "suffer fools gladly,"[124] but he rarely criticized clerks in official minutes, and if he did it was usually in terms so mild that the censure was almost lost.[125] In addition, Herbert seldom made work for himself. Instead of writing long minutes on complex questions, he preferred simply to note where he disagreed with the previous minutes, a practice which became more pronounced in the eighties because of the growing volume of work. Despite his various attempts to devolve responsibility, Herbert was wary of moving too fast in this direction; in common with many able men he attempted to do too much work himself. By nature Herbert was attracted to detail, especially honors questions and appointments. His close friend Robert Meade believed that he "revelled" in his position as chancellor of the Order of St. Michael and St. George and in being "the highest authority on all such unimportant matters!"[126] This aspect of Herbert's personality and his struggle to overcome it played an important part in the development of the Colonial Office during his term as permanent undersecretary.

Shortly after Herbert entered the office, the first Earl of Kimberley succeeded Granville as colonial secretary. Although both men belonged to the Whig branch of the Liberal party, their views on the empire were surprisingly different. Kimberley, despite his deep suspicion of further British expansion,[127] showed more sympathy than either Gladstone or Granville with colonial demands and was willing to grant concessions to the colonists. He sanctioned on his own authority the annexation of the South African diamond fields in 1871, and he looked forward to an eventual union of the Dutch republics and the British colonies under the British flag.[128] Kimberley also favored

123. For two good examples see minutes on Barkly to Carnarvon, December 3, 1874, CO 48/470; and minutes on H. Robinson to Knutsford, December 19, 1888, CO 417/24. See also Hall, The Colonial Office, pp. 22–23.

124. W. R. Malcolm's letter in the Spectator, May 13, 1905, p. 711.

125. On occasion he could be highly critical of the work of a department. Minutes on Berkeley to Kimberley, July 24, 1880, CO 152/139.

126. Meade to Ripon, September 6, 1894, Add. MS 43557, f. 203.

127. He believed that the acquisition of territory was simply "multiplying the points open to attack." Hall, The Colonial Office, p. 184. One of the chief reasons for France's weakness was, in his opinion, its Algerian and African empire. He hoped that no British government would "ever be mad enough to embark on so extravagant an enterprise" as the establishment of a West African empire. Minute of May 28, 1873, on War Office to CO, May 22, 1873, CO 96/107.

128. Kimberley to Gladstone, December 10, 1871, Add. MS 44224, ff. 221–224; Kimberley to Gladstone, October 22, 1871, ibid., ff. 212–217. He failed to see any alternative to

giving those colonies with responsible government as much power as possible. For example, although he believed that Australia and Canada would eventually become independent states, he declined to take any action which would result in an angry separation. On the question of colonial tariffs, Kimberley, a strong free trader, understood the Australian desire to promote intercolonial trade at Britain's expense.[129] Unlike Gladstone, who believed that colonial tariffs illustrated "the *reductio ad absurdum* of the colonial connection,"[130] he deprecated any attempt to coerce the self-governing colonies.[131]

Kimberley's personality differed greatly from Granville's. Whereas Granville exuded agreeableness and social charm, Kimberley presented "a somewhat hard and incisive manner."[132] Unlike Carnarvon and later Joseph Chamberlain, he did not make himself easily available to colonial visitors. He would not have been a success with the Colonial Office's "special public" in any event. By his own admission he was a very poor public speaker; his domination of any conversation and his rapid speech were the subjects of numerous jokes and complaints.[133] Kimberley frequently gave the superficial observer the impression of

---

British control over the Fiji Islands. He believed that it was "very natural that the Australians should wish to see the British flag flying in the Fijis." Kimberley to Gladstone, July 26, 1871, *ibid.*, ff. 193–194; Drus, *Transactions of the Royal Historical Society*, pp. 98–104. Although he hesitated at becoming involved in Malay politics, Kimberley also believed that it would be "a serious matter if any other European Power were to obtain a footing on the Peninsula." Kimberley to Gladstone, September 10, 1873, Add. MS 44225, f. 103; Cowan, *Nineteenth Century Malaya*, pp. 163–166.

129. Kimberley to Gladstone, May 15, 1871, Add. MS 44224, ff. 132–133.
130. Gladstone to Kimberley, copy, May 16, 1871, Add. MS 44540, f. 31.
131. Kimberley to Gladstone, December 26, 1871, Add. MS 44224, ff. 234–238.
Whenever any difficulty arises with foreign nations from our colonial possessions, or any heavy burden is laid upon the British taxpayer for colonial reasons, the question will be asked what advantage does England derive from her colonies, & it will be very difficult as regards colonies which impose heavy protective duties on British goods to show that any such advantage exists—still where as in the case of this [Australian Colonies Duties'] bill, it is clear that the colonial governments will persist in their agitation against the Imperial policy I think it is far better to give way. The question is not vital. . . . Our interests as a rule clash so little on account of their immense distance from England, that unless the Home Government is very wrong headed collisions may be avoided. For this reason I think the connexion may be maintained in time of peace—that is a connexion which is based on absolute independence of the colonies in all their local affairs. Any attempt to draw the connexion tighter would I believe soon result in separation—and notwithstanding the frothy talk occasionally indulged in on platforms by some of our public men I am not acquainted with any responsible statesman in this country who thinks otherwise.
Kimberley, *Journal*, May 24, 1873, pp. 38–39.
132. Godley, *Reminiscences*, p. 159.
133. Rogers mentions having talks "from" Kimberley. Rogers to Rev. E. Rogers, February 15, 1873, in Marindin, ed., *Letters of Blachford*, p. 347. See also Godley, *Reminiscences*, p. 158; and Sir James Rennell Rodd, *Social and Diplomatic Memories, 1884–1893* (London, 1922), p. 348.

having no real depth or ability. Sir Charles Dilke, who early in his career described Kimberley as a "chattering idiot," later changed his assessment. "He *talks* like a chattering idiot, but is a wise man."[134]

Kimberley was actually a very painstaking and thorough administrator. Arthur Godley, who worked under many secretaries of state during his long career at the India Office, placed his administrative ability only slightly lower than Gladstone's; after these two men there was a "perceptible interval."[135] Carnarvon's description of Kimberley as "an excellent man of business" was typical.[136] Although he was undoubtedly the hardest working colonial secretary during the seventies and eighties, Kimberley too often indulged his love of detail. He wanted to be responsible, actually as well as theoretically, for every decision reached.[137] Even after reaching a decision on a question Kimberley was not finished. He carefully scrutinized all important draft dispatches, correcting form as well as content. Few drafts were passed without alteration; many were almost completely rewritten. He also read many of the fair copies before signing them, and occasional complaints about the quality of the copying and the spelling attest to the thoroughness of his proofreading.

Kimberley's relations with the permanent staff of the Colonial Office were friendly, but he could be a hard and demanding master if the work was not done properly. Delays in circulating papers were frequently questioned, and he often complained of incorrect spelling, poor indexing, and sloppy drafting of dispatches.[138] Nevertheless, he had a high regard for the work of his staff, and his criticisms were frequently prefaced with praise.[139] It was clear that his criticism was

134. Dilke's Diary, August 30, 1881, Dilke Papers, Add. MS 43924, f. 59. Childers complained in a cabinet discussion on the Suakin railway in 1885 that "Kimberley has spoken nineteen times & won't let me speak *once*." Robert Rhodes James, *Rosebery: A Biography of Archibald Philip, Fifth Earl of Rosebery* (London, 1963), p. 166.

135. Godley, *Reminiscences*, p. 157.

136. Carnarvon to Sir Richard Cross (Home Secretary, 1874–1880), March 10, 1874, Cross Papers, Add. MS 51268; John Morley, *Recollections* (2 vols.; New York, 1917), II, 247.

137. When Kimberley moved to the India Office in December, 1882, he complained of the additional control imposed on him by the Board of Directors. He contrasted that system unfavorably with the Colonial Office. Kimberley to Ripon, private, March 16, 1883, Add. MS 43523, ff. 66–67.

138. Office Minutes, 878/5 and 878/6, *passim*. He was even more critical of the manner in which the work of the Home Office, Foreign Office, and Treasury was conducted. Kimberley, *Journal*, pp. 30, 34, 39.

139. For example, one minute complaining of the delay of certain West African papers began, "I have so much reason to be satisfied with the work of the office that I much regret that I am compelled . . . [to complain]." Minute of February 16, 1873, on McArthur's question for February 17, 1873, CO 96/104.

designed to make a good office even better. Of all the colonial secretaries during this period Kimberley was the most interested in civil service reform. The further reorganization of the office in 1872 was largely a result of his demands. This reorganization was designed to give the established clerks more responsibility for the work of the office. Unfortunately Kimberley was never entirely comfortable under this new system, and he continued to spend too much time deciding questions of detail.[140] He recognized the problems facing the Colonial Office in 1870 and proposed solutions to them, but unfortunately his personality and outdated ideas on the duties of the secretary of state prevented him from utilizing fully the human resources at his command.

Herbert, Kimberley, and Rogers were immediately confronted by the question of civil service reform. Prompted both by pressure from the Treasury and by their own desire to eliminate inefficiency, they conducted several new inquiries into the major administrative problems facing the Colonial Office. The first question to decide was how the Order in Council of June 4, 1870, could best be adapted to meet the peculiar requirements of the Colonial Office. Although Granville had agreed to recruitment by open competition in principle, it was necessary to frame a suitable examination and to decide which positions were to be filled in this manner. Once this had been done they then had to decide if the introduction of open competition necessitated any further changes in the organization of the office.

Shortly after Kimberley's appointment as secretary of state, the Civil Service Commission asked the Colonial Office to suggest revisions in the civil service entrance examinations.[141] Rogers, Herbert, and Kimberley each had strong, and rather different, opinions concerning the best subjects for examination. Rogers argued that the Colonial Office needed men who combined social status with ability and intellect. He therefore believed that either mathematics or the classics should be a compulsory examination subject. These were the disciplines "the majority of those whom we want to get, whether as a matter of station or as a matter of intellect are sure to have committed themselves, and in which therefore, they can be most fairly measured against each other." He also wanted to reduce the number of marks

---

140. He should certainly not have read a 238-page report on a suspension case simply because Robert Meade was too busy. Hall, *The Colonial Office*, p. 60.

141. CSC to CO, July 9, 1870, CO 323/301.

awarded for competence in the natural sciences. He feared that the existing examination which gave almost as many marks to natural science as to the classics would enable a first-class second-rate man to pass almost as high as a first-class first-rate man.[142] Herbert and Kimberley were both critical of this emphasis on the classics and mathematics. Herbert, who was an amateur naturalist, believed that the natural sciences should be rated highly; unlike history or literature, "the great strongholds of the *cram*," they offered a truer test of a man's ability and the depth of his education.[143] Kimberley argued that the examination should stress those subjects which would be of practical value to the new clerk, and for this reason he urged that jurisprudence and political economy be given more weight.[144] Kimberley recognized, however, that the British educational system, under which the classics were "unduly exalted," made his ideas difficult to implement. As long as the universities continued to neglect the study of modern languages, including English, the civil service would have to accommodate them. He therefore accepted an examination which emphasized the classics and mathematics, but for reasons different from those of Rogers.[145]

All three men agreed that it was essential for clerks to be able to express themselves clearly and concisely in minutes, and they urged that the examination rate précis writing highly.[146] They also believed that the number of subjects that a candidate could be examined on should be limited. They did not want a man with a superficial knowledge of several subjects to triumph over someone who possessed real capacity and depth of understanding in a more limited area of study.[147]

The Colonial Office also had to decide whether or not to participate in joint examinations with other departments. Again there was disagreement. Herbert believed that the office should continue to hold separate competitions. If the Colonial Office offered its clerks opportunities for overseas colonial service and "a preferable clerkship at the same rate of pay," he felt that it would continue to attract the best of the competitive market. If, however, the Colonial Office joined with

142. Rogers' minute of July, 1870, on CSC to CO, July 9, 1870, *ibid*.
143. Herbert's minute of July 23, 1870, on *ibid*.
144. Kimberley's minute of July 26, 1870, on *ibid*.
145. Kimberley's minute of August 11, 1870, on *ibid*.
146. The précis gave some test of "clearminded hardheadedness & natural method of mind, wh. is what we want particularly." Rogers' minute of July, 1870, on *ibid*.
147. CO to CSC, August 17, 1870, CO 323/301. Although this letter urged that précis writing be included, more marks be given to political economy and jurisprudence, and fewer marks be given to natural science, the Colonial Office did not propose a definitive table of marks.

such offices as the Registry of Seamen and the London Gazette Office in a joint competition, it might be left with "the twentieth man in a successful batch of twenty."[148] Kimberley and Rogers disagreed with Herbert. Kimberley argued that it would be difficult, if not impossible, to persuade able men to compete in departmental examinations filling only one or two positions. Joint competitions held at regular intervals would also be a great convenience.[149] Rogers agreed; the Colonial Office had no reason to fear a joint examination unless its inducements were less desirable than those of other departments. If the Colonial Office received "the leavings of *less important* offices," the correct policy would be to "cry out for such improvements as will put us in our right place relative to the work we do."[150] These arguments prevailed, and the Colonial Office agreed to hold joint competitions with the Treasury, the secretaries of state's offices, the Admiralty, the Council Office, and the Board of Trade.[151]

There was little debate concerning the positions which should be exempted from open competition. Herbert, Rogers, and Kimberley all agreed that the permanent undersecretary, the parliamentary undersecretary, the assistant undersecretaries, the private secretaries, and the accountant should not be required to take either a literacy or a health examination.[152]

The Order in Council of June 4, 1870, established two types of examinations. Regulation I examinations were designed to recruit university graduates for the higher posts in the civil service; Regulation II examinations were aimed at filling the lower positions.[153] Multiple exams made it possible to recruit men with different educational qualifications and to introduce into the civil service a meaningful division of labor, something which Trevelyan and Northcote had recommended almost twenty years earlier. Clerks with high educational attainments could be employed entirely on intellectual work, and those clerks with less formal education and ability could be used

148. Herbert's minute of July 23, 1870, on CSC to CO, July 9, 1870, CO 323/301. Herbert's fears proved to be unfounded, and it is difficult to see why they were ever entertained if the Colonial Office was such an attractive place in which to work. Actually, the Treasury and the Colonial Office in later years invariably obtained the top candidates.

149. Kimberley's minute of August 5, 1870, on *ibid.*

150. Rogers' minute of August 9, 1870, on CSC to CO, July 9, 1870, CO 323/301.

151. CO to CSC, August 17, 1870, *ibid.*

152. Minutes on Treasury to CO, August 4, 1870, *ibid.*

153. A copy of the Order in Council of June 4, 1870, and the Civil Service Commission's minute on it are enclosed in CSC to CO, July 9, 1870, *ibid.*

only for mechanical work such as indexing and copying. Recruitment by open competition and the elimination of political favoritism also made it possible to introduce promotion by merit. The Order in Council of June 4, 1870, did much more than introduce open competition; it made further departmental reform possible, and to a great extent necessary.

The Treasury was the first department of state to introduce a division of labor between two distinct classes of competitive clerks. The Treasury reduced the number of its upper-division clerks, giving them higher pay and more responsible work. All of the mechanical work was assigned to lower-division clerks. Charles Cox, a senior clerk at the Colonial Office, believed that the Treasury's reorganization would place the Colonial Office at a disadvantage in recruiting competent clerks. Men with university degrees would naturally prefer to compete for positions at the Treasury, where the pay was much higher and where the work was more demanding.[154] For that reason Cox proposed a reorganization of the Colonial Office on Treasury principles. He suggested replacing the five senior clerks, eight assistant clerks, and thirteen junior clerks with one principal and two first-class clerks, six second-class clerks, and ten third-class clerks. By eliminating seven positions the Colonial Office could pay its remaining clerks a higher salary and compete with the Treasury for the new university-trained clerks. The higher salaries would also enable the colonial secretary to base promotions within the office entirely on merit.[155]

Herbert was interested in the Treasury's innovations, and he requested that William Robinson, the senior clerk of the general department, study Cox's minute and submit his own views on reorganization. Robinson's report was highly critical of Cox's proposals. In common with many of the older clerks he believed that copying and indexing provided a good training for junior clerks, and he regarded the Treasury's salaries as "unnecessarily high." Compared with the opportunities provided in law, medicine, and the church, a salary of £100 rising by £20 a year to £450 was sufficient for new members in the Colonial Office. Although Robinson did recommend a reduction in the size and cost of the Colonial Office, he did not provide any additional at-

154. A new second-class Treasury clerk began at £250 and rose by annual increments of £20 to £600. The initial salary at the Colonial Office was still only £100 a year. Cox's minute of June 29, 1870, CO 537/22.
155. Cox's minute of June 29, 1870, *ibid.*

tractions for young men considering a career in the civil service.[156] He failed to see that if the number of upper-division clerks was reduced then they would no longer have time to assist with the copying and indexing. They would have to be given more responsible work and thereby earn a higher salary.

The debate between Cox and Robinson in the summer of 1870 failed to produce any specific plan for reorganization. The Treasury, which naturally considered its own constitution a good model to follow, continued to press the Colonial Office,[157] but Herbert and Rogers refused to be hurried. They believed that "long and careful consideration" was necessary before a final decision could be reached. Kimberley, who was new to the office, agreed, but he regarded the Treasury's suggestions as sound.[158]

Kimberley's commitment to reform was greatly strengthened by the admittedly deplorable condition of the copying department. William Robinson reported that the size and cost of this department had increased more rapidly than the volume of its work. Moreover, the growth of the copying department had not been accompanied by any reduction in the number of junior clerks; instead the juniors, avoiding as much copying as possible, did little or nothing. Robinson, who was undoubtedly exaggerating the problem, felt that this situation demanded correction. The juniors, despite their educational qualifications, should be required to perform much of the Colonial Office's mechanical work. The Foreign Office required its new clerks to copy, and many able men "passed unhurt through this disagreeable process." In fact, Robinson doubted whether new clerks could become familiar with the details of their departments in any other way.[159]

The expense of the copying department appalled Kimberley. "It would be most extravagant policy," he argued, "to pay for copyists, if there is no corresponding reduction of skilled clerks." He also opposed wasting the talents of the new junior clerks by employing them on mechanical duties. "I cannot concur with [Mr. Robinson] in thinking that mechanical work tends to fit a man for more important business. I think on the contrary that it has a deadening effect &

156. Robinson's minute of July, 1870, *ibid.*
157. Treasury to CO, August 30, 1870, CO 323/301.
158. Minutes on Treasury to CO, August 30, 1870, CO 323/301.
159. Robinson's minute of October 7, 1870, CO 537/22. He had expressed similar views earlier in the year. See his minute of February 10, 1870, *ibid.*

that every effort should be made to avoid employing those who are destined for responsible offices in such work."[160] It was better to train a junior by "exercising his mind."[161] The desire to promote both economy and efficiency in his department led Kimberley to support the adoption of the Treasury reforms. He, not Rogers, who was about to retire, or Herbert, who seemed unable to come to a decision without further study, was the primary force behind the subsequent reorganization.[162]

In early 1871 the Colonial Office inquired whether the Treasury would facilitate its reorganization by dealing graciously with clerks who might choose to retire.[163] The Treasury agreed that if the number of Colonial Office clerks was reduced it would consider an addition to the length of actual service in computing pensions for clerks who had served more than thirty years.[164] Herbert was very gratified by this response. In his opinion, it cleared the way for a detailed consideration of the reorganization of the Colonial Office.[165]

In private discussions, Treasury officials had already urged Herbert to adopt a plan of reorganization similar to their own. They hoped that this would encourage similar reforms in other offices.[166] Being assured of the Treasury's cooperation, Herbert prepared a long memorandum on office reform, which was similar to Cox's minute of June, 1870.[167] The basic premise of Herbert's memorandum was that the Colonial Office had too many highly educated clerks relative to the amount of its intellectual work. Assigning them to routine work was not the solution, and he therefore proposed reducing the number of upper-division clerks from twenty-five to thirteen. Because of the smaller staff he believed that the number of geographical departments would have to be reduced from four to two. Each geographical department would contain one principal clerk, two first-class clerks, and two

160. Kimberley's minute of November 16, 1870, on Robinson's minute of October 7, 1870, CO 537/22.
161. Kimberley's marginal comments of November 16, 1870, on Robinson's minute of October 7, 1870, *ibid.*
162. It is interesting to compare Kimberley's interest in these affairs to Joseph Chamberlain's view in 1895 that the permanent officials, "who know the inner workings of the office," must decide on how the office was to be staffed and organized. Chamberlain's minute of May 19, 1895, on draft of CO to Treasury, May 22, 1895, CO 323/407.
163. CO to Treasury, February, 4, 1871, CO 323/305.
164. Treasury to CO, February 14, 1871, *ibid.*
165. Herbert's minute of February 15, 1871, *ibid.*
166. Herbert's undated notation on his memo of February 14, 1871, CO 537/22. Lowe appears to have taken a personal interest in the organization of the Colonial Office.
167. Herbert's memo of February 14, 1871, CO 537/22.

second-class clerks. The general department needed only one clerk from each class.[168] Herbert also proposed to set the initial salaries of the second-class (junior) clerks at £250 a year. This was essential if the Colonial Office was to compete on an equal footing with the Treasury for the new university-trained clerks and to rank as a "first class office."[169] The second-class clerks would earn their higher salaries by minuting dispatches, preparing drafts and précis, and supervising the work of the supplementary (lower-division) clerks attached to each department. Herbert believed that his plan of reorganization would not only improve the efficiency of the office but would also save approximately £4,850 a year.[170]

During the long discussion that followed, first among the senior officials in the Colonial Office and then between the Colonial Office and the Treasury, the basic principles of Herbert's plan of reorganization were never seriously challenged. The primary topics of debate were the size of the office, the best way to employ the several classes of clerks, and the way in which the new system was to be introduced. Although matters of detail, the manner in which these questions were resolved frequently had considerable importance to the future structure of the Colonial Office. Rogers, although permanent undersecretary until May, 1871, took little part in these discussions, permitting Herbert and Henry Holland to arrange the details.

The first important question to decide was the number and size of geographical departments in the Colonial Office. Prior to the reorganization of 1872, there were four geographical departments, each employing at least four upper-division clerks. These clerks frequently had little to do because of the infrequent and irregular mail deliveries,[171] but it was still very difficult to reduce the size of the departments. Smaller departments had difficulty functioning when the work was heavy or when a part of the staff was absent on leave, on colonial service, or because of illness. Too small a department was simply not

168. These three classes were to replace the old senior, assistant, and junior clerks. This new classification was patterned on the Treasury system.

169. Herbert's minute of February 14, 1871, CO 537/22. The second-class clerks were to rise by annual increments of £20 to £500. The recommended pay for the other two classes was somewhat lower than in the Treasury.

170. *Ibid.* He also made several minor recommendations including the abolition of special pay to the chief clerk and the increase of the senior assistant undersecretary's salary from £1,200 to £1,500.

171. Barrow's minute of February 20, 1869, CO 537/22; Hamilton, *Nineteenth Century and After*, p. 600.

flexible enough to be efficient. In 1871 everyone recognized that the proposed reduction in the number of clerks would make the maintenance of four geographical departments impossible. Either they would have to be consolidated or the entire principle of geographical division of work would have to be abolished. Herbert chose the first alternative, proposing the creation of two large geographical departments with five clerks each. This would afford the necessary flexibility, and it would enable the work, which came in cycles, to be more evenly distributed.[172] Henry Holland disagreed and pointed out the obvious disadvantage of Herbert's plan. If there were only two geographical departments, the clerks would have to deal with many more colonies and lose the detailed knowledge necessary for the formation of correct policies. Holland proposed the retention of three geographical departments,[173] a plan which Herbert felt had the fatal disadvantage of requiring a larger number of clerks. The Treasury expected a reduction in the size and cost of the Colonial Office.

Another possible solution was simply the abolition of geographical departments. Instead, the work would be arranged "with reference to the arrival & departure of Mails, so as to secure, as far as possible, a constant supply of work for every Clerk."[174] This plan solved the problems created by the intermittent mail deliveries, but it would have made it difficult to maintain continuity of policy and to fix responsibility for decisions. In addition, the proposal would never have satisfied the senior clerks, who were used to supervising departments with clearly defined duties and responsibilities. There was some support, however, for a variation of this plan. Herbert, Holland, and Robert Meade, a newly appointed assistant undersecretary, considered employing one unattached principal (senior) clerk. He and an assistant would be responsible for a few colonies, but their primary duty would be to handle complex questions requiring considerable study and compression. It was also suggested that some of the smaller colonies, such as Heligoland, St. Helena, and the Falkland Islands, could also be assigned to first-class (assistant) clerks. This would relieve the pressure on the principal clerks who supervised the geographical depart-

172. Herbert's minute of February 14, 1871, CO 537/22.
173. Holland's minute of March 11, 1871, *ibid.* It is interesting to note that Holland chose to eliminate the African and Mediterranean department. This shows how little the Colonial Office foresaw the tremendous increase in African work in the seventies. By the time Herbert retired in 1892 there were two African departments.
174. Holland's minute of June 24, 1871, *ibid.*

ments.[175] These proposals, which in reality involved the revival of the office of précis writer, received no support from the principal clerks. Charles Cox feared that the unattached principal clerk would remove many important questions from the knowledge and control of the departmental heads. Questions which required considerable study could be assigned to first-class clerks under the supervision of the principal clerks.[176] Partly because of the Colonial Office's unhappy experiences with Strachey, the old précis writer,[177] this plan was dropped.

The result was a victory for the principle of geographical departments. The reorganization proposals which the Colonial Office submitted to the Treasury for approval on March 8, 1872, provided for the establishment of two large geographical departments and a smaller general department. The number of upper-division clerks filling these departments was to be reduced from twenty-six to eighteen, a somewhat smaller reduction than Herbert had first proposed. The secretary of state retained, however, the power to make any departmental adjustments he thought necessary.[178]

The continued employment of second-class (junior) clerks as private secretaries was also discussed. Prior to this time four juniors had been appointed to these positions and had received an additional £150 a year. In 1871 they cost the Colonial Office £1,480, a cost which Herbert believed was excessive. He proposed that private secretaries be drawn from outside the civil service and receive a straight salary of £200 a a year. This would reduce by four the number of highly paid second-class clerks, and it would prevent the interruption of the "official education" of the remaining clerks.[179] Holland, Meade, and most of the senior clerks had serious reservations about Herbert's plan. They argued that it was convenient for departmental heads to deal with private secretaries who were familiar with office routine. Private secretaries who were drawn from within the office could also be used on departmental work in an emergency.[180] Herbert, who was primarily

175. *Ibid.*
176. Cox's minute of December 19, 1871, CO 537/22. William Dealtry stressed the necessity of keeping the junior members of each department subordinate to their chiefs. If all letters and dispatches of any importance were not passed through the principal clerk his knowledge would be "inconveniently imperfect." Dealtry's minute of December 27, 1871, *ibid.*
177. Meade's marginal comments on Cox's minute of December 19, 1871, *ibid.*
178. CO to Treasury, March 8, 1872, *ibid.*
179. Herbert's minute of February 14, 1871, *ibid.*
180. Holland's minute of March 11, 1871, and Cox's minute of December 19, 1871, *ibid.*

concerned with the increasing costs of the Colonial Office's reorganization, remained adamant. He continued to support his own position, but he left the final decision to the secretary of state.[181] Kimberley sought a compromise, and the final proposals submitted to the Treasury provided for the appointment of only three second-class clerks as private secretaries. They were not, however, to receive any additional remuneration.[182]

The Colonial Office's final recommendations concerning salaries did not differ greatly from those proposed by Herbert in his minute of February 14, 1871. Herbert desired to raise the pay of everyone as much as possible, but he was mainly interested in improving the financial prospects of the new second-class clerks. He recommended that they receive salaries identical to those offered at the Treasury, £250 a year, rising by annual increments of £20 to £600. Herbert did not believe, however, that the Colonial Office's first-class and principal clerks required the high salaries paid to these ranks by the Treasury.[183] His object was not to encourage the older clerks to remain at the Colonial Office but to attract a new and abler class of clerks who could assume more responsibility.

One of the greatest obstacles to reorganizing the Colonial Office in 1872 was persuading some of the older clerks to retire. After all, no open competition clerks could be appointed to the office until the number of upper-division clerks was reduced from twenty-six to eighteen. The new system could not be put into operation until enough money had been saved by retirements to pay the higher salaries of the remaining clerks, and Herbert feared that the transitional period might last several years.[184] A sufficient sum would be saved if two senior clerks, presumably Henry Taylor and George Barrow, could be persuaded to retire.[185] Despite his references to the valuable services of the senior clerks, "whose retirement would in each case be a great disadvantage and source of weakness to the office,"[186] Herbert obviously hoped that some of them would take advantage of the Treasury's liberal retirement allowances. He even instructed the accountant to calculate the pension each clerk would receive if he chose to

181. Herbert's minute of January 13, 1872, *ibid.*
182. CO to Treasury, March 8, 1872, *ibid.*
183. *Ibid.*
184. Herbert's minute of January 13, 1872, CO 537/22.
185. Herbert's minute of July 3, 1872, on Treasury to CO, June 22, 1872, CO 323/309.
186. Herbert's minute of January 13, 1872, CO 537/22.

retire to facilitate reorganization.[187] Eventually Taylor and Barrow did accept the special allowances, retiring on September 30, 1872, the day the new system was brought into operation.

There are numerous indications that the senior clerks did not support the proposed changes. They continued to believe that the old system of examining nominated candidates was preferable to open competition, and despite Herbert's attempts to enlist their support and assistance, the minutes of the senior clerks show that they had little or no interest in reorganization. Certainly, they contributed nothing to the discussion. Taylor and Barrow had no important recommendations to make.[188] William Robinson added nothing to his earlier condemnation of the scheme.[189] Charles Cox and William Dealtry were primarily concerned with protecting their claims to pay as chief clerk.[190] These five men were really the last of the Colonial Office's old guard. By May, 1871, Elliot, Strachey, Gordon Gairdner, and Rogers had already retired. Barrow and Taylor retired in 1872, and Dealtry followed soon afterward. Robinson accepted a colonial governorship, leaving only Charles Cox to serve for any great length of time under the new system. As a result, the important positions in the Colonial Office in the seventies and eighties were held primarily by men who had entered the office by means of limited competition between 1855 and 1871.[191] The secretariat of the Colonial Office also continued to receive a rapid infusion of new blood in the early seventies. The newest addition was Robert Henry Meade, who was appointed assistant undersecretary when Herbert replaced Rogers as permanent undersecretary in May, 1871.

Meade secured his appointment to the Colonial Office in a manner much different from Herbert's. Both men had influential contacts, but Herbert had made a reputation before he entered the civil service. Meade's reputation was built after his appointment, and his career illustrates a second common method of entering the higher civil service in the late nineteenth century. Meade, whose landholdings were

187. Herbert's minute of July 3, 1872, on Treasury to CO, June 22, 1872, CO 323/309. Herbert hinted that if there were not enough voluntary retirements the Treasury's suggestion of "enforcing whatever retirements may be judged to be at once necessary" might be considered.
188. Taylor to Herbert, December 8, 1871, CO 537/22.
189. Robinson's minute of July, 1870, ibid.
190. Minutes by Dealtry of December 27, 1871 and Cox of December 19, 1871, ibid.
191. The first open competition clerks did not enter the Colonial Office until 1877. They did not permeate the positions of authority until the nineties.

the envy of the other permanent Colonial Office officials,[192] was the second son of the third Earl of Clanwilliam. In 1859, after attending Eton and Exeter College, Oxford, he was appointed a junior clerk in the aristocratic Foreign Office. He was not unduly burdened with the usual mechanical tasks, however: during his first three years at the Foreign Office he accompanied Lord Dufferin, Earl Russell, the Prince of Wales, and Lord Granville on various foreign tours and missions.[193] He also served for a short time as a groom of the bedchamber to the Prince of Wales.[194] When Granville became colonial secretary in 1868 Meade accompanied him as his private secretary. Meade, who was now over thirty and anxious to receive a permanent position, attempted to learn as much as possible about the Colonial Office's work, hoping to qualify for a position in the secretariat. In January, 1870, Granville considered appointing him assistant undersecretary, but he selected Herbert instead. Meade was promised the next vacancy, and Kimberley, who felt bound to honor Granville's promise, gave him this position in May, 1871.[195]

Meade's personality was similar to Granville's, helping to explain the close bond between the two men.[196] He was very well liked by the office staff. Algernon West explained that his charm and softly modulated voice "enabled him to speak his mind without giving offense."[197] His bearing and social graces, however, gave the impression of "aristocratic indifference," and despite the fact that he worked hard at his job, one of his friends believed that he was "naturally indolent."[198] Although he was less addicted to London society than Herbert, his social contacts, especially among Liberal politicians, were

192. Herbert's minute of January 16, 1878, on Bowen to Carnarvon, November 28, 1877, CO 309/116.

193. *DNB*, XXII (Supplement), 1031.

194. Sidney Lee, *King Edward VII: A Biography* (2 vols.; New York, 1925), I, 154.

195. Kimberley to Gladstone, March 14, 1871, Add. MS 44224, ff. 111–113. Gladstone had recommended one of his own private secretaries for the post, but he agreed to Meade's appointment. Gladstone to Kimberley, copy, March 15, 1871, Add. MS 44539, f. 178. The practice of rewarding private secretaries with appointments to the civil service was subjected to increasing public criticism. Between 1869 and 1890 twenty-one private secretaries were appointed to high administrative posts, seventeen of whom carried salaries of over £1,000 a year. Cohen, *British Civil Service*, p. 137. See also R. K. Kelsall, *Higher Civil Servants in Britain from 1870 to the Present Day* (London, 1955), pp. 106–107.

196. West, *Recollections*, I, 336. Meade was named executor of Granville's will in 1891, not a happy task, as Granville was greatly in debt at the time of his death. Meade to Gladstone, October 12, 1891, Add. MS 44513, f. 208.

197. Horace G. Hutchinson. ed., *Private Diaries of the Rt. Hon. Sir Algernon West* (London, 1922), p. 343.

198. West, *Recollections*, I, 336–337.

excellent. He frequently dined with Granville, Gladstone, and Rosebery. To these men, as well as to the "knot of official Liberals who formed a little coterie in the service of the Crown from about 1870 to 1890,"[199] he was affectionately known as "Bobsy."[200]

Meade, who did not possess any legal training, supervised much of the Colonial Office's general work. He was especially interested in African affairs[201] and questions involving imperial defense,[202] and after 1872 he was primarily responsible for the organization and routine of the office. Of all the members of the secretariat Meade was the most willing to delegate authority and responsibility to the clerks. Later, during his term as permanent undersecretary (1892–1896) office discipline and routine were relaxed, sometimes more than even he desired.[203] Perhaps because of the casual and relaxed attitude he displayed toward his work, Meade's reputation as an administrator was never as high as Herbert's. When Herbert announced his retirement in December, 1891, Lord Knutsford promoted Meade partly because he "could not properly be passed over" and because the Colonial Office had promised the Treasury, for financial reasons, not to appoint anyone from outside of the office.[204] It has also been suggested that his relations with the aggressive and domineering Chamberlain could not have been very smooth.[205]

Meade's appointment in 1871 was not received with complete approbation by the Colonial Office clerks. In the case of Henry Taylor, the appointment of Meade and the approaching reorganization combined to produce bitterness and a feeling that he had outlived his usefulness. Taylor, who had declined the permanent undersecretaryship in 1847, believed that Meade's position should have gone to a member of the department. Richard Eben, who had done excellent work in the West Indian department, would have been a good

199. *DNB*, XXII (Supplement), 1031. Meade's Liberalism was the subject of frequent jokes by the conservative members of the Colonial Office. See Malcolm's minute of January 15, 1878, and Herbert's minute of January 16, 1878, on Bowen to Carnarvon, November 28, 1877, CO 309/116.

200. Granville to Rosebery, April, 1886, PRO 30/29/213; Sanderson to Hervey, October 17, 1884, PRO 30/29/120; West, *Recollections*, I, 336–337.

201. Derby to Granville, October 16, 1884, PRO 30/29/120.

202. Herbert's minute of October 29, 1885, on War Office to CO, October 28, 1885, CO 323/362.

203. Meade to Ripon, private, October 11, 1892, Add. MS 43556, ff. 75–78; Meade to Ripon, private, October 6, 1894, Add. MS 43558, f. 6.

204. Knutsford to Salisbury, December 2, 1891, Salisbury Papers.

205. *Times* (London), January 10, 1898, p. 9f; R. B. Pugh, "The Colonial Office, 1801–1925," *The Cambridge History of the British Empire*, ed. E. A. Benians *et al.* (9 vols. in 8; Cambridge, 1929–1959), III, 745.

choice.[206] In addition, Herbert, Holland, and Meade were not only new to the office, but they were young, ambitious, and determined to run the Colonial Office along somewhat different lines. Taylor, who worked at home, was accustomed to having considerable freedom in dealing with subjects which interested him, such as penal code reform and hospital and prison administration, but by 1872 this freedom was being undermined.

There are now in full activity one permanent Under-Secretary and two Assistant Under-Secretaries,—all three decidedly competent and able men, all somewhat recently appointed, and each naturally desirous to make his efficiency felt and to have an opinion of his own on every question. This lays the Secretary of State open to some of the evils which are said to attend a multitude of councillors. I think it is but rarely that the present Secretary of State has been the better for my advice.[207]

Kimberley suggested that Taylor continue to handle certain subjects after his retirement. Although he eventually did offer his advice,[208] at the time of his retirement he did not believe that it would be wanted or needed.[209] The office was already well staffed: "The Under Secretary and the Assistant Undersecretaries are all three able and industrious, and there are some clerks who are not less so."[210]

Sir Frederic Rogers' resignation in 1871 probably made Taylor's own retirement easier. Nevertheless, it must have irritated Barrow and Taylor to be urged to retire to "facilitate the reorganization" of the office, an implication that their departure would somehow improve its efficiency. After his retirement, Taylor continued to take an active interest in the Colonial Office, and he and Rogers carried on a lively correspondence on colonial matters.[211] Nor was he forgotten by the Colonial Office staff, which sent flowers to his funeral in 1886.[212] Taylor in many ways—his ideas, his methods of work, and his personality—exemplified the best traditions of the old Colonial Office. Certainly the office would never be the same without Taylor, Barrow, and Rogers. Whatever the faults and shortcomings of their approach to colonial

206. Taylor, *Autobiography*, II, 291.
207. *Ibid.*
208. For example, see the minutes on Berkeley to Hicks Beach, March 11, 1880, CO 152/138.
209. Taylor, *Autobiography*, II, 292.
210. *Ibid.*, II, 296.
211. Taylor to Blachford, February 25, 1879; Taylor to Blachford, January 22, 1885, in Edward Dowden, ed., *Correspondence of Henry Taylor* (London, 1888), pp. 386–388, 421. There are also several letters from Blachford to Taylor in Marindin, ed., *Letters of Blachford*, pp. 364 ff.
212. H. A. Taylor to Granville, March 31, 1886, PRO 30/29/213.

administration, we must agree with Rogers that at the time of parting the "retrospective and rather sad side is uppermost."[213]

The Treasury wasted little time in considering Herbert's reorganization proposals embodied in the letter of March 8, 1872. Robert Lowe was anxious for the Colonial Office to confirm the principles of the Treasury's own constitution and thus strengthen his negotiating position with the Home Office and the Foreign Office, which still refused to accept open competition. The details of the Colonial Office's proposals were discussed first in private by the permanent officials of the two departments.[214] Lingen, the permanent secretary of the Treasury, had no important criticisms, believing that Herbert's plan would be accepted by the Treasury as "very good." Herbert regarded the suggestions Lingen did offer as unobjectionable.[215] The matters of dispute between the two departments were minor, involving the Colonial Office's practice of defining its constitution by means of an Order in Council, the use of the term "establishment," the salaries of certain minor officials, and the division of the supplementary clerks into two classes. The Treasury did not, however, criticize the general plan, appreciating "the regard for economy and efficiency which are apparent throughout the proposals made by Lord Kimberley."[216] The Colonial Office was equally anxious to implement the new system, and its reply, which Herbert showed to Lingen before its dispatch,[217] agreed to most of the Treasury's recommendations.[218] The only unresolved question concerned the salaries of some minor officials. The Treasury agreed that this question could be resolved when the estimates for the new year were considered. The Colonial Office's new constitution could go into effect on September 30, 1872.[219]

Herbert's new office regulations drafted on September 28 mark the conclusion of the reorganization of 1872. These regulations summarized almost three years of discussion and established certain general

213. "Notes of Autobiography," 1885, in Marindin, ed., *Letters of Blachford*, p. 295.
214. Lingen to Herbert, May 16, 1872; Lingen to Herbert, May 30, 1872, CO 537/22.
215. Lingen to Herbert, May 16, 1872, and Herbert's minute of June 29, 1872, on Treasury to CO, June 22, 1872, *ibid.*
216. Treasury to CO, June 22, 1872, CO 323/309.
217. Herbert's marginal comment on CO to Treasury, September 10, 1872, *ibid.*
218. CO to Treasury, September 10, 1872, *ibid.* The Colonial Office agreed to drop its practice of defining its constitution by an Order in Council. This was inconvenient when only minor changes were required, and none of the other offices of state followed that procedure. CO to Lord President of the Council, October 5, 1872, *ibid.* The Colonial Office also agreed that the term "establishment" included the supplementary or lower-division clerks. For convenience the supplementary clerks would be divided into two classes.
219. Treasury to CO, September 23, 1872, *ibid.*

principles of organization and routine which were followed for the next two decades. The principle of geographical division of work was confirmed. Charles Cox was appointed principal (senior) clerk of the combined Eastern and West Indian departments. William Dealtry supervised the combined North American and Australian, and African and Mediterranean departments. William Robinson was appointed principal clerk of the general department, being also placed in charge of the library and the printing of parliamentary papers.[220] The fourth principal clerkship was kept vacant to reduce the cost of the office. The Colonial Office planned to fill this clerkship as soon as the number of upper-division clerks was reduced from twenty-six to eighteen.[221]

Second, the clerks were assigned more demanding work. No class of upper-division clerks could claim a monopoly on minuting and drafting. The minutes of second-class (junior) clerks on anything except routine business were, however, to pass through a first-class (assistant) clerk or a principal clerk before being sent to the undersecretaries. Certain routine papers, such as returns of shipwrecks, meteorological reports, simple acknowledgements, and arrear returns, could be handled by the principal clerks on their own authority. Only in cases of doubt should an undersecretary be consulted on those questions. All draft dispatches were also to pass through a first-class clerk or a principal clerk before being sent to the secretariat.[222]

Herbert also attempted to improve office discipline and routine. He directed that one clerk from each department be at the office by 11:15. Each department was also to keep a clerk in attendance in the evenings, unless excused, as long as the secretary of state or any of the undersecretaries remained at work. To secure uniformity of action on certain subjects, Herbert appointed Richard Ebden to deal with all ecclesiastical questions and those involving coolie emigration, and Edward Fairfield was assigned all prison, asylum, and hospital questions. Finally, although the distribution of work in each department was the responsibility of the principal clerks, Herbert requested that these arrangements be submitted to him from time to time.[223]

The introduction of open competition in 1870 and the reorganization of the Colonial Office in 1872 were the final results of twenty

220. Herbert's minute of September 28, 1872, CO 878/5, Vol. 5, No. 40. These regulations were approved by Kimberley on September 29 and went into effect the following day.
221. CO to Treasury, September 10, 1872, CO 323/309.
222. Herbert's minute of September 28, 1872, CO 878/5, Vol. 5, No. 40.
223. *Ibid.*

years of discussion. Men such as Stephen and Rogers had recognized the inefficiencies of the old Colonial Office, but it was the Treasury, and to a lesser extent the men who joined the office after 1868, that provided the real impetus for reform. In the period after 1872, however, the Colonial Office was to a great extent a satiated establishment, primarily concerned with maintaining the status quo as exemplified by its prestigiously high salaries. The Treasury was in a similar position, and consequently most of the pressure for further civil service reform in the seventies and eighties came from the two well-known commissions that investigated this question, the Playfair and the Ridley.[224] Changes naturally occurred in the organization and routine of the Colonial Office during this period, but they cannot be explained primarily in terms of the influence of the Treasury or civil service reformers. Instead it is necessary to consider such factors as the rapid increase in the volume and complexity of the work of the office, faster methods of communication, and the changes in the Colonial Office's relations with its subdepartments, the Crown Agents for the Colonies and the Colonial Land and Emigration Commission.

224. The Colonial Office was free from formal Treasury inquiries during this period. Only the Foreign Office among the other departments of state was so fortunate. Wright, *Treasury Control of the Civil Service*, pp. 195–197.

CHAPTER III

New Problems and Opportunities,
1872-1882

THE REORGANIZATION
of 1872 attempted to correct only the most immediate and apparent
weaknesses of the old Colonial Office. Unfortunately, Herbert and his
staff based their reforms on several assumptions that proved later to
be mistaken. They determined the size of the office on the erroneous
belief that the volume of work would remain constant, and they had
little appreciation of the problems and opportunities created by the
improvements in transportation and communication, especially the
telegraph. Finally, most of the officials erroneously assumed that the
Colonial Office's function would not significantly change. The result
was that the 1872 reforms had to be modified during the seventies.

The first indications of a rapid growth in the Colonial Office's business were visible, at least in retrospect, by the end of 1872. The con-
solidation of British interests on the Gold Coast had begun, interests
which clashed with those of the Ashanti and dragged the British ever
deeper into West African politics. In Malaya the pattern was similar—
a clash of interests, a war, and a deepening of British responsibilities
in the peninsula. In the South Pacific the problems of Fiji and the
labor trade demanded solutions requiring greater British involvement.
Finally, Kimberley's annexation of the diamond mines in 1871 opened a new phase in the tragic relations among Boer, Briton, and
Bantu in South Africa. The additional work created as a result of
these and other questions was not recognized at the time of the 1872
reorganization.

The introduction of the telegraph as a common method of communication also influenced the organization and routine of the Colonial Office. The telegraph was used before 1872, but its real potential
was not appreciated until after the Ashanti (1873–1874) and Perak
(1875) wars. The more frequent use of the telegram, which was no

respecter of office hours, made the leisurely circulation of papers increasingly impracticable, and promptness no longer was a luxury but a necessity. The emphasis on speed which was promoted by the telegraph gradually changed the entire atmosphere of the office.

Third, the Colonial Office gradually came to accept a responsibility for assisting the colonies, especially the crown colonies, in their economic and social development. Although the steps taken in this direction were tentative and unsystematic during the seventies and eighties, they did represent an important development in the work of the office. For example, Herbert, who retained his interest in railroads, became concerned with improving communications in the colonies and spent considerable time discussing railway development with the crown agents and colonial representatives. Other members of the department, including many second-class clerks, tended to specialize in other areas or problems. The Colonial Office's organizational changes in the seventies and eighties reflected primarily the increasing volume of work, the greater emphasis on speed, and the growing specialization among the clerks.

Herbert and his staff in 1872 had little reason to anticipate a rapid increase in the office's work. In 1853 the total number of letters received at the office was 11,519, ten years later it was 12,579. By 1868, when the subject of reorganization was first seriously discussed, the number of letters had risen to only 14,327,[1] figures which supported the Treasury's argument that the cost of the Colonial Office had grown more rapidly than its work.[2] The volume of business remained unchanged throughout the period when reorganization was under consideration, and in 1873 the number of letters received was only 14,001, a decrease over 1868.[3] In view of these statistics, Herbert assumed that a substantial reduction in the size of the staff represented no great danger to the efficiency of the office.

There were ominous signs of growth as early as 1873, however; the number of letters received by the African department increased from 2,910 in 1870 to 3,587 in 1873, although the work of the other depart-

1. W. A. Nunes' chart of 1868, CO 323/292.
2. The salaries of the Colonial Office staff increased from £19,464 in 1840–1841 to £29,484 in 1869–1870. The Treasury also argued that the granting of responsible government to so many colonies should have resulted in reduced expenses. Treasury to CO, February 28, 1870, CO 323/302. The Colonial Office stressed the increased *number* of colonies and denied that responsible government always decreased its work. CO to Treasury, March 28, 1870, CO 323/302.
3. Chart bound with Herbert's minute of July 29, 1880, CO 323/346.

ments remained almost constant or even declined.[4] Beginning in 1874, largely as a result of the Ashanti War, the disturbances in Malaya, and the new problems in South Africa, the Colonial Office's work began to increase steadily. The office received 16,942 letters in 1878 and 20,524 in 1879, largely because of the Zulu War in South Africa.[5] The trend was firmly established by this last date. In 1890 the number of registered dispatches reached 25,313,[6] and by 1900 the number had reached an astounding 42,620.[7]

The work of the various departments did not increase uniformly. The West Indian department's work grew only 13 percent during the seventies. The North American and Australian department's work grew by only 16 percent. The work of the Eastern department increased 40 percent. It was the African department, which Henry Holland had considered abolishing in 1871,[8] however, that felt the most pressure; its work increased a phenomenal 100 percent during the same period.[9] Those different rates of growth made it necessary to shift the smaller colonies, such as Malta, Gibraltar, Heligoland, and the Falkland Islands, from department to department to balance the work.[10]

4. The work of the Australian and North American department fell from 3,798 letters to only 3,280. *Ibid.*

5. *Ibid.*

6. J. C. Braddon's chart of January 16, 1891, CO 323/386.

7. W. F. Westbrook's chart of January 25, 1901, CO 323/469. Beginning about 1880, the Colonial Office's general department prepared frequent reports on the number of dispatches received and sent by each department. Chart bound with Herbert's minute of July 29, 1880, CO 323/346; Chart bound with Kimberley's circular dispatch of December 14, 1882, CO 323/353; Braddon's chart of January 14, 1886, CO 323/366; Braddon's chart of January 14, 1889, CO 323/378; Braddon's chart of January 14, 1890, CO 323/382; Braddon's chart of January 16, 1892, CO 323/391; and Westbrook's tables of January 23, 1893, CO 323/395. The figures in these returns must be used with care, however, because of the shifting of some colonies from department to department. The figures give only an approximation of the number of dispatches concerned with a specific geographical area. To determine the exact number of yearly dispatches for a specific colony it is necessary to consult the appropriate register of correspondence.

8. Holland's minute of March 11, 1871, CO 537/22.

9. Meade's minute of June 8, 1880, CO 323/346.

10. To determine which specific colonies were included within a geographical department at any given time, it is necessary to consult the appropriate *Colonial Office List*. For example, Heligoland, assigned to the African and Mediterranean department in 1872, was shifted to the West Indian and Eastern department in 1873, returned to the African and Mediterranean department in 1875, and finally reassigned to the West Indian and Eastern department in 1877. Heligoland eventually achieved a permanent home with the West Indian department, or its equivalent the "No. 1 department," in 1881— at least until it was traded to Bismarck in 1890. Rationally conceived geographical departments were so difficult to create that the Colonial Office simply began to refer to them by number in 1889. Better to do this than to offend a colony such as Malta by referring to it in printed papers as an "African" colony. Meade's minute of January 2, 1889, CO 323/378.

Although the Colonial Office's work increased, the size of its staff decreased. Because of financial commitments to the Treasury, no new second-class clerks could be appointed until all of the redundant clerks had been absorbed into the smaller establishment. The result was that the first open competition clerk was not selected until 1877. Despite various attempts to expedite the work, by 1880 Robert Meade feared that the office would collapse in the event of any serious illnesses. Herbert agreed that additional help was urgently required.[11]

The introduction of the telegraph as a common method of communication in the seventies and the use of faster and more reliable steamships for the delivery of the mails also increased the pressure on the Colonial Office staff. Back in 1834 a voyage to India took approximately twelve weeks.[12] The average passage to Sydney in 1846 consumed 124 days, with the return averaging 138 days.[13] Service was also infrequent and irregular, and a dispatch that missed the mail packet might be delayed for weeks or even for months.[14] Under these conditions, it was not surprising that as late as 1870 the Colonial Office staff geared its work to the departures of the mails.[15]

Gradually, however, as steamships were improved and the colonies grew in population and wealth, communications became more frequent and reliable. The competition among the various steamship companies for the lucrative government mail contracts also improved the service. By 1879 the average passage time to Australia was only fifty-one days. Weekly service between Southampton and Capetown was inaugurated in 1876, with the trip taking only four weeks compared with the six weeks in 1857.[16] One result of the improved mail service was that the Colonial Office staff began to work under continual, rather than periodical, pressure. By 1880 there was little talk about meeting a specific mail deadline; the emphasis was on answering dispatches as quickly as possible and sending the replies by the *first* mail. Another effect of the improved steamship communications was an increase in the number of colonial visitors to London. Interviews

11. Meade's minute of June 8, 1880, and Herbert's minute of July 29, 1880, CO 323/346.
12. George O. Trevelyan, *The Life and Letters of Lord Macaulay* (rev. ed.; 2 vols.; New York, 1909), I, 329. Macaulay had time on his journey to read all seventy volumes of Voltaire, Gibbon's *Decline and Fall,* seven folios of the *Biographia Britannica,* and numerous Greek and Roman classics.
13. Howard Robinson, *Carrying British Mails Overseas* (New York, 1964), p. 188.
14. Young, *Colonial Office,* pp. 142–144.
15. Rogers' minute of March 14, 1870, CO 878/5, Vol. 4, No. 21A.
16. Robinson, *Carrying British Mails Overseas,* pp. 182, 239.

with these dignitaries consumed a substantial portion of the time of the permanent undersecretary and the secretary of state.[17]

The telegraph had an even more immediate impact on the organization and routine of the office. The first successful transatlantic cable in 1866 was quickly followed by cables to India (1870), Singapore (1870), Adelaide (1872), Wellington (1876), and Capetown (1879).[18] The Colonial Office's growing telegraphic expenses reflect its increased use of this new means of communication. In 1870–1871 only £800 was placed on the estimates for telegrams. Ten years later, despite the introduction of cost reducing codes, the amount was £2,800.[19] By 1892, the year Herbert retired, the Colonial Office received over one thousand telegrams, a number which quadrupled by 1900.[20]

The need for improved communications was clearly shown by the Ashanti War of 1873–1874. At this time the cable reached only to the Canary Islands, and it still took almost two months to send instructions to Cape Coast Castle and to receive a reply. Not only was West African mail service slow, but because the postmaster general had no control over the two steamship companies that carried the mails, it was also very irregular. The steamships frequently arrived at the Cape Coast at an unusual hour and gave the administrator or governor as little as fifteen minutes to "close his despatch case."[21] At the height of the crisis in November, 1873, when Sir Garnet Wolseley was preparing an advance on Kumasi, one steamship left without even waiting for the mail.[22] This situation, together with the fact that British traders were supplying arms to the Ashantis, was very disturbing to Herbert. "It is commercial freedom run mad," he minuted, "for us to be fighting our own merchants as well as the Ashantees."[23] Lord Car-

17. In donating a bust of Edward Gibbon Wakefield to the Colonial Office, the Bank of South Australia suggested placing it outside Herbert's room because "as all colonists come to the Permanent Under Secy's. room, they would all see it as well as if placed in the front hall." Meade's minute of July 10, 1876, on Bank of S. Australia to CO, July 5, 1876, CO 323/329.

18. George Johnson, ed., *The All Red Line: The Annals and Aims of the Pacific Cable Project* (Ottawa, 1903), pp. 47–49.

19. The actual cost of the telegrams was frequently in excess of the estimate. In 1880 and 1881, largely because of the Zulu and Transvaal wars, telegrams cost £4773 and £9642, respectively. For a detailed analysis of these expenses see the tables bound with Kimberley's minute of March 25, 1882, CO 323/353. See also Sir John Bramston, "The Colonial Office from Within," *Empire Review*, I (April, 1901), 281–282.

20. Westbrook to Ommanney, January 30, 1901, CO 323/469.

21. Harley to Kimberley, June 4, 1873, CO 96/99.

22. Wolseley to Commodore Hewett, November 21, 1873, enclosed in Wolseley to Kimberley, November 27, 1873, CO 96/103.

23. Herbert's minute of October 1, 1873, on FO to CO, September 29, 1873, CO 96/106.

narvon, who succeeded Kimberley in 1874, believed that improved telegraphic communications were essential to the military security of the British Empire.[24] It was not until after the disasters of the Zulu War, however, that a direct cable to Capetown was laid.

The telegraph promised ways of simplifying and improving colonial administration, but it also created new problems for the Colonial Office staff. Telegrams, if they were to be used effectively, naturally had to be disposed of quickly, often on the day of their arrival. This gave the clerks and assistant undersecretaries little time to look up previous correspondence and to record their suggestions. Kimberley, for example, wanted "all telegrams of any importance" sent to him immediately, unless of course they were received after ten o'clock in the evening.[25] The secretary of state and Herbert were increasingly forced to make decisions on important questions quickly, sometimes based on only the barest of information. As one authority on South Africa has stated, "The calming effect upon the most excited despatch of lying unread for a month in the darkness of a mailbag was lost."[26] As Herbert and his political chiefs attempted to use the telegraph to exercise a closer control over events in the troublesome colonies, such as the Malay states, the Gold Coast, and South Africa, they were forced to rely increasingly upon the other clerks to deal with the more mundane affairs of state, especially in the smaller colonies.

Although no thorough study has been made of the impact of the telegraph on the formation of colonial policy after 1870, it appears that the Colonial Office's control over its officials in the colonies was never as complete as Herbert would have liked. Actually, the Colonial Office was never able to control the activities of some of its representatives. Strong and forceful governors such as Sir John Pope Hennessy, Sir Bartle Frere, Sir Arthur Hamilton Gordon, or Sir Andrew Clarke frequently made decisions first and then sought the approval of the Colonial Office. "For God's sake don't try to govern Fiji in detail from Downing St."[27] The most extreme example of the Colonial Office's inability to control its servants was the case of Malaya from 1867 to 1876. Three successive governors precipitated crises by exceeding their instructions, leading eventually to the establishment of a system of

24. Carnarvon to Northcote, copy, May 23, 1877, PRO 30/6/7.
25. Kimberley's minute of February 17, 1873 CO 878/5, Vol. 5, No. 57.
26. Cornelius W. de Kiewiet, *The Imperial Factor in South Africa: A Study in Politics and Economics* (Cambridge, 1937), p. 293.
27. Gordon to Carnarvon, private, July 2, 1875, in Legge, *Britain in Fiji*, p. 270.

British resident advisers. C. D. Cowan has concluded that one of the most notable features of Malayan history in the seventies was "the extent to which events were precipitated by the uncontrolled action of successive governors, and this despite the fact that for most of the period the telegraph line from Europe was in operation."[28] Too often the telegraph was used as a quick means of announcing a *fait accompli*, as in Queensland's annexation of New Guinea in 1883, rather than as an improved method of asking for instructions. The Colonial Office disallowed Queensland's action, but it was very reluctant to overrule the decisions of its own colonial officials. Herbert and his colleagues realized the difficulties of administering a large empire from London, and when presented with an unauthorized action, their first reaction was usually to support the governor or administrator on the assumption that he had detailed knowledge which necessitated his action. In addition, the Colonial Office recognized the importance of upholding the dignity and authority of the representative of the crown whenever possible. If an unauthorized policy did not prove successful, however, the Colonial Office's support evaporated quickly, especially if Parliament became aroused. The difference between a "strong, forceful" governor and an "irresponsible" one frequently depended upon circumstances beyond the control of either the governor or his superiors in London. The telegraph was also less useful than Herbert had anticipated because of its unreliability during the seventies. During both the Perak War and the first Transvaal War the cables broke. The cables to the West Indies were still in an "uncertain state" as late as 1880.[29] The imperfect coding systems also caused considerable misunderstanding.[30]

The Colonial Office's reorganization had been designed to attract clerks capable of making decisions, and Herbert's minute of September 28, 1872, had given the principal clerks the authority to dispose of certain types of business.[31] The growing volume of work and the increasing pressure resulting from the use of the telegraph made it imperative that the secretary of state and Herbert devolve more responsibility and authority onto the other members of the office. Herbert and his political superiors saw relatively few dispatches from small colonies like Labuan, an island off the northwestern coast of Borneo.

28. Cowan, *Nineteenth Century Malaya*, p. 266.
29. Minutes on Berkeley to Hicks Beach, April 10, 1880, CO 152/138.
30. Minutes on Mitchell to Knutsford (tel.), March 8, 1890, CO 427/8.
31. Herbert's minute of September 28, 1872, CO 878/5, Vol. 5, No. 40.

Robert Meade, the assistant undersecretary in charge of the Eastern department, disposed of hospital and criminal statistics, mine reports, the annual estimates, land grants, suspension cases, and even some dispatches dealing with relations with foreign powers. It is more difficult to determine which dispatches were handled by the principal clerks because many of the less important papers were destroyed under statute after 1874.[32] Nevertheless, the principal clerk, Charles Cox, did dispose of simple acknowledgments, replies to circular dispatches, and certain classes of reports. Herbert and the secretaries of state confined their attention primarily to dispatches concerning foreign affairs.[33]

Herbert, despite his confidence in the Colonial Office's new constitution, requested additional clerical assistance in 1873. He argued that the retirement, death, illness, or transfer to the colonial service of five upper-division clerks within a single year, coupled with the additional work created by the Ashanti War, had "severely taxed the strength of the Office." To meet the emergency, Herbert suggested the immediate recruitment by open competition of a new second-class clerk. This new clerk would not be a permanent addition to the staff; he would be absorbed in the Colonial Office establishment as quickly as possible, and the reduction in the number of upper-division clerks would simply be delayed.[34]

The Treasury recognized the difficulties facing the Colonial Office. Robert Lowe agreed to grant Herbert a new clerk if he accepted a redundant member of another department instead of a new open competition clerk.[35] Herbert was not, however, that desperate for assistance, and he and Meade questioned the wisdom of accepting a clerk from an overstaffed office. The Colonial Office's high salaries were designed to attract able young university men and not clerks who had been engaged in copying and less intellectual work.[36] Herbert argued that the Treasury's proposal was actually "a declaration against bringing into practical operation, for a long time to come, the principle of appointing to the higher branch of the public service by open competition."[37] In the end, Herbert assigned his own private secretary to

32. Only about one-half of the 102 Labuan dispatches for 1878 were saved.
33. CO 144/40–46, *passim.*
34. CO to Treasury, October 31, 1873, CO 323/314.
35. Treasury to CO, November 20, 1873, *ibid.* The Treasury had filled a vacancy by taking a redundant clerk from the Admiralty.
36. Meade's minute of November 21, 1873, on *ibid.* Meade admitted that this objection also applied to the Colonial Office clerks who had recently received large salary increases. It was impossible, however, for the office to appoint an entirely new staff.
37. Herbert's minute of November 25, 1873, on *ibid.* Kimberley did not believe that

departmental duties instead of accepting a redundant clerk.[38] Without the colonial secretary's solid support Herbert could do little to overcome the intransigence of the Treasury. Kimberley, having carried through one major reorganization of the office, was not prepared to alter his work this quickly.

In February, 1874, the Conservatives won a decisive victory at the polls, and Benjamin Disraeli secured the political power which had eluded him for so long. Lord Carnarvon, who had been colonial secretary in 1866–1867, returned to his old post in the new ministry. Disraeli was more interested in foreign policy than in colonial questions per se, and he gave Carnarvon considerable freedom of action. This freedom, together with the grand and "showy" schemes which he was disposed to promote,[39] made Carnarvon the best known colonial secretary between Earl Grey and Joseph Chamberlain.

Herbert believed that Carnarvon differed in two major respects from most of his predecessors. He was one of the first important public figures "to have always present with him a strong and unquestioning belief in the value—to this country and to the Colonies equally—of Imperial expansion and cohesion."[40] Carnarvon saw this tie largely as a military bond. He had vigorously opposed the Cardwell reforms, and once in office he attempted to persuade his colleagues in the cabinet, as well as the colonists, to restore the imperial garrisons in the larger colonies. He received little support, however, and his proposals came to nothing.[41] After his resignation in 1878, he served as the chairman of the Royal Commission on Colonial Defense, which met until 1882,[42] and in later years he was a strong advocate of imperial federation.

Carnarvon also differed from his predecessors in that he had a deep

---

the Treasury meant to abandon open competition except in cases of an *addition* to the staff. "They leave us to choose between the inconvenience of extra pressure, and the inconvenience of having a less efficient clerk than we should have if we obtained him by competition." Kimberley's minute of November 26, 1873, *ibid.*

38. CO to Treasury, December 4, 1873, *ibid.*

39. Rogers, "Notes of Autobiography," 1885, in Marindin, ed., *Letters of Blachford,* p. 263.

40. Earl of Carnarvon, *Speeches on Canadian Affairs,* ed. Sir Robert Herbert (London, 1902), p. xiv.

41. Carnarvon to Disraeli, copy, private, November 30, 1875, and March 16, 1876, PRO 30/6/11, ff. 104–105, 121–122. Carnarvon to Hardy [secretary of state for war], copy, private, December 12, 1875, PRO 30/6/12. Hardy to Carnarvon, private, March 6, 1876, PRO 30/6/12. Robinson [governor of New South Wales] to Carnarvon, private, September 22, 1875, PRO 30/6/25. Dufferin [governor-general of Canada] to Carnarvon, private, February 23, 1875, in C. W. de Kiewiet and F. H. Underhill, eds., *Dufferin-Carnarvon Correspondence, 1874–8* (Toronto, 1955), p. 132.

42. For Carnarvon's correspondence on this subject see PRO 30/6/52.

personal interest in the colonies and their future.[43] He did not attempt
to isolate his private life from his public life, as Kimberley had done,
and he frequently entertained colonial guests at Highclere, his Berk-
shire home. Carnarvon's voluminous private correspondence with colonial governors and statesmen reflected not only a desire to do his
work well but also a deep interest in the empire.[44] This interest continued even after his resignation. He visited Canada in 1883, and in
1887–1888 he traveled to South Africa and Australia.[45] Unlike Kimberley, Carnarvon was greatly assisted in his relations with the Colonial
Office's "special public" by the warmth of his personality, his eloquence as a public speaker, and his wide range of interests. He could
converse on almost any subject.[46]

Carnarvon's relations with the Colonial Office staff were excellent.
He was a warm and friendly individual and was always willing to lis-
ten to advice from his subordinates.[47] He expected the staff to match
his own diligence, but as his private secretary stated, "the Colonial
Office in those days was a happy family. There was no internal friction,
and all were united in a common devotion to the chief."[48] Preferring
to concentrate on larger questions of policy, Carnarvon delegated a
greater share of the less important business to his subordinates. He
was frequently slow to reach a decision, but once he had decided a
question he seldom changed his mind.

Carnarvon's relations with his colleagues in the cabinet were rather
strained. Although Disraeli gave Carnarvon considerable freedom in
deciding colonial questions, he did not really trust his colonial secretary. Carnarvon's excitable temperament had earned him the nick-
name of "Twitters,"[49] and Disraeli always feared that Carnarvon's
idealism and unwillingness to compromise would lead to a crisis, as

43. Carnarvon, *Canadian Speeches*, pp. xiv–xvi.

44. He wanted to see all articles of interest appearing in colonial newspapers. Fairfield's minute of September 28, 1875, CO 878/6, Vol. 6, No. 11.

45. Sir Henry Parkes, a leading Australian politician, believed that Carnarvon "was
regarded in many respects, by the best-informed men in the colonies, as a true friend
of Australia." Sir Henry Parkes, *Fifty Years in the Making of Australian History* (2 vols.;
London, 1892), II, 95. This was a considerable achievement in a period when Downing
Street was still an odious term in many colonies.

46. For the breadth of his interest see Earl of Carnarvon, *Essays, Addresses and Translations*, ed. Sir Robert Herbert (3 vols.; London, 1896), *passim*.

47. Rogers, "Notes of Autobiography," 1885, in Marindin, ed., *Letters of Blachford*,
p. 263.

48. Sir Arthur Henry Hardinge, *The Life of Henry Howard Molyneux Herbert,
Fourth Earl of Carnarvon, 1831–1890* (3 vols.; London, 1925), III, 318.

49. Disraeli to Lady Bradford, September 27, 1878, in W. F. Monypenny and G. E.
Buckle, *The Life of Benjamin Disraeli, Earl of Beaconsfield* (rev. ed.; 6 vols. in 2; London, 1929), II, 1292.

they did in 1878. Disraeli may also have been somewhat jealous of his colonial secretary. The Colonial Office was still regarded as a minor office, but Carnarvon's successes, as well as his mistakes, became increasingly matters of public interest and concern. "Talking of Carnarvon, I am extremely amused that, while all the Government are attacked in the metrop. papers for their blundering, etc., little Carnarvon, who feeds the Radical press, is always spared, and really he is the only one who has made mistakes, and committed a series of blunders."[50] Disraeli and most of the other members of the cabinet still regarded a colonial debate as a burden.[51] Even worse, "little Carnarvon's" series of blunders made the government's other polices more difficult to implement. Lord George Hamilton, the parliamentary undersecretary of the India Office, reflected the feelings of many Conservative politicians toward Carnarvon.

Possessed as he was by a great charm of manner, of eloquence and industry and courage, yet he had a microbe of incurable fidgetiness in his composition. Three times in twenty years did he resign office. There was on his part an inability to weigh or give adequate consideration to influences, however important or pressing they might be, if they were outside the ken of his immediate job. Though loyal and straightforward in all his transactions, he was a constant worry to his colleagues, and at times to his officials. ... He was a high-minded and lovable gentleman with strong moral ideals, but not the stamp of man to deal with a crisis or to fall into the team work necessitated by our party system. . . .[52]

Disraeli was probably relieved when Carnarvon resigned in 1878 over the government's eastern policy.[53] Carnarvon himself always complained that the cabinet did not appreciate the importance of colonial questions or the work he was attempting to do. According to him, Disraeli would not even read the colonial materials sent to him.[54] He grumbled that a colonial secretary was expected "to make bricks

50. Disraeli to Lady Bradford, April 26, 1876, in *ibid.*, p. 815.
51. Disraeli to Lady Bradford, June 25, 1874, in Marquis of Zetland, ed., *The Letters of Disraeli to Lady Bradford and Lady Chesterfield* (2 vols.; London, 1929), I, 108. "I might be at Evelyn's [Lady Carnarvon's] tonight and see you! And I am detained by an infernal debate on the Gold Coast Policy of Evelyn's husband. Such is life! No wonder people go mad!"
52. Lord George Hamilton, *Parliamentary Reminiscences and Reflections, 1886–1906* (London, 1922), p. 10.
53. Disraeli to Carnarvon, January 31, 1878, PRO 30/6/11, ff. 218–219. Disraeli had twice offered Carnarvon new positions. Hardinge, *Life of Carnarvon*, II, 94–95.
54. Carnarvon to Hardy, copy, private and personal, July 19, 1877, PRO 30/6/12. Disraeli's opinion was that Carnarvon, "the greatest fidget in the world," worried him to death with his four-page telegrams. Disraeli to Lady Bradford, December 29, 1875, in Zetland, ed., *Letters of Disraeli*, I, 312–313.

without straw or to live in a chronic wrangle with his colleagues."[55]

Carnarvon's unwillingness to compromise and his inability to see all sides of a question are reflected in his attitudes toward the organization of the Colonial Office. Carnarvon, who prefaced many of his private letters with complaints of overwork,[56] was concerned with the weakened condition of the Colonial Office. He felt that Kimberley had approved too large a reduction in the size of the staff; the précis writership should certainly not have been eliminated.[57] Several of the reforms which he proposed to strengthen the office were inconsistent with the principles of the 1872 reorganization. The result was that considerable friction developed between the Treasury and the Colonial Office over questions of office organization.

Carnarvon first attempted to solve some of the problems created by the increased use of the telegraph. He and the undersecretaries were frequently awakened at night because of the arrival of a cypher telegram. These telegrams often turned out to be of little importance. Carnarvon therefore proposed that two second-class (junior) clerks be appointed resident clerks, as was the practice at the Foreign Office. He also suggested that one of the copyists, F. J. Villiers, be promoted to supplementary clerk and placed in charge of all telegraphic work during the regular office hours.[58] The Treasury reluctantly agreed, but it instructed the resident clerks to record the number of important telegrams received out of office hours in order to determine if the experiment should be continued during "time of ordinary quiet."[59]

Edward Fairfield and A. A. Pearson received the first appointments. Because of a delay in the preparation of their rooms, they continued to live at their private residences. During their first year of work they received only seventy-one telegrams, one of which was intended for Dutch colonial officials; Carnarvon sent only nine telegrams after office hours.[60] Although the need for resident clerks had not been clearly demonstrated, Herbert proposed that the experiment be con-

55. Carnarvon's minute of March 22, 1876, on Bulwer to Carnarvon, December 31, 1875, CO 179/118. He also complained that his South African Bill was endangered because of the lack of government support in the Commons. Carnarvon to Northcote, copy, private, July 18, 1877, PRO 30/6/7, ff. 216–217.
56. Carnarvon to Cairns, copy, private, October 22, 1874, PRO 30/6/6, ff. 18–19; Carnarvon to Disraeli, copy, private, December 10, 1875, PRO 30/6/11, ff. 106–107; Carnarvon to Salisbury, copy, private, September 3, 1875, PRO 30/6/10.
57. Carnarvon to Northcote, copy, private, June 11, 1874, PRO 30/6/7, f. 21.
58. CO to Treasury, March 14, 1874, CO 323/319.
59. Treasury to CO, March 21, 1874, ibid.
60. Fairfield's and Pearson's minute of December 28, 1874, ibid.

tinued.[61] The Treasury agreed as long as the colonial secretary was convinced of its necessity.[62] Eventually the resident clerks received rooms on the third floor of the new Colonial Office and became a permanent part of the establishment.[63]

Carnarvon was less successful in correcting the shortcomings of the Colonial Office's printing department. This department had been placed under the control of the senior clerk of the general department in 1870, and at that time its work had consisted primarily of preparing papers for presentation to Parliament.[64] After 1870, when the volume of work began to increase rapidly, the Colonial Office also began the practice of printing bulky or important correspondence for office use. These "confidential prints" date almost entirely from the period after 1870.[65] Most of these prints are very complete and show little or no signs of editing. For the sake of convenience, long dispatches were frequently printed immediately upon their arrival at the Colonial Office, before they were circulated through the office. Parliamentary papers were usually important nonconfidential papers selected from these confidential prints.[66] This new procedure led to increased printing costs and to inevitable disputes with the Stationery Office and the Treasury.

Carnarvon was primarily concerned with eliminating the delays in the printing of the Colonial Office's parliamentary papers. The India Office and the Foreign Office each had its own printing press, but the Colonial Office was still required to send its work to the Stationery Office, which was known for its manufacture of red tape.[67] Carnarvon therefore proposed that a small printing press be installed in the basement of the new Colonial Office building. The press could be operated

61. Herbert's minute of December 31, 1874, *ibid.*
62. Lingen to Meade, January 4, 1875, *ibid.*
63. Tables bound with Office of Works to CO, June 15, 1874, CO 323/320. Originally the competition for these positions was very keen. In the twentieth century, however, the increased popularity of marriage made them less attractive, and it was necessary to establish a "rota system." Charles Jeffries. *The Colonial Office* (London, 1956), p. 130.
64. Sidney Joseph's minute of February 22, 1869, CO 537/22.
65. Public Record Office, *List of Colonial Office Confidential Print to 1916* (London, 1965), *passim.*
66. For the details of the printing and registration of these prints see R. B. Pugh, *The Records of the Colonial and Dominions Offices* (London, 1964), pp. 39–40. Some parliamentary papers, such as the proceedings of the Colonial Conference of 1887, underwent considerable editing before presentation. Holland to Salisbury, May 7, 1887; Salisbury to Holland, copy, May 8, 1887; Holland to Salisbury, May 21, 1887; Salisbury to Holland, copy, private, May 22, 1887; Salisbury to Holland, copy, private, June 25, 1887, Salisbury Papers.
67. William Robinson's minute of June 25, 1873, on Stationery Office to CO, June 24, 1873, CO 323/316.

by Harrison, who did the Foreign Office's Work.[68] The Treasury, already alarmed at the rising cost of printing, refused his request, and the proposal was dropped.[69] The Treasury's decision led, however, to many acrimonious disputes between the two offices. In the seventies the Colonial Office sent most of its confidential and parliamentary work to Harrison at the Foreign Office, who was somewhat more expensive than the Stationery Office.[70] The Stationery Office and the Treasury continually complained that Harrison's cost was excessive, and eventually only confidential papers of great importance were printed by Harrison. The remainder of the work was farmed out by the Stationery Office to Eyre and Spottiswode, an arrangement that was never really accepted at the Colonial Office.[71]

The increased telegraphic and printing costs produced some departmental friction, but the Treasury was even more disturbed by Herbert's and Carnarvon's attempts to increase the size of the Colonial Office's staff and to raise some salaries. The Treasury argued with considerable justice that this was inconsistent with the spirit of the Colonial Office's reorganization in 1872. Carnarvon was forced to use all of his personal influence in order to raise the salaries of the supplementary clerks, appoint a third assistant undersecretary, and fill the vacant fourth principal clerkship. The Treasury eventually approved all of these changes, but its relations with the Colonial Office during Carnarvon's secretaryship, at least on civil service questions, were seldom smooth.

Before 1870 the Colonial Office's supplementary clerks had been used almost exclusively on such mechanical work as the registration of dispatches. They were eligible, however, for promotion to staff positions such as assistant librarian, parliamentary clerk, and superintendent of the copyists, appointments that carried salaries ranging from £400 to £800 a year. In 1870 most of these lucrative staff appointments were eliminated. The supplementary clerks naturally complained,

68. CO to Treasury, April 8, 1874, CO 323/319.

69. Treasury to CO, May 26, 1874, ibid.

70. Harrison had a very good reputation for secrecy in the printing of confidential papers. Sir Edward Hertslet, Recollections of the Old Foreign Office (London, 1901), pp. 46, 50–51. Harrison was also much faster than the Stationery Office. In addition, all papers sent to the Stationery Office were kept on file there. Meade objected to this practice because the head of that department was a frequent contributor to the newspapers. Meade's minute of February 26, 1875, on Stationery Office to CO, February 8, 1875, CO 323/324.

71. Ebden's minute of February 4, 1882, CO 323/353; minutes on Courtney to Herbert, November 13, 1884, CO 323/358.

arguing that it was unfair to use these savings to increase the salaries of the other members of the office.[72]

Kimberley, who was primarily interested in improving the financial prospects of the upper-division clerks, did not see any real justification for granting the supplementary clerks higher salaries. When the Treasury rejected Herbert's plan to reduce the number of supplementary clerks in order to give the remainder a small raise, Kimberley allowed the question to drop.[73] The following year Carnarvon, who believed that the entire office needed strengthening, supported another appeal to the Treasury. This time the Colonial Office requested a raise in pay for the supplementary clerks without agreeing to a reduction in their numbers.[74] The Treasury refused to alter its earlier decision,[75] and the question was again shelved while the Playfair Commission inquired into the entire subject of civil service economy and efficiency.

The Order in Council of February 12, 1876, which embodied some of the recommendations of the Playfair Commission, established a new class of lower-division clerks for the entire civil service. These new clerks would gradually replace the Colonial Office's supplementary clerks as vacancies occurred. Herbert and Meade hoped, however, that the Treasury would treat the present supplementary clerks generously and give them the higher salaries that had been recommended.[76] Carnarvon discussed the question privately with Sir Stafford Northcote, but he had little success. The chancellor of the exchequer simply reminded Carnarvon that members of the cabinet should "bear in mind that the cry of extravagance is one which is always worked with effect against a Conservative Govt., and that a Conservative Ch. of Exch. cannot afford to disregard it."[77] Officially the Treasury reiterated its position that an increase in the salaries of the supplementary clerks was incompatible not only with the recent Order in Council but also with the 1872 reorganization of the Colonial Office. A strict division between the mechanical work of the supplementary clerks and the intellectual work of the upper-division clerks would be

72. Supplementary Clerks to Herbert, November 11, 1872, CO 323/310; Supplementary Clerks to Herbert, October 28, 1873, CO 323/314.
73. Kimberley's minute of November 20, 1872, on Supplementary Clerks to Herbert, November 11, 1872, CO 323/310. Herbert proposed that the maximum salary of each class be raised £50 and that the number of supplementary clerks be reduced from eight to six. CO to Treasury, April 10, 1873, *ibid*; Treasury to CO, June 7, 1873, CO 323/314.
74. CO to Treasury, July 21, 1874, CO 323/316.
75. Treasury to CO, August 17, 1874, CO 323/319.
76. CO to Treasury, July 14, 1876, CO 323/328.
77. Northcote to Carnarvon, private, October 6, 1876, PRO 30/6/7, f. 162.

maintained only by supporting two distinct salary scales. The Treasury did propose, however, further informal negotiations between the two departments.[78]

Negotiations between Meade and Sir Ralph Lingen, the permanent secretary of the Treasury, finally resulted in a compromise. Lingen refused to grant the supplementary clerks a general increase in salaries, but he did suggest that some of them might be given "staff appointments." Meade accepted this offer,[79] and five staff appointments were created. They included supervisory positions in the registry, the copying department, the parliamentary printing department, and the library, and the assistant to the legal assistant undersecretary. These appointments carried a maximum salary of £400 a year.[80] Meade believed that this compromise secured "provisions more favourable than that for which we had contended."[81]

The creation of these supervisory positions was really a return to the pre-1870 arrangements which the Treasury had then regarded as chaotic and unduly expensive. Although the Treasury officials hoped that these staff positions would be abolished in the near future, they were probably not surprised when they became an established part of the Colonial Office's constitution. These positions did prove to be rather valuable, however. By assigning supplementary clerks to the supervision of the routine work, the second-class (junior) clerks were freed for more important duties. These positions also provided some incentive for the members of the Colonial Office's lower division. The Treasury never really accepted the idea of staff appointments or duty pay, and these questions proved to be a perennial source of conflict between the two departments.[82]

The Treasury was also very hostile to Carnarvon's plan to strengthen the upper division and the secretariat of the Colonial Office. Carnarvon believed that the office was dangerously undermanned because of the abolition of the position of précis writer in 1870 and the reduction in the size of the staff in 1872. He therefore recommended the appointment of a third assistant undersecretary of state.[83] The "multiplication of mail services" and the extension of the telegraph to most of the col-

78. Treasury to CO, October 21, 1876, CO 323/328.
79. Meade's minute of January 13, 1877, ibid.
80. Treasury to CO, January 26, 1877, CO 323/332.
81. Meade's minute of February 8, 1877, on Treasury to CO, January 26, 1877, ibid.
82. CO to Treasury, April 19, 1880, CO 323/346; Treasury to CO, June 18, 1880, CO 323/344.
83. Carnarvon to Northcote, copy, private, June 11, 1874, PRO 30/6/7, f. 21.

onies made it impossible, in his opinion, for Herbert and only two assistant undersecretaries to give careful attention to the many delicate and difficult questions requiring prompt consideration. Unless the Treasury sanctioned his proposals, it ran the risk of placing "undue strain" on individuals and of receiving "imperfect work."[84]

The Treasury agreed to give the Colonial Office a third assistant undersecretary because of the "strong representations" made by Carnarvon. Northcote and his advisers believed, however, that the appointment of another assistant undersecretary raised serious questions concerning the entire constitution of the Colonial Office. They argued that the recent reorganization had been based on the premise that the highly paid first-class and principal clerks would prove competent to perform many of the duties previously falling to assistant undersecretaries. The Treasury informed the Colonial Office that no new principal clerks were to be appointed without its approval.[85] Herbert of course defended the constitution of his office and argued that, in addition to the three assistant undersecretaries, four principal clerks were essential "for the safe and punctual despatch of business." He did hold out some hope of future reductions, however: "If the anticipations which have been formed as to the superior capacity of clerks entering the office after open competition on a comparatively high salary should be realised, it might become possible again to reduce the number of clerks, but years must elapse before the effect of this method of appointment can be ascertained."[86]

The Treasury's approval of the appointment of a third assistant undersecretary initiated a long and bitter debate over the proper method of selecting and rewarding these officers. The Superannuation Act of 1859 allowed men who entered the civil service with special professional qualifications to add a certain number of years to their period of service when computing their pensions. The permanent undersecretary of the Colonial Office, for example, received an addition of ten years, and Herbert believed that the assistant undersecretaries should receive the same privilege.[87] He did not believe that

84. CO to Treasury, June 11, 1874, CO 323/319. Carnarvon sent this letter privately to Northcote. Carnarvon to Northcote, copy, private, June 11, 1874, PRO 30/6/7, f. 21. Although Northcote promised that the question would be considered on its merits, he could do nothing "without full discussion with [his] departmental advisers." Northcote to Carnarvon, June 12, 1874, PRO 30/6/7, f. 22.
85. Treasury to CO, July 6, 1874, CO 323/319.
86. CO to Treasury, July 9, 1874, ibid.
87. Herbert's minute of December 2, 1876, on Audit Office to CO, November 30, 1876, CO 323/329.

these positions could be filled by promotions from within the civil service. The introduction of unrestricted open competition might eventually make this possible, but for the present at least Herbert maintained that trained lawyers had to be recruited from private life to handle the Colonial Office's complex legal work.[88]

The Treasury could not understand why all three assistant undersecretaries required legal training; only one, the legal assistant undersecretary, needed seven years added to his actual time of service. The other two assistant undersecretaries should be recruited from the civil service.[89] Despite Colonial Office objections, the Treasury issued a formal minute affirming this decision.[90] The Colonial Office then retreated slightly, agreeing that only two of the three assistant undersecretaries required legal training and therefore an addition of years in the computation of their pensions. In the future the other undersecretary would be recruited from within the office.[91] When this compromise was rejected, the Colonial Office was forced to rely upon the secretary of state's private negotiations with the chancellor of the exchequer.[92]

These proved futile; the Treasury continued to argue that

the perusal of a Legislative Act for the purposes of approval or disapproval by a Secretary of State belongs rather to the province of a politician or administrator rather than to that of a professional lawyer. . . . Most of the work of the Colonial Office requires no more knowledge of the law than "any well-educated man of sufficient ability to rise to a principal post in a Secretary of State's office, must, almost of course, have acquired."[93]

This slur upon the work of the Colonial Office naturally provoked several heated minutes from the assistant undersecretaries. They maintained that at least two lawyers were essential for the smooth working of the office.

The Treasury know more of the working of this office than either Sir Michael Hicks Beach or his predecessor [Carnarvon], therefore they adhere to their previous opinion. All the same if the "well educated men of sufficient ability to rise to principal posts in the Treasury" were to try their

88. Minutes on Treasury to CO, March 16, 1877; CO to Treasury, April 18, 1877, CO 323/332.
89. Treasury to CO, March 16, 1877, *ibid.*
90. Treasury to CO, July 1, 1878, CO 323/337. "It is just like the usual Treasury practice to try & override the Secy. of State in this way as if he was one of their subordinates." Meade's minute of July 5, 1878, on *ibid.*
91. CO to Treasury, July 30, 1878, *ibid.*
92. Minutes on Treasury to CO, July 30, 1878, *ibid.*
93. Treasury to CO, January 11, 1879, CO 323/340.

hands at the St. Lucia Codes, & the procedure & criminal Laws that come from other colonies they would not write such letters as this.[94]

When further informal negotiations between the political heads of the Colonial Office and the Treasury failed to produce any agreement, Herbert and his colleagues employed their second great weapon against an intransigent Treasury—blackmail. In 1880, the Treasury and the Foreign Office were both extremely anxious for the Colonial Office to accept responsibility for Cyprus, which Disraeli had acquired in 1878. Herbert and Lord Kimberley, who returned to the Colonial Office in 1880, refused to consider this transfer unless the question of the assistant undersecretaries was settled.[95] This time the Treasury capitulated. "My Lords" agreed to extend the privileges of the Super-annuation Act of 1859 to the three present assistant undersecretaries. No vacancy was to be filled without a reconsideration of the question, however.[96] When a vacancy finally did occur in 1892, the Colonial Office promoted a member of the office, Edward Fairfield. Because Fairfield was a qualified barrister both departments were satisfied.[97]

The assistant undersecretaries appointed to the Colonial Office in the seventies are good representatives of the higher civil service of the period. Their backgrounds were very similar, and their community of interests also helps to explain the smooth operation of the office under Herbert. William R. Malcolm was appointed the new third assistant undersecretary in 1874.[98] He supervised the general legal work of the office and the work of the North American and Australian department. Malcolm, like Herbert, was educated at Eton and Balliol College, Oxford.[99] At Balliol he received a first class at the final examination (1860) and was elected a fellow of All Souls in 1865. He was also called to the bar at Lincoln's Inn in 1865. Before entering the Colonial Office he served for a time as an assistant secretary at the Board of Trade.

Shortly after Malcolm's appointment, Henry Holland resigned to

94. Bramston's minute of January 13, 1879, on *ibid.*
95. Minutes on Treasury to CO, September 14, 1880, CO 323/344.
96. Treasury to CO, December 3, 1880, *ibid.*
97. In 1897 a legal assistant at £750 a year was added to the establishment. CO to Treasury, May 17, 1897, CO 323/417. The following year the Treasury approved the appointment of a fourth assistant undersecretary. Treasury to CO, September 7, 1898, CO 323/431. These additions simply reflected the constantly increasing volume of the Colonial Office's work.
98. Carnarvon to Malcolm, July 17, 1874, CO 323/319.
99. Malcolm was the third son of John Malcolm, M. P. of Poltalloch, Argyll. *Colonial Office List* (1877), p. 355; Sir Ivo Elliott, ed., *The Balliol College Register, 1833–1933* (2nd ed.; Oxford, 1934), p. 23.

stand for Parliament for Midhurst.[100] Although the Colonial Office still had a legal assistant undersecretary in Malcolm, Carnarvon believed that he needed at least two assistant undersecretaries with legal training.[101] He therefore appointed Sir Julian Pauncefote, a trained barrister, as Holland's replacement. Pauncefote also possessed considerable colonial experience. He was attorney general in Hong Kong from 1865 to 1872, and in 1872 he was appointed chief justice of the Leeward Islands, helping to establish the administration of justice in that newly created colony. When he returned to England, he was rewarded with an assistant undersecretaryship at the Colonial Office.[102] Pauncefote remained at the Colonial Office for only a brief period; a man of his ability and experience could not have enjoyed being the junior assistant undersecretary.[103] When a parliamentary committee recommended the creation of the position of legal assistant undersecretary at the Foreign Office in 1876, Pauncefote received the post because of his age and experience.[104]

Pauncefote's successor was Herbert's old Balliol and Queensland friend, John Bramston.[105] Bramston had remained in Australia after Herbert's departure in 1866, serving as attorney general of Queensland from 1870 to 1873. In 1873 he accepted a similar position at Hong Kong. At the Colonial Office Bramston supervised most of the South African and North American work until his retirement in 1897.

Edward Wingfield was the last assistant undersecretary to enter the Colonial Office during this period. He replaced Malcolm, who resigned in 1878 to become a partner in Coutt's Bank.[106] Wingfield received his education at Winchester and New College, Oxford, and he was called to the bar at Lincoln's Inn in 1859. Before entering the

100. The death of Holland's father in 1873 improved his financial position so that he could afford to enter politics. His gamble was not great because, as his son remarked, Midhurst was "almost a pocket borough of Lord Egmont of Cowdray." Holland held this seat until 1885 when Midhurst ceased to be a separate constituency. *DNB*, XXIV (1912–1921), 262; Sidney Holland, *In Black and White* (London, 1926), p. 71.

101. Carnarvon's minute of September 5, 1874, CO 878/5, Vol. 5, No. 92; Carnarvon to Northcote, copy, private, August 28, 1874, PRO 30/6/7, f. 54.

102. R. B. Mowat, *The Life of Lord Pauncefote* (London, 1929), pp. 15–25.

103. There is also some evidence that the ultraconservative Pauncefote was not entirely in sympathy with the "orthodox departmental line" on many issues. Hamilton, *Barbados and Confederation, 1871–1885*, pp. 20–23.

104. Carnarvon to Malcolm, copy, June 13, 1876, PRO 30/6/45, ff. 255–256; Malcolm to Carnarvon, June 13, 1876, PRO 30/6/45, ff. 253–254. Pauncefote later became permanent undersecretary of the Foreign Office and British ambassador to the United States. Mowat, *Life of Pauncefote*, pp. 27–121.

105. Bramston's father, T. W. Bramston, represented South Essex in the House of Commons for over thirty years. Bowen to Cardwell, September 15, 1865, CO 324/13.

106. Elliott, *Balliol College Register*, p. 23.

Colonial Office, he practiced for several years on the home circuit.[107] As a lawyer, he supervised much of the general legal work of the office and also the work of the West Indian department. In 1897 he succeeded Sir Robert Meade as permanent undersecretary.[108]

After Wingfield's appointment in 1878, the secretariat of the Colonial Office remained unchanged until Herbert's retirement in 1892. Herbert, Meade, Bramston, Wingfield, Holland, and Malcolm all worked well together. This was partially the result of the similarity of their backgrounds. They were all Oxford graduates except Holland, who attended Trinity College, Cambridge. They all attended good public schools such as Harrow (Holland), Eton (Herbert, Meade, and Malcolm), and Winchester (Bramston and Wingfield). They all entered the British civil service at the highest level with very little previous administrative training. All of them except Meade were lawyers, helping to explain their emphasis on the legal aspects of any colonial problem. Finally, they were all conservatives except Meade, and Herbert believed that Meade, because of his landholdings, might be developing some of the "prejudices of a squatter."[109] Only Pauncefote, who received his early education in Paris and Geneva and who thought at one time of making a career in the Indian Army, [110] did not conform to this general pattern, and he remained in the office less than two years. Because of these common factors in their backgrounds, the members of the secretariat of the Colonial Office were able to communicate easily with each other and to discuss questions on the basis of a number of common ideals and assumptions.

The Treasury's reluctance to appoint a third assistant undersecretary with expensive legal qualifications was partially due to Carnarvon's decision to fill the vacant fourth principal clerkship. In 1872 Kimberley had agreed to keep that position vacant until all of the redundant clerks had been absorbed into the establishment. Carnarvon insisted, however, that the work of the Colonial Office was too voluminous for only two geographical departments. Three departments were absolutely essential. He therefore decided to give William

107. *Colonial Office List* (1891), p. 496.
108. Although Wingfield was known as a very hard and consciencious worker, his appointment as permanent undersecretary was regarded by Sydney Buxton, the parliamentary undersecretary from 1892 to 1895, as a stopgap measure and "not a very brilliant appointment." Buxton to Ripon, February 25, 1897, Add. MS 43555, f. 68.
109. Herbert's minute of January 16, 1878, on Bowen to Carnarvon, November 28, 1877, CO 309/116.
110. He spent only two years at the newly founded Marlborough College, Oxford. Mowat, *Life of Pauncefote*, pp. 5–8.

Robinson, the principal clerk of the general department, a colonial governorship.[111] Henry C. Norris replaced Robinson as the third principal clerk, and Richard Eben was appointed acting fourth principal clerk.[112] The Treasury in sanctioning the appointment of the third assistant undersecretary raised serious doubts concerning the necessity of employing so many principal clerks.[113] Carnarvon was surprised and angered because he was now forced "to carry on a controversy with the Treasury on a matter of the smallest detail in order to secure the bare means of discharging in a proper manner the work of [the Colonial Office.]"[114] Carnarvon, who could on occasion be extremely intolerant of opposition, appealed directly to the chancellor of the exchequer to avert an interdepartmental controversy. The private communications between these two ministers superseded the official correspondence.

Carnarvon assured Northcote that he, not Herbert, had decided that the appointment of an acting fourth principal clerk was necessary. He stressed the need of having "a sufficient and thoroughly effective staff with which to administer from home." "All my wishes and tendencies—though I see no object in proclaiming them—are towards economy, but I perceive in this what I have perceived in so many other matters, public and private, the penny wise and pound foolish view, which leads ultimately to great and unnecessary expense." To avoid an interdepartmental quarrel, Carnarvon proposed an informal meeting with Sir Ralph Lingen, the permanent secretary of the Treasury. If Lingen, the "genius of official economy," could be convinced of the Colonial Office's needs, then Northcote would also be put at ease.[115] Carnarvon also trusted that Northcote's "candour & breadth of view" would enable him to see the merits of the Colonial Office's position.[116]

Apparently the expected deficit in the annual budget restricted Northcote's "breadth of view." He reiterated that the principal clerks' high salaries had been granted on the assumption that they

111. Robinson accepted the governorship of the Bahamas on August 30, 1874. Robinson to Carnarvon, August 30, 1874, PRO 30/6/41, No. 67.
112. Carnarvon's minute of September 5, 1874, CO 878/5, Vol. 5, No. 97; CO to Treasury, September 11, 1874, CO 323/319.
113. Treasury to CO, October 26, 1874, CO 323/319.
114. Carnarvon's minute of October 29, 1874, on *ibid.*
115. Carnarvon to Northcote, copy, confidential, November 4, 1874, PRO 30/6/7, ff. 70–71.
116. Carnarvon to Northcote, copy, private, December 1, 1874, PRO 30/6/7, f. 78.

would perform duties which had previously fallen upon the secretariat. Carnarvon's appointment of a third assistant undersecretary disproved the validity of this supposition.[117] With a strengthened secretariat there was no need for a fourth principal clerk. Northcote also objected to the constant alteration of the Colonial Office's constitution.

There is great inconvenience in one head of a department [Kimberley] improving its force in one way and his successor [Carnarvon] improving it in another; because if the first says, I don't want more secretaries provided you raise my clerks, and the second says, It is not the clerks but the secretaries that want strengthening, the advance is made double.[118]

Carnarvon could only reply that without the extra assistance the Colonial Office would have "broken down." Economy in large questions could be obtained only by "an effective and therefore liberally paid administration at home."[119] Northcote again backed down, and the Colonial Office obtained a fourth principal clerk. This clerk did not, however, receive the full pay of his class.[120] The creation of a third geographical department necessitated a redistribution of the Colonial Office's work. Charles Cox's West Indian and Eastern department remained essentially unchanged. A separate North American and Australian department was created and placed under the supervision of William Dealtry. With the exceptions of Western Australia and Fiji, this department dealt exclusively with colonies with responsible government. Henry Norris supervised the new African and Mediterranean department, and Richard Ebden headed the unchanged general department.[121]

This debate over the appointment of a fourth principal clerk is typical of the petty disputes clouding the relations between the Colonial Office and the Treasury throughout the seventies. The Treasury officials became convinced that Carnarvon's demands for more principal clerks was simply a ruse to extort higher salaries from the public funds which they were pledged to defend. The Colonial Office staff placed all of the blame on the Treasury. The "genius of official econ-

117. Herbert had admitted in a private conversation with Northcote that the principal clerks were not competent to perform the duties of the assistant undersecretaries.
118. Northcote to Carnarvon, private, December 2, 1874, PRO 30/6/7, ff. 79–81.
119. Carnarvon to Northcote, copy, private, December 6, 1874, PRO 30/6/7, ff. 82–83.
120. Carnarvon to William Smith, copy, January 1, 1875, PRO 30/6/17, ff. 1–2.
121. The distribution of the work can be determined from the various editions of the *Colonial Office List*.

omy" did not appreciate the growing responsibilities of the Colonial Office, the diverse nature of its work, and, most importantly, the time required to make the 1872 reorganization effective.

The Colonial Office was handicapped throughout the seventies because it could not recruit any new competitive clerks until the office's redundant clerks had been absorbed into the establishment. The number of upper-division clerks had to be reduced from twenty-six to eighteen,[122] and it was not until 1877 that the first of the new university men entered the Colonial Office. Herbert anticipated that these new clerks would be assigned more responsible work and reduce the pressure on the secretariat. In general they fulfilled his expectations. Until they entered the office in significant numbers and advanced to positions of authority, it was necessary, however, to rely on a reduced number of older clerks to perform an increasing amount of work. Some of the older members such as Richard Ebden, A. W. L. Hemming, and Edward Fairfield met the challenge; others did not.

The recruitment of open competition clerks was facilitated to some extent by the Treasury's decision to permit the Colonial Office to enlarge its upper-division staff. In 1878 a new second-class clerk was recruited because of the absorption of the old Emigration Office into the Colonial Office.[123] Another second-class clerk and a first-class clerk were added in 1880 because of the additional work resulting from the disturbances in South Africa and the transfer of Cyprus from the Foreign Office.[124] Another second-class clerk was appointed in 1881. The upper division of the Colonial Office then comprised twenty-two clerks: four principals, seven first-class clerks, and eleven second-class clerks. This distribution remained unchanged until 1891 when the upper division was reduced to only twenty-one members.[125]

Between 1877 and 1892, when Herbert retired, eleven open competition clerks entered the office. In selecting these men the Colonial Office naturally attempted to recruit men who possessed both station in life and ability. Rogers, who believed that every clerk should have "received the education of a gentleman, & presumably among gentle-

122. There were to be four principal clerks, five first-class clerks, and nine second-class clerks.

123. Treasury to CO, June 26, 1878, CO 323/337. See chapter iv.

124. Treasury to CO, September 14, 1880, CO 323/344. A fourth geographical department was also established by dividing the Eastern and West Indian department. This meant that one of the five departments in the Colonial Office was placed under the supervision of a first-class clerk.

125. CO to Treasury, September 15, 1891, CO 323/387.

men," had stressed the first quality.[126] Herbert tended to emphasize ability. If capable men could not be obtained, he did not think that the smaller Colonial Office staff would be able to function effectively.[127]

The Civil Service Commission was responsible for filling vacancies in the Colonial Office. Upon receiving notification of such a vacancy, the commissioners advertised the position and announced the date of the examination in various newspapers and journals.[128] The examination was still divided into two parts, and it continued to stress the classics. Frequently a candidate received almost half of his marks in Latin and Greek. The examination therefore insured that most of the Colonial Office's new clerks possessed a public school and university education. Only one of the eleven second-class clerks who entered the office between 1877 and 1889, Sidney Webb, was not a university man. Seven were from Oxford, two attended Cambridge, and one, John Anderson, was a product of the University of Aberdeen. Although the educational attainments of the new clerks were more impressive, most of them came from the same ranks of society as earlier. There were five sons of clergymen. H. J. Read's father owned a drapery store, while C. P. Lucas' father was a doctor. W. H. Mercer's father was a university-trained designer. Again, the only exception to the general rule was Sidney Webb, whose father was a public accountant.[129]

Each examination usually filled vacancies in several different offices. The winning candidate had his choice of the available positions. The person who finished second could then choose from among the remaining offerings, a process which was continued until all of the openings had been filled. The top candidates invariably chose either the Colonial Office or the Treasury,[130] and when neither of these two offices had vacancies the quality of the men competing for positions in

126. Rogers' minute of February 17, 1870, on Treasury to CO, December 23, 1869, CO 323/297.
127. CO to Treasury, November 17, 1876, CO 323/309; CO to Treasury, April 21, 1877, CO 323/332.
128. CSC to CO, March 11, 1881, CO 323/350. The Colonial Office also attempted to do some recruitment. Notices of vacancies were sent to all of the Oxford and Cambridge colleges and to the other English and Irish universities.
129. This information was drawn primarily from the biographical sketches in the *Colonial Office List* and from the correspondence between the Colonial Office and the Civil Service Commission.
130. C. P. Lucas and R. L. Antrobus were the top candidates in the 1877 examination. "Reports of Her Majesty's Civil Service Commissioners; with Appendices: Twenty-second, 1878," C. 2178, p. 177, *Parl. Paps. 1878*, XXVII. H. W. Just finished second in the April 9, 1878, examination. The top candidate chose a Treasury clerkship. "Twenty-third, 1878," C. 2439, p. 163, *Parl. Paps. 1878–79*, XXII.

the civil service was lower.[131] The popularity of these two offices is easy to explain; these departments had the highest salaries and the most prestige. In the early nineteenth century the Board of Trade had been a distinguished office,[132] but by 1886 some people regarded it as "the least desirable of the Public Offices."[133] The decline in the popularity of the Board of Trade was largely because its initial salary was only £200 compared with the £250 offered by the Treasury and the Colonial Office. Many offices paid much less than the Board of Trade. The reorganization of 1872 had made the Colonial Office one of the most prestigious, if not important, departments in the British civil service.[134]

A candidate's personality and future ambitions usually determined his choice between the Colonial Office and the Treasury. Sir Reginald Welby, the permanent secretary of the Treasury, admitted that candidates who desired "a more varied service" generally preferred the Colonial Office.[135] The first three candidates at the February 1, 1881, examination, G. V. Fiddes, Sidney Webb, and G. W. Johnson, selected the Colonial Office, and Welby had to be content with the candidate who finished fourth.[136] The opportunities for overseas colonial service certainly contributed to the popularity of the Colonial Office. G. W. Johnson chose the Colonial Office because he wanted "to see a little of the world outside the little duck-pond Cambridge."[137] Some of the

131. Meade's minute of January 29, 1886, on Bishop of Dover to Stanley, January 25, 1886, CO 323/366.

132. Bernard Mallet, *Sir Louis Mallet: A Record of Public Service and Political Ideals* (London, 1905), pp. 15–16.

133. Edward Hardcortte to Col. F. A. Stanley, n.d., 1886, CO 323/366. Hardcortte asked Stanley to arrange a transfer of his nephew from the Board of Trade to the Colonial Office.

134. Sir Lionel Earle, Lord Crewe's private secretary in 1908, has written, "The Colonial Office was staffed with the most brilliant set of men of any Department of State at that time. This was largely due to the prestige of Mr. Joseph Chamberlain, who not only by his personality had attracted the young men who passed highest, into the service, but had also raised the scales of salaries to those of Treasury officials." *Turn Over the Page* (London, 1935), p. 82. This exalted and mistaken view of Chamberlain's importance in the staffing of the Colonial Office has been frequently repeated. The Colonial Office was a prestigious office long before his appointment. Chamberlain may have inspired the clerks to greater effort, but the staff he inherited was equal to any in the entire civil service.

135. "Second Report of the Royal (Ridley) Commission," C. 5545, p. 3, *Parl. Paps. 1888*, XXVII.

136. "Reports of Her Majesty's Civil Service Commissioners; with Appendices: Twenty-sixth, 1882," C. 3245, p. 190, *Parl. Paps. 1882*, XXII.

137. G. W. Johnson to A. Johnson, November 22, 1878, in Alice Johnson, *George William Johnson: Civil Servant and Social Worker* (Cambridge, 1927), p. 23. Another clerk remarked that the main advantage of the Colonial Office was "the well-paid opportunities for committing gentlemanlike suicide . . . on the West Coast of Africa." W. A. B. Hamilton, *Mr. Montenello: A Romance of the Civil Service* (3 vols.; London, 1885), I, 29.

new clerks expected too much adventure and excitement, and they later objected to the restrictions placed upon them by departmental routine. Many of them did, however, see service in the colonies.[138]

The first three competitive clerks to enter the office were C. P. Lucas, R. L. Antrobus, and H. W. Just. All three men had received a classical education at Oxford. In addition to academic distinction, they possessed the "tact, manners, and *savoir faire*" which were regarded as important to a clerk.[139] Perhaps for this reason, they frequently served as private secretaries. Lucas was Herbert's private secretary for almost ten years. Antrobus was private secretary to both Lord Derby (1882–1885) and Lord Granville (1886), and Just was assistant private secretary to most of the colonial secretaries during the eighties.[140] Until Chamberlain's term as colonial secretary these three men spent relatively little time on departmental work.

Of these three clerks Lucas was perhaps the most able and also the most interesting. Herbert obviously appreciated his ability, and when an Emigrants' Information Office was established in 1886 Lucas was appointed to serve on its managing council.[141] Lucas handled most of the new office's important business. He enjoyed his work as a publicist, and his vigorous promotion of emigration earned him the praise of his superiors.[142] In later years Lucas became the Colonial Office's strongest advocate of imperial unity, becoming increasingly critical of what he considered the Colonial Office's lack of imagination.

Lucas was appointed to supervise a new Dominions Department in 1907. He attempted to use this new department to promote imperial unity and preference and to educate the people at home and in the colonies to the value of the empire and the problems facing it. He suggested the publication of pamphlets dealing with such topics as Asian immigration and defense. After a visit to Australia in 1909, he became convinced that the dominions actually desired the Colonial Office to exercise stronger leadership.

138. Antrobus administered the government of St. Helena from November 5, 1889, to June 8, 1890. John Anderson went on a mission to Gibraltar in 1891. Charles A. Harris investigated the civil establishments of the West Indies in 1892. For Meade's comments on the use of clerks in the colonies see "Second Report of the Royal (Ridley) Commission," C. 5545, pp. 75–76, *Parl. Paps. 1888*, XXVII.
139. Hamilton, *Nineteenth Century and After*, p. 608.
140. In 1872 Herbert had hoped to limit continuous service as a private secretary to one year, a rule which was never enforced. Herbert's minute of January 13, 1872, CO 537/22.
141. Herbert to Lucas, September, 1886, CO 384/162. For the establishment of this office see chap. iv.
142. Minutes on Lucas' memo of November 12, 1886, CO 384/162; minutes on Treasury to CO, February 1, 1887, CO 384/166.

The danger is not that the Colonial Office will interfere too much. On the contrary, one of the first men in Australia told me that he thought it would be well if the Colonial Office on occasion spoke more strongly. The danger is that the Australians should think that they are being ignored and kept in the dark, without any obvious reason.[143]

Lucas' position encountered strong opposition from within the Colonial Office. H. W. Just, the permanent secretary to the Imperial Conference, argued that the dominions could be retained within the empire only if the Colonial Office maintained its policy of noninterference.[144] Just emerged victorious from the struggle, and Lucas retired in 1911 at the early age of fifty-five. Largely because of his outspoken views on the empire and its administration, he had been passed over twice for the permanent undersecretaryship.[145] Lucas probably felt that the work of promoting imperial unity would be easier if carried on from outside of the confines of Downing Street.[146] Just replaced him as assistant undersecretary of the Dominions Department. Despite this promotion, Just was never as highly regarded as Lucas, possessing none of Lucas' imagination.[147]

The remainder of the new second-class clerks were employed almost exclusively on departmental duties. They were all permitted to minute

143. J. A. Cross, "The Dominions Department of the Colonial Office: Origins and Early Years, 1905–14" (doctoral thesis, University of London, 1965), pp. 59–60.
144. *Ibid.*, p. 223.
145. *Ibid.*, p. 218.
146. After his retirement, Lucas, supported by an All Souls' fellowship, continued to devote his life to writing about the empire. His most important works include a multivolume *Historical Geography of the British Colonies* (1888–1901), *A History of Canada, 1763–1812* (1909), *Greater Rome and Greater Britain* (1912), and *Religion, Colonising, and Trade* (1930).
147. Cross, "The Dominion Department," p. 223. One member of the office described Just as "a gay, little, gentle, lovable figure" who fluttered around his colleagues like "a shy but friendly bird round someone with crumbs on a plate." Sir Ralph Furse, *Aucuparius: Recollections of a Recruiting Officer* (London, 1962), p. 25. Just's own efforts at publicizing the empire were confined to a short volume of incredibly bad verse. His most interesting poem is perhaps "Ballade of Red Tape" which concludes:

> He [the clerk] sits with his quill of the grey goose feather
>   By an inkpot; to train his thoughts to flow
> His freeborn soul to a desk they tether
>   Whilst messengers entering in dumb show
>   Deposit the bundles row on row
> For this dull-eyed hermit in his retreat.
>   Away from the fields and flowers that blow
> It is all red tape in Downing Street.
>
>   . . . .
>
> Clerk, if you find the Office slow,
>   If the Press with a gibe your labours greet,
> Forget not the days of your boyhood, though
>   It is all red tape in Downing Street.

Sir H. W. Just, *Verses* (Cambridge, 1930), p. 15. An example of his political poetry, "Britanniae Omnes," may be found in the *Saturday Review*, CIII (April 13, 1907), 459.

dispatches and to undertake other responsible duties shortly after their appointment to the Colonial Office.[148] C. A. Harris, the senior second-class clerk in the West Indian department, played an especially important role in colonial administration. The principal clerk of his department, John Hales, was probably the least able of the older clerks; Herbert and Bramston were both disturbed by his inefficiency.[149] Because of Hales' administrative shortcomings, Harris and later Sydney Olivier did much of the West Indian work.[150] The second-class clerks working under able men such as Fairfield and Ebden had fewer opportunities to distinguish themselves. All of them did, however, take an active and important part in the work of the office.[151]

Three of these new clerks, G. W. Johnson, Sidney Webb, and Sydney Olivier, are especially interesting. They were all extremely idealistic, and their dissatisfaction with the routine of the Colonial Office says much about its strengths and weaknesses. G. W. Johnson, who entered the office in 1881, was born "to an inheritance of upright, liberal Nonconformity."[152] His religious outlook on life continued to develop, and he spent most of his free time working for various social movements. He was associated for a short time with the Fabians. Later he served as editor of the *Christian Socialist*. From 1887 to 1898 he was chairman of Morley College for Working Men and Women. Johnson was also a director of the London Missionary Society, active in the Women's Suffrage Movement, and "a tower of strength" to the Association for Moral and Social Hygiene.[153]

148. G. W. Johnson to Alice Johnson, July 7, 1881, in Johnson, *G. W. Johnson*, p. 41; Sydney Olivier to Graham Wallas, May 10, 1882, in Olivier, ed., *Sydney Olivier*, p. 52.

149. Minutes on Berkeley to Kimberley, July 24, 1880, CO 152/139.

150. CO 152/156–68, *passim*. See especially the minutes on Lees to Derby, September 9, 1884, CO 152/158. Olivier, perhaps because of his experiences with Hales, called attention to the differences between the "old stagers" and the "younger more distinctly intelligent class of men." M. Olivier, ed., *Sydney Olivier*, p. 31.

151. Sidney Webb's work on African financial questions was especially appreciated by Herbert. Herbert's minute of September 5, 1891, on Webb to Ebden, August 20, 1891, CO 323/387. Lucas handled the estimates of Labuan the year after his appointment. His superiors added nothing beyond their initials to his suggestions. The second-class clerk who served as assistant private secretary to the secretary of state had great power in the appointment of minor officials to the overseas colonial service. Antrobus' minute of March 12, 1883, on Rev. W. Wright to Derby, March 5, 1883, CO 429/2; Just's minute of November 23, 1886, on R. A. Freeman to Stanhope, October 3, 1886, CO 429/3. Such examples are typical of the eighties, as Meade indicated in testimony before the Ridley Commission. "Second Report of the Royal (Ridley) Commission," C. 5545, p. 75, *Parl. Paps. 1888*, XXVII.

152. His father was only the second dissenter to receive a degree from Cambridge. G. W. Johnson, *The Evolution of Woman, from Subjugation to Comradship, with a Memoir* (London, 1926), p. 13.

153. *Ibid.*, p. 24. He and his wife were close friends of Josephine E. Butler, the foremost suffragette of the day, and they later edited her memoirs.

Within the Colonial Office, Johnson was regarded as a man of high principle. His work was confined to the Eastern department, where he became very concerned about the social problems arising from the use of indentured labor and the exploitation of prostitution and opium smoking for revenue purposes.[154] Although he remained at the Colonial Office until 1917, Johnson was never admitted to the inner circle of power. This was partly because of his very poor eyesight, but more important was the fact that secretaries of state preferred the "clear logical brain" of a George Fiddes[155] to the idealism of a Johnson.

Sidney Webb and Sydney Olivier, the Colonial Office's most famous dropouts, shared Johnson's concern for the great social problems of the day. Unlike Johnson, however, they eventually left the office. Webb's background was unusual for a Colonial Office clerk. His father was a public accountant "in a very modest way," and Sidney did not therefore possess an Oxford or Cambridge education. He entered the civil service at the age of eighteen, becoming a lower-division clerk at the War Office. Three years later, in 1881, he competed for and secured a second-class clerkship in the Colonial Office.[156] Webb was immediately put to work in the West Indian department; a "globular little Napoleon III"[157] had little chance of serving as a private secretary.

Webb found his life's work outside the civil service. In 1879 he met George Bernard Shaw and, like J. S. Mill and his friends forty years earlier, they formed a debating club. Webb later interested Sydney Olivier in their discussions, which usually dealt with some aspect of socialism or Marxism.[158] In 1885 Shaw, Webb, and Olivier all joined the budding Fabian Society, and after that date leading Fabians, such as Graham Wallas, were frequent visitors at the Colonial Office.[159] Most of the secretarial work of the Fabian Society was done before the Colonial Office opened. The political neutrality of a civil servant could be stretched only so far, however, and in 1891 Webb resigned to stand for the London County Council.[160] Although few members of the

154. Johnson, G. W. Johnson, pp. 41–52.
155. Furse, Aucuparius, p. 24. Fiddes received the permanent undersecretaryship in 1916 instead of Johnson.
156. DNB (1941–1950), pp. 935–936.
157. L. S. Amery, My Political Life (3 vols.; London, 1953), I, 230. "Sidney Webb was a robust little man with a goatee beard who peered at you shrewdly through thick eyeglasses and spoke with a strong lisping Cockney accent." Ibid., I, 229.
158. Webb to G. B. Shaw, November 4, 1884, Shaw Papers, Add. MS 50553, ff. 67–68.
159. C. H. Harris, "Recollections," in M. Olivier, ed., Sydney Olivier, pp. 227–228.
160. He served as a Progressive member of the LCC until 1910. In 1929 Webb, now

Colonial Office agreed with Webb's politics, they were all sorry to see him leave, especially Herbert, who respected his ability. Herbert did not, however, feel that the Colonial Office should be surprised or disappointed at Webb's decision "to enter upon a wider field of labor."[161]

Sydney Olivier remained at the Colonial Office for several more years. He continued to take an active interest in socialism, and in 1889 he contributed to the *Fabian Essays in Socialism*. In 1893 he used his leave to travel to Zurich and to deliver a major speech before the International Socialist Congress. This speech was fully reported in the *Times*, and Sydney Buxton, the parliamentary undersecretary, was worried that Olivier might involve the Colonial Office. Although Olivier was not ordered to return to London, Buxton did believe that he needed a good "wigging."[162]

Even if Olivier had discontinued his political activities, he would still have been unpopular with his colleagues. He was sarcastic, self-assured, and intolerant of people less intelligent than himself. He "never dreamt of considering other people's feelings."[163] To Olivier, George Fiddes was "a rabid narrow-minded Jingo," Milner was a "*booby*," and the colonial service was a veritable wasteland of talent.[164] After about eight years at the Colonial Office, he applied for overseas service. The absence of any contact with "realities and the people" distressed him. He was also convinced that "most Governors were exceedingly stupid."[165] The Colonial Office appointed him colonial secretary of British Honduras, probably relieved to deal with him at a distance. Until his "retirement" in 1913 Olivier alternated work in the Colonial Office with what he considered the more important work in the colonies.[166]

The new second-class clerks who entered the Colonial Office after 1877 were in general extremely able men. In fact, it has been suggested that perhaps the staff was "too intelligent to be imaginative."[167]

Lord Passfield, became secretary of state for the dominions and colonies. See Sir Drummond Shields, "Sidney Webb as a Minister," *The Webbs and Their Work*, ed. Margaret Cole (London, 1949), pp. 201–218.

161. Minutes on Webb to Ebden, August 20, 1891, CO 323/387.

162. Buxton to Ripon, August 10, 1893, Add. MS 43553, ff. 128–133; Olivier, ed., *Sydney Olivier*, p. 11.

163. G. B. Shaw, "Some Impressions," in Olivier, ed., *Sydney Olivier*, p. 9; Robert V. Kubicek, *The Administration of Imperialism*, p. 19.

164. Olivier to Shaw, 1899, Shaw Papers, Add. MS 50553, ff. 121–132.

165. Olivier, ed., *Sydney Olivier*, p. 36.

166. Shaw stated that Olivier never understood that his political ideas and personality were offensive to the Colonial Office and retarded his advancement. "Some Impressions," in Olivier, ed., *Sydney Olivier*, p. 14.

167. *CHBE*, III, 768.

Some of the new clerks, however, possessed abundant enthusiasm. Lucas, Johnson, Webb, and Olivier were all highly idealistic and eager to champion a cause. Lucas worked with varying degrees of success within the Colonial Office. The others found their causes elsewhere, partly because of the bureaucratic inflexibility of their department. To these men their most important work was done outside the Colonial Office. The greatest failing of Herbert, Meade, and Wingfield was their inability to harness effectively the restless energy of the Webbs and the Oliviers. If the charge of unimaginativeness is valid, the secretariat of the Colonial Office must take most of the blame.[168] Although Herbert's term in office was primarily a training period for the new clerks, many of them soon expressed annoyance with the restrictions of departmental routine. Chamberlain later lost many of his best clerks to the overseas colonial service.[169]

There were several alterations in the Colonial Office's constitution in the seventies. These changes resulted primarily from the increased amount and urgency of the work. Resident clerks were appointed to meet the problems created by the telegraph. The secretariat was strengthened by the addition of another assistant undersecretary. The supplementary clerks were given staff appointments designed to relieve the second-class clerks of all mechanical work. Finally, the number of upper-division clerks in the Colonial Office was increased from eighteen to twenty-two. These clerks were recruited by open competition and given a greater role in the formation of policy. Unlike Herbert and the colonial secretaries, who dealt primarily with crisis questions, these new clerks specialized in the affairs of one colony or a group of colonies or on a specific problem such as finance, defense, or social reform. Whereas in 1870 the secretary of state had only four or five advisers, by 1892 when Herbert retired most of the upper division of the office was serving in an advisory capacity. After 1882 there were very few important changes in the organization and routine of the office. In fact, between 1882 and 1889 no new clerks were appointed to the upper division of the Colonial Office. Herbert's department had secured a good class of clerks with high salaries, and it was primarily interested in maintaining the status quo.

168. From Herbert's point of view, the unimaginativeness of the Colonial Office was probably more of a strength than a weakness. The colonies with responsible government would not have appreciated vigorous direction from London.
169. Kubicek, *The Administration of Imperialism*, p. 21.

CHAPTER IV

The Crown Agents and the Colonial Land and Emigration Commission

THE COLONIAL OFFICE'S two most important subdepartments were the Crown Agents for the Colonies and the Colonial Land and Emigration Commission. Both of these offices had been established in the 1830's and in 1870 they still retained a considerable amount of autonomy. Herbert and his political superiors in the seventies attempted to tighten their control over these departments, a plan which was facilitated by the completion of the new Colonial Office building in 1876. After that date, the Colonial Office and its two subdepartments were housed under the same roof.

Relations between the Colonial Office and the Crown Agents for the Colonies were complicated in the seventies by the fact that the Treasury also possessed some supervisory powers over the actions of the crown agents. It was not until 1880 that the Colonial Office assumed sole responsibility for them. In the same year, the crown agents were prohibited from undertaking any work for colonies with responsible government. The crown agents' department became, at least in theory, simply a means by which the Colonial Office could promote the economic and social development of the crown colonies.

The Colonial Land and Emigration Commission also underwent great changes in the seventies. With the full cooperation of the Treasury, Herbert and his superiors transferred the commissioners' duties to the Board of Trade, the Crown Agents for the Colonies, and the Colonial Office itself. The Colonial Land and Emigration Commission was completely abolished in 1878, and its reduced staff was absorbed into the Colonial Office. In 1886, however, it became necessary to establish a new Emigrants' Information Office to assist the growing number of emigrants. This new office, which was responsible to the colonial secretary, proved very useful, and it functioned virtually unchanged throughout the nineties.

I

THE origins of the modern Crown Agents Department are to be found in the eighteenth century. Most of the colonies discovered that it was advantageous to send resident agents to London to protect their financial, commercial, and political interests. The British government also appointed officials to supervise the expenditure of parliamentary grants to the colonies. After 1763 warrants were issued to several "crown agents," who helped in the financial administration of the recently conquered territories. These officials placed loans, collected overpayments, and provided materials requisitioned by the colonial governments. By the early nineteenth century, the appointment of these "crown agents" was a prerogative of the colonial secretary, and he frequently used these positions to reward elderly clerks in the Colonial Office. The inefficiency of this system led to numerous complaints and eventually to the appointment of an investigating commission. In 1833 the Colonial Office and the Treasury decided, in the interests of both economy and efficiency, to retain only two agents. These two men, George Baille and Edward Barnard, were forced to retire from the Colonial Office and to concentrate on the work of the new consolidated Crown Agency Office.[1]

The Crown Agency was a good idea, but unfortunately the inefficiency of its personnel reduced its value and aroused considerable discontent in the colonies. The West Indian colonies continued to employ their own agents, and the new office's work was restricted to those crown colonies required to use its services. Immediately upon receiving representative institutions, the Australian colonies established their own agencies in London. Finally, in 1858 (Sir) Penrose Julyan, an ex-army man with considerable financial ability, was appointed senior agent general. Julyan reorganized his department and improved the efficiency of his staff.[2]

The Colonial Office and the Treasury facilitated Julyan's reforms by granting his department a formal constitution. The primary responsibility for supervising Julyan's agency was given to the Colonial Office in 1860; the Treasury was to be consulted only on "extraordi-

1. Lillian M. Penson, "The Origins of the Crown Agency Office," *English Historical Review*, XL (April, 1925), 196–206; A. W. Abbott, *A Short History of the Crown Agents and Their Office* (London, 1959), pp. 11–18; Young, *Colonial Office*, pp. 29–32.
2. Abbott, *Crown Agents*, pp. 17–18.

nary occasions." The Colonial Office sanctioned an increase in the commission which the Crown Agents for the Colonies, as Julyan's department was now called, could charge for the issue and payment of colonial loans. This additional revenue was used to establish an office reserve fund. Finally, the crown agents were directed to submit half-yearly returns to the Colonial Office for inspection.[3]

The business of the Crown Agents for the Colonies increased rapidly after Julyan's appointment. Its average annual disbursement rose from £817,000 in 1858–1860 to £9,481,000 in 1875–1877, and its average annual income rose from £12,000 in 1863–1869 to £21,645 in 1876–1882.[4] The size of the crown agents' staff almost doubled during the seventies.[5] Julyan's success initially won the respect and admiration of all of the Colonial Office officials. Speaking from colonial experience, Herbert attested to the crown agents' "great superiority in honesty, efficiency, & economy over any other system of Agency."[6] Rogers attributed their success primarily to Julyan's "remarkable energy."[7]

The crown agents' success was largely the result of their growing loan business with colonies with responsible government. The average annual disbursement for these colonies in 1875–1877 was £7,533,000 compared to only £1,948,000 for the crown colonies. Julyan's intimate knowledge of the City and the efficiency of his department gave him many advantages over the financial representatives of individual colonies. Queensland purchased its railway supplies through Julyan and his associates in 1868, and New Zealand invariably had the crown agents negotiate its loans. By 1878 the agents had issued eighty-eight loans representing a total sum of £33,750,000.[8] Julyan's office was also

3. *Ibid.*, pp. 18–22; Newcastle's circular dispatch of December 31, 1863, "Papers Relating to the Functions of the Crown Agents for the Colonies," C. 3075, pp. 3–4, *Parl. Paps. 1881*, LXIV; Sir Penrose Julyan, "Memorandum on the Origins and Functions of the Department of the Crown Agents for the Colonies," p. 2, CO 323/336.

4. Crown Agents to CO, March 3, 1870, CO 323/299; Crown Agents to CO, April 2, 1886, CO 323/364.

5. Crown Agents to CO, March 3, 1870, CO 323/299; Chart enclosed in Crown Agents to CO, February 1, 1882, CO 323/351. In 1878 the crown agents pioneered in the employment of lady clerks. Crown Agents to CO, January 17, 1879, CO 323/339. Women typists were not appointed to the regular civil service until 1888. Hilda Martindale, *Women Servants of the State, 1870–1938* (London, 1938), pp. 28–29; 205–206.

6. Herbert's minute of March 4, 1870, on Crown Agents to CO, March 3, 1870, CO 323/299.

7. Rogers' minute of March 5, 1870, on Crown Agents to CO, March 3, 1870, *ibid.* If anything, Julyan might know "a shade too much abt the Stock Exchange," and have "too much of contrivance & speculation in the management of finance." Rogers' memo of May 11, 1869, enclosed in Meade to Gladstone, May 11, 1869, Add. MS 44420, f. 240.

8. Abbott, *Crown Agents*, pp. 22–23; Julyan, "Memorandum on the Crown Agents," p. 3, CO 323/336.

strengthened by the 1874 requirement that all goods imported for the public service of crown colonies had to be purchased through the crown agents.[9] This monopoly later became a source of considerable complaint in the crown colonies.

The duties of the crown agents in the seventies and eighties were numerous and diverse. Besides acting as purchasing and loan agents for the colonies, they assisted the Colonial Office in the administration of the empire. They were responsible for the payment of half-pay and pensions to colonial officers.[10] The crown agents also helped to recruit officers requiring technical qualifications.[11] When the Colonial Land and Emigration Commission was abolished in 1878, most of its emigration and convict work was transferred to the crown agents.[12] Because the crown agents retained the services of several consulting engineers, the Colonial Office frequently consulted them on technical questions. They advised on the design of hospitals and jails, the construction of railroads and harbor facilities, communication questions, and countless other problems.[13] The crown agents were also the "financial advisers" on all crown colony loans.[14] Occasionally they were employed on overseas service. William Sargeaunt, the junior crown agent, went to the Transvaal in 1877 in a vain attempt to straighten out its finances.[15] The crown agents were frequently employed by departments and governments not under the direct control of the Colonial Office. During the Ashanti War, for example, the crown agents procured most of Wolseley's supplies and 250 cases of gin, "at the lowest possible price," for Captain Glover's expedition.[16] In 1881, with the permission of the Home Office and the Treasury, they were appointed financial agents for the Isle of Man.[17]

Despite their financial success, the Treasury and the Colonial Office

9. Abbott, *Crown Agents*, p. 24.
10. Julyan, "Memorandum on the Crown Agents," p. 4, CO 323/336.
11. Hall, *The Colonial Office*, p. 43.
12. Stephen Walcott to Crown Agents, March 30, 1878, enclosed in Walcott to Herbert, March 30, 1878, CO 384/121.
13. For their suggestions on Natal railroads see Julyan to Herbert, April 30, 1872, CO 179/109, and minutes on E. Wood to Kimberley (tel.), October 30, 1881, CO 179/138.
14. "Second Report of the Royal (Ridley) Commission," C. 5545, p. 83, *Parl. Paps. 1888*, XXVII.
15. Herbert's minute of November 21, 1877, on Bartle Frere to Carnarvon, October 15, 1877, CO 48/483. Julyan went on a similar mission to Mauritius in 1873. J. K. Chapman, *The Career of Arthur Hamilton Gordon, First Lord Stanmore, 1829–1912* (Toronto, 1964), pp. 144–148.
16. CO to Crown Agents, November 12, 1873, Colonial Office, "Ashantee Invasion: Further Correspondence," p. 302, *Confidential Print, 1873*, CO 879/5, Sec. 36. See also CO 96/106, *passim*.
17. Crown Agents to CO, January 29, 1881, CO 323/348.

became increasingly suspicious of Julyan and his associates. The Treasury was alarmed at the agents' anomalous relationship with the colonies with responsible government, whose internal affairs were not under British control. The Colonial Office was dismayed by a series of questionable financial transactions. The result was that during the seventies several attempts were made to alter the constitution of the Crown Agents for the Colonies. The Treasury argued that the agents' functions should be severely restricted; the Colonial Office, which desired an effective agency, preferred simply to subject Julyan and his department to tighter controls. The Treasury and the Colonial Office finally reached a compromise in 1880. The crown agents were prohibited from undertaking work for colonies with responsible government, but they were allowed to assist, under the strict supervision of the Colonial Office, in the development of the crown colonies.

The constitution of the crown agents' department was partially responsible for the indecision of the Colonial Office and the Treasury during the seventies. Neither department was certain who had the ultimate responsibility for Julyan's actions. The reorganization of the crown agents' department in 1863 had placed the primary responsibility on the Colonial Office, but two years later the Treasury decided that it should also inspect the office returns. "My Lords" later explained that it was necessary for them to be informed regarding "all investments made by the Crown Agents of Balances in their office account."[18] Usually, however, Herbert and his staff simply informed the Treasury of the decision taken by the colonial secretary.[19] Occasionally the crown agents invested their money without securing the approval of either department.[20] All alterations in the size and cost of the crown agents' department originally required the approval of both the Treasury and the Colonial Office. In 1870 Julyan appointed several new clerks, and the salaries of the two crown agents, Julyan and Sargeaunt, were raised to £1,200 and £1,000, respectively. Julyan also received a personal allowance of £200 in recognition of his unique services.[21] The Treasury never showed much interest in the structure of the Crown Agents for the Colonies, however, and after 1873 it attempted to repudiate all responsibility for Julyan's actions.

The laxness of the Colonial Office's control over the work of the

18. Treasury to CO, October 11, 1867, CO 323/288.
19. CO to Treasury, January 29, 1872, CO 323/308.
20. Minutes on Crown Agents to CO, January 23, 1872, *ibid.*
21. CO to Treasury, March 21, 1870; Treasury to CO, April 23, 1870, CO 323/299.

crown agents was clearly illustrated in 1873. In that year Julyan and Sargeaunt purchased the lease on a house in Spring Gardens without obtaining the permission of the secretary of state. They anticipated that their purchase would be routinely approved and that the house would be used for additional office space. Kimberley disliked the transaction, however. He did not attribute bad motives to the crown agents, but he saw no excuse for Julyan's failure to consult with the Colonial Office. He argued that the Colonial Office had to be very careful to avoid "anything which would seem to give sanction to officers of a public department engaging in a private speculation & getting the Govt to take their bargain off their hands."[22] To the annoyance of the Colonial Office, the Treasury refused to become embroiled in the controversy. Meade questioned whether their intervention was really necessary,[23] but Herbert and Kimberley were more cautious. They believed that the Treasury had an obligation to assist the Colonial Office in the financial supervision of the Crown Agents for the Colonies. As Herbert stated: "The status of the Agents in relation to the Government is undefined & anomalous; in the event of serious losses occurring in their office, I doubt very much whether the Colonies would not be entitled to hold this government responsible."[24] The Colonial Office eventually approved the purchase. In 1876 the crown agents' department moved into the new Colonial Office building, the Treasury reluctantly agreeing that it could occupy twenty-three rooms in the basement and on the ground floor for an annual rent of £400. The crown agents provided their own furniture and assisted in defraying the cost of the fuel, lighting, and special fixtures.[25]

The Colonial Office's concern over the "undefined & anomalous" position of the crown agents was intensified as a result of some questionable financial transactions. In 1875 Herbert discovered that Julyan and Sargeaunt had received an honorarium in return for negotiating a New Zealand loan. Herbert first assumed that the honorarium was the standard percentage paid to the office fund, but Julyan later admitted that it was a personal remuneration.[26] He argued that his position as loan agent was "entirely independent" of his position as

22. Kimberley's minute of February 21, 1873, on Crown Agents to CO, January 22, 1873, CO 323/313.
23. Meade's minute of March 23, 1873, on Treasury to CO, March 13, 1873, CO 323/314.
24. Herbert's minute of March 26, 1873, on *ibid.*
25. Treasury to CO, April 25, 1873, CO 323/314; Crown Agents to CO, July 13, 1875, CO 323/322; CO to Treasury, March 23, 1876, CO 323/328.
26. Meade's minute of December 28, 1875, CO 537/157.

crown agent and that the honorarium had been "spontaneously offered" by the government of New Zealand,[27] an explanation which
did not satisfy the Colonial Office. Meade pointed out that the crown
agents' salaries had been raised in 1870 on the condition that they
would refuse all personal fees for negotiating loans. Besides, in requesting permission to act as loan agent, Julyan had not mentioned any
honorarium. Meade could not understand how a public official could
receive pay for services as a private individual. The New Zealand government had employed Julyan as loan agent because of his position
as crown agent.[28]

Herbert was equally disturbed. In an earlier interview Sir Julius
Vogel, a former New Zealand official, had expressed surprise that the
Colonial Office permitted the crown agents to accept personal honorariums. Being unaware of the transaction, Herbert had assured him
that all money received for negotiating loans was paid into the crown
agents' office fund. Now Herbert feared that the Colonial Office had
been "seriously compromised," and he recommended that the agents
be "severely reprimanded and substantially punished." Unless Julyan
furnished a suitable explanation the last honorarium of £3,333 should
be paid into the office fund.[29] Carnarvon agreed that the agents had
"deliberately violated" the regulations.[30]

Julyan explained that he and Sir Julius Vogel had been appointed
independent agents with the power to determine when, where, and in
what form the New Zealand loans should be issued. After much consideration, they had decided that the crown agents should offer the
loan. The Crown Agents for the Colonies received the usual percentage for doing this work; his own gratuity was for services "entirely
independent" of the work of his department.[31] Meade and Herbert,
who were undoubtedly embarrassed by their ignorance of the honorarium, accepted this explanation.[32] Carnarvon, however, still argued
that Julyan had committed a "very serious error" by serving both as a
member of a government department and as a private loan agent.
In addition, Julyan's reasons for not reporting the acceptance of the

27. Julyan to Meade, December 3, 1875, ibid.
28. Meade's minute of December 28, 1875, ibid; Crown Agents to CO, March 3, 1870,
CO 323/299.
29. Herbert's minute of January 19, 1876, CO 537/157.
30. Carnarvon's minute of January 26, 1876, ibid.
31. Julyan to Herbert, February 17, 1876, ibid.
32. Meade's minute of February 22, 1876, and Herbert's minute of February 22,
1876, on Julyan to Herbert, February 17, 1876, ibid.

honorarium were still not clear. Carnarvon felt that Julyan and Sargeaunt should pay a fine of £1,000 into their office fund.

An office like this [the Colonial Office] cannot keep itself too jealously removed from the slightest shade of suspicion in money matters. Any doubt on this point is fatal to it: and it is impossible to lay down too strict a rule of conduct with regard to a department of it [Crown Agents for the Colonies] which is brought into daily contact with commercial transactions and people amongst some of whom it is notorious that a considerable laxity of ideals on this subject prevails. I therefore feel bound to express my great regret that the Crown Agents should have allowed themselves so far to depart from what I must hold to have been their duty.[33]

Despite appeals by Meade and Herbert,[34] Carnarvon refused to alter his position, and the fine was eventually paid.[35]

In view of this irregularity, the Colonial Office naturally attempted to tighten its control over the crown agents. In 1876 Julyan and Sargeaunt requested permission to hire seven new clerks to handle their growing work. They also asked for increases in their own salaries.[36] Meade and Herbert approved these requests, proposing that Julyan receive an increase of £300 to £1,700 a year, and that Sargeaunt rise from £1,000 to £1,200. They also recommended the appointment of a third crown agent with a salary of £800 rising to £1,000.[37] Carnarvon, who was disturbed by the great increase in the cost,[38] reluctantly agreed, but he stipulated that the crown agents must devote their entire time to official work.[39] They were forbidden to act in a private capacity for any colony or to receive any personal remuneration.[40]

The Colonial Office attempted to keep the financial irregularities

33. Carnarvon's minute of March 4, 1876, on Julyan to Herbert, February 17, 1876, *ibid.*

34. Meade's minute of June 5, 1876, and Herbert's minute of June 18, 1876, on Julyan to Herbert, May 23, 1876, *ibid.*

35. Julyan to Herbert, December 8, 1876, *ibid.*

36. Crown Agents to CO, July 25, 1876, CO 323/327.

37. Meade's minute of December 7, 1876, and Herbert's minute of December 8, 1876, on Crown Agents to CO, July 25, 1876, *ibid.*

38. Carnarvon's minute of December 12, 1876, on Crown Agents to CO, July 25, 1876, *ibid.*

39. CO to Crown Agents, December 22, 1876, *ibid.*

40. Richard Ebden's minute of February 22, 1881, CO 537/217. This minute paraphrased an official letter to the crown agents of January 30, 1877. The letter was also communicated to the governor of New Zealand. Carnarvon appointed his private secretary, M. F. Ommanney, third crown agent. Ommanney had received a commission in the royal engineers, and Carnarvon had a high regard for his abilities as an engineer and draftsman. Carnarvon to Northcote, copy, private, August 30, 1876, PRO 30/6/7, ff. 156–159. Besides being of great use in furnishing technical advice, Carnarvon probably hoped that Ommanney would serve as a link between the Colonial Office and the crown agents. In 1900 he was appointed permanent undersecretary of the Colonial Office.

of the crown agents secret,[41] and the officials at the Treasury were
probably unaware of them. The Treasury was, however, suspicious of
the crown agents for another reason. In the past the British government had guaranteed numerous colonial loans. The guarantees were
supposedly confined to loans for imperial projects, but frequently they
were of benefit only to a particular colony. Some colonists came to regard these guarantees, which facilitated the floating of loans, as one of
the privileges of membership in the empire. In England, however,
many people came to object to them on the same grounds that they
opposed the maintenance of imperial troops in the colonies. It was
also argued that the guarantees encouraged the colonists to engage in
reckless borrowing. Finally, each guaranteed loan had to be approved
by Parliament, allowing the opposition to express views which might
be damaging to the government.[42]

Despite the vigorous objections of the Treasury, in 1875 the British
government was still committed to guaranteeing a New Zealand loan of
£1,000,000. W. H. Smith, the secretary to the Treasury, was concerned
about a "serious loss to the Exchequer" if New Zealand's expenditures
could not be reduced.[43] Northcote, the chancellor of the exchequer,
was equally alarmed at the fiscal irresponsibility of some colonies, and
he objected to the British government's being asked to guarantee any
additional loans.[44] The officials at the Treasury also feared that a loan
negotiated by the Crown Agents for the Colonies might be interpreted
as having an imperial guarantee. This concern explains most of the
Treasury's hostility toward the crown agents in the seventies.

The Treasury showed its displeasure with existing arrangements
by suddenly denying any responsibility for the actions of the crown
agents. When the Colonial Office requested that the Treasury approve
the reorganization of the crown agents' office in 1876, the Treasury

41. The correspondence was marked secret and bound separately. Only Julyan, Sargeaunt, Meade, Holland, Herbert, and Carnarvon appear to have been parties to the
controversy.
42. Farr, *The Colonial Office and Canada*, pp. 64–65, discusses this problem in relation
to Canada.
43. Smith to Carnarvon, private, March 24, 1875, PRO 30/6/17, ff. 19–20. Carnarvon
was more sanguine regarding New Zealand's finances. Carnarvon to Smith, copy, private,
March 25, 1875, PRO 30/6/17, f. 21.
44. Northcote to Carnarvon, private, March 3, 1875, PRO 30/6/7, ff. 86–87; Northcote
to Carnarvon, private, October 24, 1875, PRO 30/6/7, f. 95; Northcote to Carnarvon,
private, January 20, 1876, PRO 30/6/7, ff. 113–114. In 1875 the Treasury refused to
guarantee a Griqualand West loan, and the Colonial Office therefore decided not to
raise the question of a loan guarantee for Natal railroads. Minutes on Bulwer to Carnarvon, December 31, 1875, CO 179/118.

refrained from making any comments on the proposals.[45] Despite further attempts by the Colonial Office to persuade the Treasury to accept some responsibility for the Crown Agents for the Colonies,[46] Lingen and his colleagues refused. The Treasury "neither claim any authority over, nor acknowledge any responsibility in connection with this office."[47] The Colonial Office was naturally angered and concerned at the Treasury's refusal to accept a traditional responsibility.

> It may save the Treasury officers some little trouble but their refusal to assist the Sec. of State by maintaining in financial matters that control over other Depts. which I always imagined to be one of their most useful functions will not absolve Her Majesty's Govt. from the responsibility incurred by the acts of the Secretary of State in dealing with the C. Agents Dept. unassisted by the experience of the chief financial Dept. of the Govt. ... If The Treasury are allowed to shuffle off their responsibility, there may be some great disaster which the Treasury may have to repair, & for which they will only have to thank themselves.[48]

The Treasury's obstinacy did, however, impress upon the Colonial Office the inconsistencies in the crown agents' position. In September, 1878, Sir Penrose Julyan prepared a long memorandum on the origins and functions of his department. Unfortunately, he emphasized the difficulty in determining the extent to which the British government was responsible for the crown agents' financial transactions.[49] Richard Ebden, the principal clerk of the general department, argued that Julyan had exaggerated the problem by overestimating his own authority. In actuality, the colonial secretary appointed the crown agents, controlled the size and cost of their department, and sanctioned all purchases by crown colonies of over £100. All loans were backed by the revenue and assets of the various colonies. The only serious difficulty arose because of the crown agents' work for responsible government colonies, which were not under the strict control of the secretary of state.[50]

Meade and Herbert agreed with Ebden, but they were reluctant to force the agents to abandon their lucrative loan business with colonies with responsible government. They feared that this would necessitate

45. Treasury to CO, January 10, 1877, CO 323/332.
46. CO to Treasury, October 25, 1878, CO 323/337. See also Meade's minute of October 13, 1878, on Treasury to CO, April 3, 1878, ibid.
47. Treasury to CO, August 26, 1879, CO 323/340.
48. Herbert's minute of November 28, 1879, on Treasury to CO, August 26, 1879, ibid.
49. Julyan, "Memorandum on the Crown Agents," pp. 5–6, CO 323/336.
50. Ebden's marginal comments on Julyan's memorandum, ibid.

a reduction of nearly one-half in the crown agents' establishment.[51] Hicks Beach, the colonial secretary from 1878 to 1880, decided to allow the crown agents to continue to negotiate colonial loans, feeling that the political advantages outweighed any financial risk.[52] He did, however, anticipate a gradual reduction in this type of work. When Julyan retired in 1879, Hicks Beach did not fill the vacancy.[53] A final decision on the status of the crown agents was postponed until 1880.

In July, 1880, the Treasury, which had "long felt grave doubts respecting the indeterminate relations in which the Crown Agents and their transactions stand toward Her Majesty's Government," suggested the appointment of an interdepartmental committee to inquire into its constitution.[54] Meade believed that the inquiry would be useful. His only concern was that Sir Ralph Lingen, the permanent secretary of the Treasury, would attempt to abolish the crown agents' department, and he therefore hoped that Herbert would represent the Colonial Office. "No one else would be able to cope with Sir R. Lingen. At least I certainly could not do so."[55] Herbert believed that the inquiry would also be useful in determining whether official trustees for the crown agents should continue to be appointed. Lingen was one of the trustees, and Herbert attributed much of the Treasury's hostility to Lingen's concern with these duties. He also believed that the crown agents' business with responsible government colonies could be restricted. Herbert would not, however, permit an interdepartmental committee to abolish the Crown Agents for the Colonies. This department was essential as long as the crown colonies were retained. "The Colonial Office must continue to supervise thoroughly & control in all its details the finance & expenditure of Crown Colonies; and if this control is relaxed we know by experience that there will be danger of demands for assistance from Imperial Funds to the mismanaged Colonial Treasuries."[56]

An official inquiry was avoided when Meade, Herbert, and Lingen

51. Meade's minute of January 13, 1879; Herbert's minute of June 26, 1879, on Julyan's memorandum, *ibid.*
52. Hicks Beach's minute of August 3, 1879, on Julyan's memorandum, *ibid.*
53. Hicks Beach's minute of February 20, 1880, on Fairfield to Hicks Beach, January 6, 1880, CO 323/347. In January, 1881, Kimberley, who succeeded Hicks Beach, appointed Ernest Blake, a first-class clerk at the Colonial Office, third crown agent. Sargeaunt was ill, and Ommanney was unable to transact all of the business unaided. Herbert to Blake, January 28, 1881, CO 323/349. The number of crown agents was later reduced to two.
54. Treasury to CO, July 8, 1880, CO 323/344.
55. Meade's minute of July 19, 1880, on Treasury to CO, July 8, 1880, *ibid.*
56. Herbert's minute of July 20, 1880, on Treasury to CO, July 8, 1880, *ibid.*

agreed informally to prohibit the crown agents from transacting business for colonies with responsible government.[57] This decision was communicated to the governors of the Cape and New Zealand, the only such colonies still employing the crown agents.[58] Herbert also assumed Lingen's duties as official trustee of the crown agents' securities.[59] Finally, the Colonial Office assumed full responsibility for the agents' department.[60]

Unfortunately, these reforms came too late to prevent another disagreeable discussion concerning honorariums. In June, 1879, the New Zealand government appointed Sir Julius Vogel, Julyan, and Ommanney to act as its loan agents. Julyan and Ommanney were bound by official regulations to act only in an official capacity and to receive no personal remuneration. Julyan, however, retired on November 30, 1879, twelve days before the loan had been fully subscribed. He then informed the government of New Zealand by telegraph that, as a private individual, he expected a personal commission of one-eighth of one percent on the £5,000,000 loan. Not wishing to jeopardize the success of its loan, the government of New Zealand agreed, and on December 19, 1879, Julyan received an honorarium of £6,250.[61] The Colonial Office did not learn of this payment until 1881.

Herbert, Meade, and Kimberley were naturally angry at not having received a formal communication from the crown agents. Sargeaunt and Ommanney were reprimanded for their negligence, and they were distinctly told not to undertake any new loan business without the approval of the secretary of state.[62] Even more serious, however, was Julyan's "acceptance" of a personal fee for an appointment which he owed to his official position. Kimberley believed that the entire transaction had an "ugly appearance."[63] Although Herbert was convinced that Julyan had been aware of the irregularity, there was little the Colonial Office could do except to ask for an explanation.[64]

57. Herbert's minute of October 19, 1880, on Treasury to CO, July 8, 1880; CO to Treasury, November 26, 1880, *ibid.*
58. Kimberley to Hercules Robinson, May 19, 1881; Kimberley to A. H. Gordon, May 19, 1881, "Papers Relating to the Functions of the Crown Agents for the Colonies," C. 3075, pp. 10–11, *Parl. Paps. 1881*, LXIV.
59. Treasury to CO, July 27, 1880, CO 323/344.
60. CO to Treasury, January 10, 1881, *ibid.*
61. Ebden's minute of February 22, 1881, CO 537/217; Crown Agents to CO, confidential, April 29, 1881, CO 537/218.
62. CO to Crown Agents, secret, June 2, 1881, CO 537/218.
63. Kimberley's minute of March 11, 1881, CO 537/217.
64. Herbert's minute of March 10, 1881, *ibid*; Herbert to Julyan, May 16, 1881, CO 537/218.

Julyan had no explanation to offer. He simply argued that the Colonial Office had no legal right to question his private actions, and he trusted that Kimberley would apologize.[65] When the Colonial Office refused to recant,[66] Julyan merely recited his past services and condemned the "unfairness of the Colonial Office and their desire to get a conviction rather than to hear explanations." He also argued that the value of his services should be assessed by looking at the remunerations secured by the great financial houses in the City.[67]

The Colonial Office allowed the correspondence to drop. Herbert and Meade did not believe that Julyan had a moral right to obtain a personal honorarium from a public service, but his legal right to the payment could not be questioned. Meade summed up the problem very well when he minuted that "Sir P. Julyan thinks that if we knew more about the City Practices we should not be surprised at the rate of remuneration He obtained. This is very possible but we do not admit the City Standard of Morality in such matters." It was a matter of deep regret to Meade that Julyan should "terminate his career of great usefulness by an act as I think of sharp practice."[68]

The restriction of the crown agents' activities in 1881 and Julyan's questionable financial transactions should not obscure the solid achievements of the crown agents during this period. Although the loss of business in 1881 necessitated a reduction in the size of the Crown Agents for the Colonies,[69] its period of decline was brief. By 1885 the revenue of the agency nearly equalled that of 1881. In the same year, the crown agents established a branch office in the City to enable them to issue inscribed stock for the crown colonies more easily.[70] The prohibition against doing business for colonies with responsible government was strictly enforced,[71] but with that exception the crown agents' duties continued to be the same. Their reputation for efficiency also remained high. In 1892 Kitchner asked the

65. Julyan to Herbert, June 25, 1881, CO 537/219.
66. Herbert to Julyan, August 1, 1881, *ibid.* Herbert minuted that "Sir P. J. is probably unconscious of the degree of the impropriety of his action in this matter. He is honest, but fond of money." Herbert's minute of July 28, 1881, on Julyan to Herbert, June 25, 1881, *ibid.*
67. Julyan to Herbert, September 21, 1881, CO 537/220.
68. Meade's minute of September 30, 1881, on Julyan to Herbert, September 21, 1881, *ibid.*
69. Crown Agents to CO, April 2, 1886, CO 323/364; CO to Crown Agents, April 15, 1886, *ibid.*
70. Crown Agents to CO, January 25, 1885, CO 323/360.
71. When Western Australia received responsible government in 1890, it was forced to sever its relations with the crown agents. Kimberley to Sir W. C. F. Robinson, September 19, 1890, CO 323/382.

Colonial Office to allow the agents to serve as supply agents for the Egyptian army. The Colonial Office refused the request because such work would not be consistent with the regulations laid down in concert with the Treasury.[72]

When Herbert retired in 1892, the annual receipts of the crown agents' department exceeded its requirements, the reserve fund established in 1863 amounting to almost £300,000.[73] The Colonial Office therefore reduced the charges levied on the crown colonies. Herbert believed that this would please the colonists and also give "confidence that the Sec. of State watches the course of the Cr. Agents' business."[74] The status and duties of the crown agents remained essentially unchanged in the nineties. Their business, especially for the African colonies, grew very rapidly. A third agent was appointed in 1895, and by 1903 the department was too large to remain within the Colonial Office building. The crown agents and their monopoly on the purchases of crown colonies did come under increasing criticism, however. Joseph Chamberlain attempted to stifle this criticism by a thorough investigation of the department. This inquiry produced only minor changes, major reforms being postponed until the twentieth century.[75]

II

The Colonial Land and Emigration Commission declined steadily in importance during the early years of Herbert's secretaryship. The commission had been established in 1836 on the recommendation of a select parliamentary committee. This committee was influenced by Wakefield's ideas, and it proposed the creation of a central agency in London to control the sale of crown lands in the colonies and to regulate the flow of emigrants. An expanded Colonial Land and Emigration Office, under the supervision of the colonial secretary, was established in 1840. Its duties included the collection

72. Minutes on Kitchner to Ripon, September 6, 1892; Bramston to Kitchner, October 8, 1892, CO 323/389.

73. Meade's minute of June 10, 1891, CO 323/387.

74. Herbert's minute of August 20, 1891; CO to Crown Agents, November 26, 1891, ibid.

75. Kubicek, The Administration of Imperialism, pp. 62–66. For the Crown Agents for the Colonies in the twentieth century see Sir George Fiddes, The Dominions and the Colonial Office (London, 1926), pp. 28–30; W. E. Simmett, The British Colonial Empire (London, 1949), pp. 153–159; Charles Jeffries, The Colonial Empire and Its Civil Service (Cambridge, 1938), pp. 191–194, 221–223.

and diffusion of accurate statistical information regarding emigration, the sale of crown lands, the sending out of emigrants, and the rendering of periodical accounts of their activities.[76] Frederic Rogers, who was an emigration commissioner from 1847 to 1860, also reported on the legality of colonial acts.[77]

The work of the new commission grew rapidly, receiving 42,891 letters in 1848. In 1849 its staff consisted of three commissioners, eleven established clerks, and approximately thirty temporary clerks.[78] The commission's work began to diminish after 1855, however. This was due partially to a general decline in emigration from the British Isles.[79] Even more important was the decision of the Australian colonies to appoint their own emigration agents in London.[80] The board also lost its legal business when Rogers was appointed permanent undersecretary of the Colonial Office in 1860.

In 1872 the Colonial Land and Emigration Commission sent out only 490 emigrants,[81] and there was a growing belief that the office should be abolished. It still had several important functions, however. The commissioners supervised voluntary emigration and administered the passengers acts, which regulated the conditions of health and comfort on British passenger ships. They also advised the Colonial Office on colonial land questions, dealt with Indian and Chinese immigration matters, and published information for people considering emigration.[82] All of these duties would have to be transferred to other departments before the commission could be abolished.

As part of his plan for reorganizing the Colonial Office in 1872, Kimberley requested that Sir Clinton Murdoch, the senior emigration commissioner, recommend ways of reducing the size of his office. Murdoch replied that much of his office's work could be transferred to the Board of Trade, the crown agents, and the Colonial Office itself.[83] Unfortunately, the large pensions which Murdoch and the other emigration clerks would receive in the event that their offices were

76. Fred H. Hitchens, *The Colonial Land and Emigration Commission* (Philadelphia, 1931), pp. 20–57.
77. Tyler, "Sir Frederic Rogers," pp. 25–27.
78. Hitchens, *Colonial Land and Emigration Commission,* p. 76.
79. W. A. Carrothers, *Emigration from the British Isles* (London, 1929), pp. 207–224, 305–306.
80. Hitchens, *Colonial Land and Emigration Commission,* pp. 77–80. With the granting of responsible government the British government also lost control of the waste lands in the colonies.
81. *Ibid.,* p. 82.
82. Sir Clinton Murdoch's memo of February 3, 1872, CO 384/100.
83. *Ibid.*

abolished made it virtually impossible to implement this plan. It was almost as expensive to abolish the Colonial Land and Emigration Commission as it was to keep it in operation,[84] and the Colonial Office therefore recommended that Murdoch's valuable services be retained.[85] The Treasury agreed, urging however that the commission's staff be reduced as soon as possible. The Treasury also suggested that Murdoch and his staff move into the Colonial Office building.[86] The Colonial Office was too crowded for this transfer to take place immediately,[87] and it was not until 1874 that the remnants of the board were assigned six rooms on the ground floor of the new Colonial Office.[88]

Although the Colonial Land and Emigration Commission was not suddenly abolished, its responsibilities and the size of its staff were gradually reduced between 1872 and 1878. The Merchant Shipping Act of 1872 transferred its duties and powers under the passengers acts to the Board of Trade. The responsibility for preparing emigration returns was also given to the Board of Trade.[89] In 1875 Richard B. Cooper, the assistant secretary, died, and his position was not filled.[90] When Murdoch decided to retire in 1876, he again suggested that some of his department's duties be transferred to other offices.[91] After consulting Murdoch, the Colonial Office decided to give the Crown Agents for the Colonies all of the board's financial business.[92] After Murdoch's retirement, the board's staff consisted of only six men: the commissioner (Stephen Walcott), the accountant, two clerks, a messenger, and a porter.[93] Walcott retired in 1877, and the Colonial

84. *Ibid.*; Herbert's minute of February 25, 1872, CO 537/22.
85. CO to Treasury, March 8, 1872, CO 537/22.
86. Treasury to CO, June 22, 1872, CO 323/309.
87. CO to Treasury, September 10, 1872, *ibid.*
88. Tables bound with Office of Works to CO, June 15, 1874, CO 323/320.

89. One clerk, who was experienced in the administration of the passengers acts, was sent to the Board of Trade. Emigration Office to CO, copy, September 2, 1872, CO 386/119. The Colonial Office received its last emigration returns from the Emigration Office in January, 1873. Edward Knatchbull-Hugessen, the parliamentary undersecretary, did not lament the occasion, minuting that "I shall part with these returns without regret. They are of little value as affording information as to the destination & settlement of emigrants. . . . I shall regret, however, the *admirable handwriting* in which papers come from the E. Office." Knatchbull-Hugessen's minute of January 19, 1873, on Emigration Office to CO, January 18, 1873, CO 384/101.

90. Emigration Office to CO, copy, October 20, 1875, CO 386/119.
91. Emigration Office to CO, May 29, 1876, CO 384/112.
92. Emigration Office to CO, December 9, 1876, CO, 384/119; Meade's minute of November 28, 1876, on Emigration Office to CO, May 29, 1876, CO 384/112.
93. CO to Treasury, December 11, 1876, CO 384/112. The accountant retired early in 1877.

Office then proposed that the Colonial Land and Emigration Commission simply be abolished.[94] The Treasury approved the plan, and all that remained was to dispose of the remaining duties of "a Department which of late lost its importance only because its work has been accomplished."[95] The Colonial Office assumed responsibility for general land and emigration questions, and the supervision of coolie immigration to the West Indies, the arrangement of passage money for convicts' families, emigration to Natal, and certain other minor duties were transferred to the crown agents.[96] The Colonial Land and Emigration Commission was formally abolished in March, 1878.

The abolition of the commission did not radically alter the routine of the Colonial Office. For several years prior to its demise the board had functioned as a subdepartment of the Colonial Office rather than as a separate office. Beginning in 1872, all emigration correspondence was registered at the Colonial Office. The emigration commissioners minuted these dispatches first, but the Colonial Office officials made the final decisions and drafted the replies.[97] After the abolition of the board in 1878, the Colonial Office handled emigration matters no differently from its other work. J. B. Gill, a clerk transferred from the defunct board, usually minuted emigration dispatches first. They were then submitted by Richard Ebden to the secretariat for final decision.[98]

The most laborious part of the emigration work was the supervision of the coolie traffic from India and China to the various British colonies. It was necessary to inspect the ventilation and equipment of the ships transporting the coolies, to insure that the coolies received return transportation after the expiration of their contracts, and to prevent the recruitment of coolies with serious illnesses. Once the coolies were

94. To handle the increased work, the Colonial Office urged that they be allowed to appoint a new second-class clerk and to pay the principal clerk in charge of emigration work, Richard Ebden, an additional £100 a year. Ebden and the two clerks transferred from the Emigration Office to the Colonial Office were to form an emigration department within the Colonial Office. CO to Treasury, January 24, 1878, CO 323/332.

95. Meade's minute of February 22, 1878, on Emigration Office to CO, February 12, 1878, CO 384/121.

96. Emigration Office to Crown Agents, March 30, 1878, enclosed in Emigration Office to CO, March 30, 1878, CO 384/121.

97. Private letters, usually requesting information on opportunities for employment in the colonies, were disposed of at the Emigration Office. In 1872 Richard Ebden was placed in charge of all coolie immigration questions at the Colonial Office. Herbert's minute of September 28, 1872, CO 878/5, Vol. 5, No. 40.

98. CO 384/127, passim. After 1878 there was also a greater necessity to consult the crown agents on emigration questions. CO 384/131, passim.

in the colonies, they still required protection against possible mistreatment and abuse.[99] Herbert was especially concerned with this problem. He believed that the appointment of a traveling coolie inspector would be "of highest value." This inspector could also report on the condition of colonial jails, hospitals, and asylums. Although Herbert's suggestion received some support from his superiors, the plan was eventually abandoned, largely because of the difficulty in assessing the contributions required from the colonies employing coolie labor.[100]

In addition to these traditional duties, the Colonial Office was faced with new emigration problems resulting from the serious depressions in England in 1876–1877 and 1883–1886. The plight of the agricultural worker was especially serious, and a growing number of people sought economic salvation by emigrating to the colonies, Argentina, and the United States.[101] One notable feature of this new wave of emigration was the assistance rendered by private individuals and societies.[102] In addition, there was a growing demand, both in and out of Parliament, that the government attempt to relieve economic distress at home by assisting emigration to the colonies. Beginning in 1880 the Colonial Office was bombarded by the emigration schemes of "inexperienced dreamers." In Herbert's opinion there was no subject on which there was more "wilful ignorance."[103]

The Colonial Office was officially opposed to a resumption of state-assisted emigration. In 1880 W. C. Burnet, the emigration agent for the Cape Colony, inquired whether the British government planned to assist destitute Irish in emigrating to the colonies. Kimberley refused to consider the idea.

If [the] Govt. were to undertake any scheme of Emigration from Ireland, a storm would be raised against what would be styled a measure for en-

99. The Colonial Office carried on a voluminous correspondence with the Foreign Office and India Office on these subjects. CO 384/130, *passim*. Private individuals frequently reported cases of mistreatment, which also had to be checked. CO 384/131, *passim*.

100. Minutes on India Office to CO, April 26, 1880, CO 384/130.

101. J. H. Clapham, *An Economic History of Modern Britain* (3 vols.; Cambridge, 1926–1938), II, 231–234; Carrothers, *Emigration from the British Isles*, pp. 225–228. From 1881 to 1885 the net emigration from the United Kingdom was 934,000.

102. For a list of these societies see Carrothers, *Emigration from the British Isles*, pp. 319–320.

103. Herbert's minute of March 9, 1886, on Earl of Harrowby's motion of March 4, 1886, CO 384/162. Several of the schemes submitted to the Colonial Office in 1884–1885 were printed in "Correspondence on the Subject of Emigration from Great Britain to the Colonies and the Proposed Formation of an Emigrants Information Office," C. 4751, pp. 1–69, *Parl. Paps. 1886*, XLV.

abling landlords to clear their Estates. . . . It is safer to leave the matter, in my opinion, to the operation of the natural pressure in times of difficulty. The Emigration from Ireland already shows a striking increase.[104]

The official position of the British government did not change during the ensuing years. Herbert was the only Colonial Office official who showed any real interest in assisting emigration. In 1887 he recommended that the question of assisted emigration be discussed at the Colonial Conference.[105] He did not, however, think that any of the plans proposed up to that time would "hold water financially." If anything practical was to be accomplished, Herbert believed that it would cost money. He also believed that Parliament "could make a good investment" by supporting a strong colonization society.[106] When the colonies refused to support any such plan the British government definitely rejected any subsidy for emigrants.[107]

The Colonial Office was compelled, however, to extend its emigration work in one area—the diffusion of information to persons contemplating emigration. In 1880 Sir Alexander Galt, the high commissioner of Canada, asked Kimberley to use "all legitimate influence" to encourage British emigration to Canada rather than to the United States.[108] Kimberley declined to alter the well-established policy of taking "no active steps to invite Emigration to the Colonies," but, on Herbert's advice, he did agree to enlarge the annual colonization circular. This publication describing opportunities in the various colonies was sold at a low price to persons intending to emigrate.[109]

The growing unemployment in England in the eighties produced demands that the Colonial Office facilitate, if not actually promote, emigration to the colonies. In 1885 Sir William Harcourt, the home secretary, and Arnold White, a part-time social worker in east London, suggested the establishment of a central bureau in London for the dissemination of information on employment prospects overseas. This information could be collected and periodically revised by the agents

104. Kimberley's minute of July 14, 1880, on Burnet to Kimberley, July 6, 1880, CO 384/131. See also minutes on Peace (emigration agent for Natal) to Hicks Beach, March 13, 1880, *ibid.*
105. Herbert's minute of March 17, 1887, on *Daily News*, March 12, 1887, CO 384/166.
106. Herbert's minute of February 5, 1887, on Seton-Karr's motion for February 8, 1887, CO 323/367.
107. Herbert's minute of August 7, 1887, on Kimber's motion for August 8, 1887, CO 384/166.
108. Galt to Kimberley, June 8, 1880, CO 384/130.
109. Herbert's minute of June 18, 1880, on Galt to Kimberley, June 8, 1880; Herbert to Galt, June 28, 1880; minutes on Home Office to CO, September 27, 1880, CO 384/130.

general of the various colonies.[110] Herbert and Lord Derby, the colonial secretary (1882–1885), both thought that Harcourt's suggestion had considerable merit. They believed that such a bureau could be established quickly and inexpensively; all that was necessary was a room, one or two clerks, and a small grant from the Treasury.[111] The last item proved difficult to obtain.

The Treasury objected to the establishment of a separate department at public expense. Instead, the Treasury argued that the agents general should collect the information at colonial expense. The Colonial Office could then publish the information and distribute it among intending emigrants.[112] Richard Ebden, who was in charge of the emigration work at the Colonial Office, was appalled at this suggestion.

To judge from the example of the Emigration Bd. during the Emigration fever of from 30 to 40 years since, we should be besieged with inquiries, police would be required to keep order, a "queue" of unemployed would be filtering through the office all day, and it would not conduce to their good humour to find that unlike the Emigration Commrs. we could only give them information and that they must go elsewhere for their passages.[113]

Herbert and his superiors believed that the Treasury was being unreasonable, but they preferred to allow Sir William Harcourt and the Home Office to raise the matter in the cabinet and to deal officially with the Treasury.[114]

In June, 1885, the Treasury agreed in principle to providing financial support for the dissemination of emigration information. Numerous changes in personnel at the Treasury during the second half of 1885, however, made it difficult to formulate any definite plans.[115] Finally, on January 29, 1886, the Treasury agreed to provide £400 to £500 a year to maintain an information bureau,[116] but before the new office could be founded the Colonial Office and the Local Government Board had to resolve a misunderstanding over which department was

110. Home Office to CO, March 27, 1885, CO 384/157; Herbert's minute of March 31, 1885, on *ibid.*

111. Herbert's minute of March 31, 1885, and Derby's minute of March 31, 1885, on Home Office to CO, March 27, 1885, CO 384/157; CO to Treasury, April 4, 1885, *ibid.*

112. Treasury to CO, April 11, 1885, *ibid.*

113. Ebden's minute of April 14, 1885, on Treasury to CO, April 11, 1885, *ibid.*

114. Minutes on Treasury to CO, April 11, 1885, and CO to Home Office, April 18, 1885, *ibid.*

115. Colonel Stanley, the new Conservative colonial secretary (June, 1885–February, 1886), gave this explanation to a deputation of representatives from the various emigration societies in January, 1886. *Times* (London), January 18, 1886, p. 7d.

116. Treasury to CO, January 29, 1886, CO 384/162.

to control it.[117] Herbert did not want to annex this "laborious duty," but he saw no way to avoid it.[118] The parliamentary undersecretary, George Osborne Morgan, was particularly anxious for his office to accept this responsibility,[119] something which was done in March, 1886.[120]

Only one obstacle still remained; the Treasury refused to grant more than £500 a year for the new office, and Herbert doubted whether that would suffice. "The Colonial Office by no means covets the work and is callous to the Treasury scoldings. It will be for the Cabinet to decide, after the conference with Mr. Ryder, whether the scheme is to be vetoed. We clearly cannot undertake to work it unless it is put on a workable footing."[121] After several further exchanges,[122] the Emigrants' Information Office, as the new bureau was called, was finally established and staffed with a grant of £500 a year for salaries and £150 a year for rent.[123] It began work in its small offices at 31 Broadway, Westminster, in October, 1886, a year and a half after Harcourt had first suggested its establishment. Meanwhile, well over 300,000 people had left the British Isles without its assistance.[124]

The Emigrants' Information Office was supervised by an unpaid committee of management, whose president was the colonial secretary. Its other officers included members of Parliament, representatives of the emigration societies, and Colonial Office officials. Charles Lucas, a second-class clerk at the Colonial Office, was the secretary of the committee of management. He and J. B. Gill, who had been transferred to the Colonial Office from the defunct Colonial Land and Emigration Commission, spent one or two hours each day answering important correspondence and preparing reports. The full-time permanent staff consisted of a chief clerk, John Pulker, and three boy clerks. Pulker's time was spent primarily in answering oral inquiries. This small paid staff was assisted by volunteer workers from the various

117. LGB to CO, March 12, 1886; Herbert to Joseph Chamberlain, copy, March 17, 1886; Chamberlain to Herbert, March 18, 1886, ibid.
118. Herbert's minute of March 18, 1886, on LGB to CO, March 12, 1886, ibid.
119. Osborne Morgan's minute of March 19, 1886, on LGB to CO, March 12, 1886, ibid.
120. CO to Treasury, March 20, 1886, "Papers on Emigration," C. 4751, p. 80, Parl. Paps. 1886, XLV.
121. Herbert's minute of April 2, 1886, on Treasury to CO, March 31, 1886, CO 384/162.
122. CO to Treasury, April 14, 1886; CO to Treasury, May 18, 1886; Treasury to CO, June 10, 1886; CO to Treasury, June 17, 1886; Treasury to CO, June 17, 1886; CO to Treasury, July 6, 1886; Treasury to CO, July 16, 1886; CO to Treasury, July 28, 1886, ibid.
123. Treasury to CO, July 16, 1886, ibid.
124. Carrothers, Emigration from the British Isles, p. 306.

emigration societies, who periodically revised the office's information and performed other clerical tasks.[125]

The Emigrants' Information Office was instructed simply to provide prospective emigrants with accurate information on employment conditions in the colonies.[126] This information was given to persons calling at the office, and it was also distributed quarterly to post offices, emigration societies, and workmen's organizations throughout the country. It was not the function of the Emigrants' Information Office either to encourage or to discourage emigration from Britain.[127] It did, however, hope to stop "useless and superfluous inquiries as well as ill-advised emigration."[128]

The new office was immediately popular; during the year ending March 31, 1890, over 5,000 people inquired personally, and it received over 10,000 letters.[129] Herbert and Lord Knutsford, the secretary of state for the colonies (1887–1892), both believed that the work was very valuable and was being done efficiently.[130] A select parliamentary committee appointed in 1890 to inquire into the question of emigration reported that the new office was doing admirable work and urged that its annual grant be increased.[131] During Joseph Chamberlain's secretaryship the functions and the size of the Emigrants' Information Office changed very little.[132] In the twentieth century, however, its size and importance grew rapidly, and by 1911 it was receiving about

125. Lucas' memo of November 12, 1886, CO 384/162; Herbert's form letter of appointment to the managing committee, September, 1886, CO 384/162.
126. In 1890 the office was given an additional £50 a year to enable it to provide information on opportunities in foreign countries as well as in the colonies. Treasury to CO, June 4, 1890, and CO to Treasury, June 28, 1890, CO 384/178.
127. Herbert's form letter of appointment to the managing committee, September, 1886, CO 384/162.
128. "Report on the Emigrants' Information Office, for the Year ending 31st March 1890," C. 6064, Parl. Paps. 1890, XLIX. At least two contemporary writers stressed this negative feature of the office's work. Richard Mayo Smith, Emigration and Immigration: A Study in Social Science (New York, 1890), p. 196; Arnold White, Efficiency and Empire (London, 1901), p. 229. White, who took a prominent role in the agitation for the new office, remarked that "the message of this department to the people is the cry of the eternal 'Don't go.'"
129. "Report for Year ending 31st March 1890," C. 6064, Parl. Paps. 1890, XLIX.
130. Minutes on Treasury to CO, February 1, 1887, CO 384/166; minutes on EIO to CO, May 3, 1889, CO 384/174.
131. "Report From the Select Committee on Colonization," No. 152, p. xv, Parl. Paps. 1890–91, XI. "Probably no more valuable and efficient work was ever done at so small a cost to the public." This was primarily due "to the businesslike character of the direction and to the philanthropic spirit which animates its members." In 1891 the Treasury agreed to increase the annual grant from £650 to £1,000. Treasury to CO, June 4, 1891, CO 384/182.
132. "Report on the Emigrants' Information Office, for the Year ending 31st December 1898," C. 9196, Parl. Paps. 1899, LVIII. In 1898 the office received 2,323 personal inquiries and 11,038 letters.

130,000 letters a year. After World War I it was renamed the Overseas Settlement Department and placed first under the Dominions Department of the Colonial Office and then under the new Dominions Office.[133]

133. Fiddes, *The Dominions and Colonial Offices*, pp. 163–172.

CHAPTER V

The Colonial Civil Service
and Honors

THE ENGLISH ADMINIS-
trative reforms of the seventies and eighties, which emphasized the importance of open competition and a strict division of labor, had little
impact on the overseas colonial service. Throughout this period the
secretary of state retained a substantial amount of patronage, although
it was never as great as the numerous applicants and their influential
sponsors believed. The numerous applications for appointments,
transfers, passage money, pensions, and honors created considerable
work for the members of the Colonial Office's secretariat. Some responsibility for these questions was given to the clerks and private
secretaries, but much of the time and private correspondence of
Meade, Herbert, and the successive secretaries of state was necessarily
devoted to them. Although Herbert and his colleagues attempted to
select able men, recruitment by patronage frequently resulted in the
appointment of men for reasons other than ability. The Colonial
Office's recruitment problems were further complicated by the absence
of any uniform or consolidated colonial service. The appointments
at the disposal of the secretary of state varied according to a colony's
political development or its local traditions. Herbert and his colleagues attempted to professionalize the colonial service in the seventies and eighties. These limited changes, however, indicated simply
an awareness of the problems facing the colonial service rather than
any real willingness or ability to achieve fundamental reforms.

Herbert was convinced that it was "the best and the most important
of all economies to secure an efficient Governor."[1] After all, the governor and his official staff were responsible for implementing the
policies formulated in London. Theoretically governors could not

1. R. B. Joyce, "Sir William MacGregor: A Colonial Governor," *Historical Studies
Australia and New Zealand,* XI (November, 1963), 22.

have policies of their own,[2] but the Colonial Office realized that occasionally they would have to make important decisions on their own authority without prior reference to Downing Street. Carnarvon hoped to keep these instances to a minimum by the judicious use of the telegraph.[3] Once a decision was made, however, the Colonial Office usually made every effort to support the actions of their "man on the spot."[4] Herbert and his colleagues regarded any governor or administrator working in the tropics[5] or dealing directly with colonists[6] as worthy of their sympathy and understanding.

Despite the sympathy and understanding they received, the overseas colonial service was not highly regarded by the Colonial Office staff. Robert Meade believed that most crown colony governors were "very inferior persons."[7] Kimberley doubted whether anyone was "more difficult to deal with than a wrong headed Indian or Colonial judge."[8] There was a general feeling at the Colonial Office that many men entered the colonial service because they had failed in other endeavors.[9] This general lack of respect was partially the result of an

2. Kimberley to Gladstone, May 24, 1880, Add. MS 44225, ff. 167–169. When Gladstone returned to power in 1880, Sir Bartle Frere was removed as high commissioner for South Africa because his opinions clashed with the policies of the new government. Kimberley to Frere (tel.), July 28, 1880, enclosed in Kimberley to Gladstone, July 28, 1880, Add. MS 44225, ff. 206–207.

3. Carnarvon's minute of December 26, 1875, on Treasury to CO, December 11, 1875, CO 431/34.

4. Edward Knatchbull-Hugessen, the parliamentary undersecretary from 1870 to 1874, stressed the necessity "of upholding their decisions & supporting their authority whenever this can be done without an absolute departure from the principles by which our Policy is guided." Minute of January 9, 1872, on Kennedy to Kimberley, December 16, 1871, CO 96/89.

5. Kimberley's minute of June 29, 1871, on Kennedy to Kimberley, June 2, 1871, CO 96/88. "I wish some of the ardent civilizers of Africans we have at home would try their hands at the actual work of administration and civilization in these abominable pest houses." Kimberley was greatly upset when Governor Keate died two weeks after he was sent to the Gold Coast. As he confided to Edward Cardwell, "It is really nothing short of murder to send Europeans to that pestilential place." Kimberley to Cardwell, private, April 17, 1873, Cardwell Papers, PRO 30/48/5/33, f. 20.

6. Herbert's minute of January 20, 1887, on Havelock to Edward Stanhope, December 20, 1886, CO 179/165. "We must support Sir A. Havelock. He is one of our most trustworthy Governors, & anyone who has to deal with the Natal Council deserves the utmost assistance & sympathy." Herbert, upon receiving the report of the completion of new parliament buildings for Victoria, minuted, "The cage will be much finer than the animals contained in it." Herbert's minute of October 30, 1877, on Bowen to Carnarvon, August 11, 1877, CO 309/115. See also Herbert's minute of July 24, 1874, on Irving to Carnarvon, June 16, 1874, CO 152/119.

7. Meade to Ripon, October 16, 1892, Add. MS 43556, f. 88. See also Meade to Ripon, September 2, 1892, ibid., f. 5. Sydney Olivier believed that most colonial governors were "exceedingly stupid." Olivier, ed., Olivier, p. 36.

8. Kimberley to Ripon, private, October 24, 1884, Add. MS 43525, ff. 203–204.

9. For example, see Herbert's minutes of December 4 and 14, 1880, and Kimberley's minute of December 15, 1880, CO 323/346.

inadequate understanding of the difficulties in translating policy into action. In addition, some Colonial Office clerks, especially the younger ones, regarded themselves as the intellectual superiors of the officials in the colonies. There was a tendency, which had to be periodically checked, for the Colonial Office officials to make their feelings known in dispatches to erring governors.[10]

Even the most prominent and decorated governors were open to criticism and ridicule from the Colonial Office. Sir George Bowen, who served as governor of Queensland, New Zealand, Victoria, Mauritius, and Hong Kong, was regarded as nothing more than "a pompous donkey,"[11] suffering from "ridiculous egotism."[12] The most that could be said for Bowen was that he avoided any serious "scrapes."[13] This was apparently the secret of his longevity as a governor, for his egotism and incorrigible optimism earned him little respect from the Colonial Office officials.[14]

The case of Sir John Pope Hennessy, who served successively as governor of Labuan, West Africa, the Bahamas, Barbados, Hong Kong, and Mauritius, was somewhat different. Pope Hennessy's intelligence was generally admitted, but, unfortunately for the peace of the Colonial Office, he was also "vain, unscrupulous, wanting in sound judgment & common sense, and prone to quarrel with his subordinates."[15] Pope Hennessy had received his appointment to the colonial service because of his political connections.[16] It was not until he had

10. Kimberley's minute of October 15, 1880, on Berkeley to Kimberley, September 10, 1880, CO 152/140; Kubicek, *The Administration of Imperialism*, p. 46. See also Earl, *Turn Over the Page*, pp. 82–84.

11. Granville to Cardwell, confidential, September 23, 1869, PRO 30/48/5/28, f. 67.

12. Kimberley to Granville, February 27, 1881, PRO 30/29/135, f. 32. Meade to Ripon, private, October 19, 1892, Add. MS 43556, ff. 91–92. "Bowen has served a long time, & officially we say with distinction; But in truth he is nothing but a wind bag & has only been preserved during a long career by Lady Bowen's tact & popularity & by the gt. personal friendship of Herbert which he has requited with the most violent abuses."

13. E. Stanhope to Salisbury, private, November 9, 1886, Salisbury Papers.

14. Herbert's minute of August 7, 1873, on Bowen to Kimberley, June 3, 1873, CO 309/109. "Very pleasant to see always through rose coloured glasses. I think Sir G. B. would give a flourishing account of the town of Cape Coast." Malcolm's minute of August 12, 1877, on Bowen to Carnarvon, May 27, 1877, CO 309/115. "Sir G. Bowen seems by his own account to be fated to live in the midst of tremendous constitutional difficulties, wh, happily, are invariably solved to the satisfaction of all parties by the wisdom & learning of the Govr."

15. Kimberley, *Journal*, September 6, 1873, p. 42. The opinion of the permanent officials was similar. James Pope-Hennessy, *Verandah: Some Episodes in the Crown Colonies, 1867–1889* (New York, 1964), pp. 167, 187, 204. Herbert's minute of June 11, 1872, on Pope Hennessy to Kimberley, May 18, 1872, CO 96/93.

16. He served in Parliament from 1860 to 1865. When he lost his seat by seven votes, Disraeli intervened with the Duke of Buckingham, and Pope Hennessy, who was in great financial difficulty, was appointed governor of Labuan. Pope-Hennessy, *Verandah*, pp. 40–55.

helped to initiate the Ashanti War, played a major role in the Barbados riots of 1876, and created serious disturbances in Mauritius that he was finally informed that his services were no longer required by the Colonial Office.[17] When Pope Hennessy died in 1891, the *Times* appropriately observed that his career said "very little for the intelligence or discretion with which the Colonial Office [exercised] its patronage."[18]

Kimberley regarded Sir Hercules Robinson, perhaps the best known of the colonial governors, as the ablest man in the colonial service.[19] Sir Henry Bulwer, twice governor of Natal, and Sir Marshall Clarke, the resident commissioner for Basutoland from 1884 to 1893, were two other South African officials who managed to retain the confidence of the Colonial Office.[20] Most of the others were less fortunate, and even Sir Hercules Robinson came in for strong criticism because of his dispute with Sir Charles Warren.[21] It was extremely difficult to build a reputation in South Africa, but it was easy to lose one. Perhaps this was the real reason that Herbert refused a governorship in 1892.

The prestige of the overseas colonial service was not enhanced by the manner in which its members were recruited. Herbert and his colleagues made little progress toward adopting the same principles which guided appointments to the home civil service. Instead, a candidate's politics and friends remained frequently more important than his ability or experience. Defeated members of Parliament, such as Pope Hennessy, or politicians out of favor were often given administrative posts in the colonies.[22] "Impecunious peers" were also assisted with colonial positions.[23] Gladstone twice intervened with Kimberley

17. *Ibid., passim.*
18. *Times* (London), October 8, 1891, p. 11d.
19. Kimberley to Gladstone, June 29, 1880, Add. MS 44225, f. 186. See also Knutsford to Salisbury, August 22, 1890, Salisbury Papers.
20. Kimberley to Gladstone, December 2, 1881, Add. MS 44227, ff. 82–84; Meade's minute of June 18, 1874, on Bulwer to Kimberley, January 17, 1874, CO 144/42; Minutes on Robinson to Stanhope, August 10, 1886, CO 417/11.
21. Minutes on Robinson to Derby (tel.), March 11, 1885, CO 417/4.
22. In 1881 Lord Lansdowne, the undersecretary of state for India, resigned because of Gladstone's Irish policy. A short time later he was appointed governor-general of Canada. Derby to Gladstone, April 24, 1883, Add. MS 44141, ff. 70–71. *Punch* carried a cartoon showing Lansdowne dressed in heavy clothing and wearing snowshoes. The caption read: "In his new Canadian costume, specially adapted to remaining for some time out in the cold." T. W. Legh (Lord Newton), *Lord Lansdowne: A Biography* (London, 1929), p. 24. See also Salisbury to Holland, copy, confidential, May 19, 1887, and Holland to Salisbury, May 31, 1887, Salisbury Papers.
23. Salisbury to Knutsford, copy, private, April 17, 1892, Salisbury Papers. In 1888 Lord Onslow, who had previously served as parliamentary undersecretary at the Colonial Office, requested the governorship of New Zealand because of financial difficulties. He received the appointment. Knutsford to Salisbury, private, October 14, 1888, and Knutsford to Salisbury, private, October 27, 1888, Salisbury Papers.

and Derby on behalf of Sir Arthur Gordon. Gladstone admitted that Gordon was a man of "unyielding idiosyncracies,"[24] but Derby should not forget that he was still the son of Lord Aberdeen.[25] Some governors received new appointments simply because of a failure in their previous assignment which required that they be removed from a colony.[26] Religion[27] and marital status[28] were also important considerations in the selection of colonial officials. These criteria for appointment did not preclude ability, but the system assuredly was not designed to select the best man for each particular position.

The *Rules and Regulations for Her Majesty's Colonial Service* embodying legislation governing the granting of retirement pensions to colonial officials may also have hindered the Colonial Office's attempts to make effective appointments and transfers. Because of the difficulty in granting significant pensions to governors less than sixty years of age or who had served only briefly in the colonial service, Herbert was frequently reluctant to terminate the services of officials he regarded as "unfit" or "incompetent." He had no desire to leave colonial officials, and particularly governors, in financial straits. To eliminate this problem Herbert believed that it would be politic to admit when mistakes were made and to spend the money necessary to pension men who failed in their duties. He admitted, however, that there was little hope for this approach; "on this point the Treasury would at once become hard of hearing."[29] Kimberley had a different and more cynical objection to relaxing requirements for pensions. He feared that "the temptation to pension off governors assumed to be bad public servants, to make way for others possibly no better, is too great."[30] Little was done to remedy this situation until 1887 when a new pension act

24. Gladstone to Kimberley, copy, July 4, 1882, Add. MS 44545, f. 161; Gladstone to Kimberley, copy, August 2, 1870, Add. MS 44539, f. 3.
25. Gladstone to Derby, copy, December 23, 1882, Add. MS 44546, f. 57.
26. Minutes on Bowen to Hicks Beach (tel.), August 20, 1878, CO 309/118.
27. Kimberley believed that Sir C. Van Straubenzee was a good choice for Malta because his "ultramontane wife" would be harmless there. Kimberley to Cardwell, private, April 18, 1872, PRO 30/48/5/32, f. 74. Queensland objected to Pope Hennessy as governor because he was a Roman Catholic, and Kimberley withdrew the nomination. Pope-Hennessy, *Verandah*, p. 289.
28. Bulwer was handicapped in promotion because he was a bachelor. Knutsford to Salisbury, November 9, 1888, Salisbury Papers.
29. Herbert's minute of June 10, 1871, on Treasury to CO, June 8, 1871, CO 449/3. Prior to 1864 the problem of granting pensions to governors had not existed. The absence of pensions, however, was a source of considerable discontent among the governors and may have discouraged able men from entering or continuing in the colonial service. D. G. G. Kerr, *Sir Edmund Head, A Scholarly Governor* (Toronto, 1954), pp. 234–235.
30. Kimberley's minute of January 30, 1872, on A. G. Finlaison to Herbert, January 6, 1872, CO 449/4.

made it easier to grant partial pensions to governors serving short terms.[31] The Colonial Office remained, however, excessively charitable to governors striving to obtain higher pensions through longer service throughout Herbert's term in office.

Because of their lack of confidence in their colonial officials, Herbert and his colleagues frequently looked to the personnel of other departments in an emergency. Military men, especially those possessing engineering backgrounds, were in great demand.[32] Sir Andrew Clarke was selected in 1873 to initiate a more forward policy in Malaya.[33] When the situation in Natal became critical in 1875, Carnarvon requested the temporary use of Sir Garnet Wolseley as governor.[34] Wolseley, who had performed well during the Red River campaign of 1869–1870 and the Ashanti War, was popular with the Colonial Office because he was a military man without being a "red-tapist."[35] G. Gathorne Hardy, the secretary of state for war (1874–1878), disliked the Colonial Office's constant reliance on Wolseley; it created discontent among the other officers. In addition, in a period when most of England's wars were small colonial wars, Hardy feared that Wolseley's favor would come to be regarded as "the mode of purchasing advance."[36] Less important missions were also frequently intrusted to army officers. In 1875, for example, Carnarvon requested that the Duke of Cambridge allow Colonel Crossman, "a man in whose character and firmness as well as his personal ability I can entirely trust," to report on the financial condition of Griqualand West. Crossman's appointment, and others like it, also created problems with the War Office. His popularity naturally angered officers who outranked him, and Carnarvon had to use all of his influence before the Duke of Cambridge consented to Crossman's appointment.[37] The Colonial Office's extensive employment of military officers reflected poorly on the

31. "Report of the Inter–departmental Pensions Committee," CO 449/8.
32. Carnarvon to Duke of Cambridge, copy, August 17, 1875, PRO 30/6/14, ff. 153–156. Both of Carnarvon's private secretaries, Ommanney and Herbert Jekyll, were engineers. Carnarvon also admitted that members of the military were frequently the only good men who could be induced to go to places with "unwholesome" climates. Carnarvon to Duke of Cambridge, copy, October 28, 1874, PRO 30/6/14, ff. 28–29.
33. Cowan, *Nineteenth Century Malaya*, pp. 176–178.
34. Carnarvon to Hardy, copy, private, February 16, 1875, PRO 30/6/12; Hardy to Carnarvon, private, February 16, 1875, PRO 30/6/12.
35. Carnarvon to Hardy, copy, August 23, 1877, PRO 30/6/12.
36. Hardy to Carnarvon, private, December 5, 1875, PRO 30/6/12.
37. The most important pieces relative to this controversy are: Carnarvon to Duke of Cambridge, copy, August 10, 1875, PRO 30/6/14, ff. 150–151; Duke of Cambridge to Carnarvon, private, August 13, 1875, PRO 30/6/14, ff. 157–158; Carnarvon to Duke of Cambridge, copy, August 17, 1875, PRO 30/6/14, ff. 153–156; Duke of Cambridge to Carnarvon, private, August 22, 1875, PRO 30/6/14, ff. 169–170.

ability of the colonial service to produce men capable of serving in important positions.

The Colonial Office also relied heavily on officials trained in India, lowering further the prestige of the overseas colonial service. Sir George Bowen, in obtaining Kimberley's permission to apply for the governorship of Madras in 1881, complained that very few colonial governors received positions in India. Several Indian officials, the most famous being Sir Bartle Frere, had received colonial posts, however. Bowen trusted that his candidacy would produce a situation where colonial governors might "fairly submit a claim—if not to 'Free Trade'— at least to 'reciprocity' between the two services."[38] Unfortunately this was not the case. It was not until the 1930's that the colonial service, because of the approaching end of British rule in India, became supreme.[39]

Although methods of recruitment changed little, political developments in the colonies tended to professionalize the higher colonial service in the 1870's and 1880's.[40] As the Australasian colonies increased their political and economic power, they developed what Sir Edward Hamilton, the permanent secretary to the Treasury, referred to as "snob-like tendencies."[41] The governor's political duties diminished, while his social functions became increasingly important. Herbert observed as early as 1875 that an Australian governor was merely

a gentleman whom the Colonists prefer to have nominated from home *to preside over their society*—having no desire to have one of themselves entertaining half the community & excluding the other half from Government House.

Whenever they cease to wish for this, we can have an Imperial Officer to give us information on local matters for £1000 a year instead of £10,000,— he will be richer than the Governor is on £10,000, and matters will go on much as now.[42]

By 1881 Arthur Hamilton Gordon, the governor of New Zealand, was complaining that his duties were "purely prefunctory."[43] Because of

38. Bowen to Gladstone, May 25, 1881, Add. MS 44470, f. 13.
39. Robert Heussler, *Yesterday's Rulers: The Making of the British Colonial Service* (Syracuse, N.Y., 1963), p. 114.
40. For a brief analysis of the backgrounds of colonial governors in 1871, 1881, 1891, and 1901 see Hall, *The Colonial Office*, p. 89.
41. Hamilton, *Diary*, November 27, 1888, Hamilton Papers, Add. MS 48649, f. 123.
42. Herbert's minute of June 8, 1875, on Stawell to Carnarvon, confidential, April 16, 1875, CO 309/113.
43. Chapman, *Arthur Hamilton Gordon*, p. 235.

the governors' changing role in the large self-governing colonies, it became more important for them to have social status at home,[44] plenty of money to spend on entertainment,[45] and a "good wife."[46] In 1889 Queensland refused to accept Sir H. B. Blake as governor, partially because he was a "professional" governor.[47] Tasmania, which was not as pretentious as its neighbors, was easier to please.[48]

The changing role of the governors in the self-governing colonies was partly due to the growing influence of the colonial agents general. Originally the agents general[49] dealt primarily with financial and immigration work, but by the seventies they increasingly served as a direct link between the Colonial Office and the colonial governments on political questions.[50] Following the appointment of a Canadian high commissioner in 1881,[51] the quasi-diplomatic role of these colonial representatives could no longer be disputed. The files of the Colonial Office show a rapid increase in the number of letters received from agents general after 1880. These officials advised on political questions,[52] scrutinized British legislation affecting the various

44. By 1889 Hamilton noted that it was "quite the fashion" for peers to seek colonial governorships. Hamilton, *Diary*, February 13, 1889, Add. MS 48650, f. 54. In 1883 Prince Leopold, the Duke of Albany, tried to obtain a governorship, but Derby and Gladstone feared that a governor from the royal family would create problems. Queen Victoria did not approve the plan either. Derby to Gladstone, private, May 17, 1883, Add. MS 44141, ff. 82–83; Gladstone to Derby, copy, private, May 19, 1883, Add. MS 44546, ff. 115–116; Derby to Gladstone, January 16, 1884, Add. MS 44142, f. 42.

45. Governor Frederic Weld of Tasmania requested a transfer because he could not afford the expense of entertaining. Weld to Carnarvon, March 19, 1877, PRO 30/6/25, No. 50A. Lord Knutsford believed that a governor should spend all of his salary, and if possible a little more, in his colony. Knutsford to Lady Musgrave, January 9, 1889, Musgrave Papers, Duke MS Department. "In N. S. Wales you must look for a rich man who does not mind spending a couple of thousand over his salary.

Things are done on a big scale there and probably £2,000 or £3,000 has to be sunk at once in plant—Horses, carriages, wines, Footmen & other Servants etc." Meade to Ripon, December 29, 1892, Add. MS 43556, ff. 160–161.

46. Knutsford to Salisbury, May 16, 1890, Salisbury Papers. The lack of a wife to do the honors was "a fatal deficiency" in an Australian governor.

47. Hamilton, *Diary*, November 27, 1888, Add. MS 48649, f. 123. The fact that Blake was rumored to have an unemployed son who had married a barmaid did not help his chances. Knutsford to Salisbury, November 9, 1888, Salisbury Papers.

48. Meade to Ripon, September 2, 1892, Add. MS 43556, ff. 6–7; Meade to Ripon, December 29, 1892, Add. MS 43556, ff. 159–160.

49. The term "agent general" was first used officially in the *Colonial Office List* in 1875. Canada, New South Wales, Victoria, New Zealand, South Australia, and Queensland employed agents general. *Colonial Office List* (1875), p. 12.

50. In 1875 Herbert minuted that "the Colonial Ministers, either by the transmission of their minutes through the Governor, or by instructing their Agent General, *do* communicate directly with H. M. Government in their own words on most important occasions." Herbert's minute of June 8, 1875, on Stawell to Carnarvon, confidential, April 16, 1875, CO 309/113.

51. For the background to this appointment see Farr, *The Colonial Office and Canada*, pp. 253–270.

52. During the debate over the annexation of New Guinea in the mid-eighties, most of the correspondence between the Colonial Office and the colonial governments was

colonies,[53] recommended colonists for honors,[54] and even passed judgment on the performance of the colonial secretary.[55]

The increasing importance of the agents general created certain problems for the Colonial Office. Frequently they were indiscreet in their treatment of confidential communications. Bramston complained, for example, that any document given to an agent general immediately became public property.[56] In addition, the governors naturally complained that the "political prominence" given to the agents general reduced their own power and prestige.[57] The Colonial Office was not willing, however, to attempt to restrict their powers; it was often convenient to communicate through the agents general. All that Herbert and his colleagues did was to request the colonial governments "to treat their Governors a little better in the matter of information."[58] W. H. Mercer, a young second-class clerk, summarized the problem most precisely when he minuted that

the question is one of expediency, and if it is found convenient to conduct certain correspondence through the Agents General (as it now often is), the Governor must accept the situation. In a responsible government colony, the necessity of his forming the mouthpiece of the ministry is, in fact, obsolete whenever it is distinctly inconvenient. He has other functions which justify his existence; but he cannot permanently claim to conduct the negotiations of the colonial government.[59]

By the twentieth century, the self-governing colonies were arguing that it was not only inexpedient but constitutionally wrong for the

---

channeled through the agents general. When this question had been considered a decade earlier, the governors had provided the key link.

53. Saul Samuel to Kimberley, copy, July 14, 1881, enclosed in Bickersteth to Godley, July 15, 1881, Add. MS 44226, f. 193.
54. Arthur Blyth to Herbert, April 23, 1885, CO 447/44.
55. Tupper to Herbert, July 31, 1886, PRO 30/29/213.
56. Bramston's minute of October 15, 1886, on Loch to Stanhope, confidential, September 3, 1886, CO 309/130. Herbert's minute of November 9, 1886, on Loch to Stanhope, confidential, September 3, 1886, CO 309/130.

What it is desirable, but difficult, to make them understand in a friendly way is that the anxiety of each Agent General to show his superior energy and efficiency, & the eagerness of each Colony to be ahead of the others in all matters, leads to so free a publication of such liberally extended announcements as to compel H M Govt. to exercise more reserve in communicating with them than they would desire to do if a greater amount of diplomatic reticence could be practised. A conversation could no doubt be useful.

57. Loch complained that the government of Victoria had virtually ignored him on the important question of New Guinea. Loch to Derby, confidential, December 31, 1884, CO 309/127; Loch to Col. Stanley, November 27, 1885, CO 309/129; Musgrave to Stanhope, September 18, 1886, CO 234/47.
58. Herbert's minute of April 4, 1885, on Loch to Derby, confidential, December 31, 1884, CO 309/127; Granville's circular dispatch of April 8, 1886, CO 309/127.
59. Mercer's minute of February 2, 1885, on Loch to Derby, confidential, December 31, 1884, CO 309/127.

governor to serve as the channel of communications between the two governments.

The Colonial Office officials did not actively oppose the growing distinction between the professional administrators of crown colonies and the amateurs who presided over the society of the larger self-governing colonies.[60] Meade could not blame the Australian colonies for preferring amateurs, "considering what many of our governors are."[61] Herbert also argued that few professional colonial administrators were able to make the transition from crown colony government to the political conditions of the larger colonies. "I fear that very few Crown Colony Governors are able to learn late in life, the art of governing under Responsible Government. We have had in South Australia needless collisions between the Governor & his ministers in consequence of the former ventilating or pressing personal opinions which he should have kept unpublished."[62] By 1891 the distinction between the professional and amateur governors was fairly well established, and Lord Knutsford predicted that he would probably never again see "such a record of service as those of Sir H. Robinson & Sir G. Bowen."[63]

The declining opportunities for service in self-governing colonies made the professional colonial administrators extremely jealous of the chief secretaryships and governorships of the crown colonies. The Colonial Office admitted that these positions should be reserved for capable and experienced men already in the colonial service. Meade feared that if outsiders were given these appointments the colonial service would be demoralized.[64] In 1887 Salisbury sought to appoint Sir Drummond Wolff, a defeated member of Parliament, governor of Hong Kong.[65] Henry Holland, later Lord Knutsford, objected that "outsiders may well be given a Responsible Government Colony, but it is a blow to the Service to give a Crown Colony to an outsider."[66] Happily Wolff declined the appointment, and Holland selected Sir G. W. Des Voeux, a professional administrator, from "a large & anxious

60. This division was never absolute, Sir William MacGregor, who served as administrator of New Guinea and governor of Lagos, ended his career as governor of Queensland. Joyce, *Historical Studies*, XI, 18.
61. Meade to Ripon, September 2, 1892, Add. MS 43556, ff. 5–6.
62. Herbert's minute of October 6, 1888, on Musgrave to Knutsford, August 17, 1888, CO 234/31.
63. Knutsford to McDonnell, January 17, 1891, Salisbury Papers.
64. Meade to Ripon, September 2, 1892, Add. MS 43556, ff. 7–8.
65. Salisbury to Holland, copy, confidential, May 19, 1887, Salisbury Papers.
66. Holland to Salisbury, confidential, May 17, 1887, Salisbury Papers.

covey of applicants."[67] There was still no unified colonial service in the seventies and eighties, but the realization that the important posts in the crown colonies had to be reserved for able and experienced men already in the colonial service was an important step toward its establishment.

The principal administrative officer under the governor was the chief secretary, who directed the work of the colony's central secretariat. He usually possessed considerable colonial experience and anticipated becoming a governor himself. His primary duty was to advise the governor and to assist him in his correspondence with the Colonial Office. In addition, as the regular channel of approach to the governor, his position in a colony was similar to Herbert's at the Colonial Office. He also administered the colony in the governor's absence.[68] Because of the importance of his position, it was essential that the chief secretary work closely with the governor. When the two men disagreed, as they frequently did, it was extremely difficult to maintain peace in a colony's small official community, or in the Colonial Office for that matter.[69]

In addition to the governors and chief secretaries, the Colonial Office had numerous minor positions to fill, such as surveyor, coroner, postmaster, police magistrate, doctor, and treasurer.[70] The extent of this patronage varied considerably from colony to colony. In colonies with responsible government the secretary of state had virtually no patronage. In those colonies with an established European population, such as in the West Indies or Natal, the governors usually filled the lower positions in the colonial service with local candidates, the Colonial Office merely confirming these appointments.[71] The eastern colonies (Ceylon, the Straits, and Hong Kong) had a civil service modeled on the Indian civil service. Colonies with military bases, such as Malta, Gibraltar, Cyprus, or Bermuda, had a higher proportion of military

67. Holland to Salisbury, May 24, 1887, Salisbury Papers.
68. The chief secretary was frequently called the colonial secretary, but he should not be confused with the secretary of state in London. Simmett, British Colonial Empire, p. 68; Jeffries, The Colonial Empire and Civil Service, pp. 128–129; and Sir Alan Burns, Colonial Civil Servant (London, 1949), pp. 48–49.
69. Pope-Hennessy, Verandah, pp. 352–361.
70. For a detailed description of the colonial service in the 1930's see A. Bertram, The Colonial Service (London, 1930). Jeffries, The Colonial Empire, pp. 3–29; Heussler, Yesterday's Rulers, pp. 1–26; and Hall, The Colonial Office, pp. 115–154, also provide some information on the development of the service before World War I.
71. Just's minute of December 30, 1888, on R. W. Eastwick to Knutsford, December 11, 1888, CO 429/4; Harris' minute of April 4, 1881, on C. H. H. Woseley to Kimberley, January 24, 1881, CO 429/2. See also Chapman, Arthur Hamilton Gordon, pp. 87–90.

men in administrative positions.[72] Most of the Colonial Office's patronage was for the colonies in Africa, where it was most difficult to recruit able men. The African character of the colonial service became even more pronounced in the twentieth century.[73]

Before a person was seriously considered for a colonial position it was necessary for him "to be known to the Secy of State, or to someone of position, or to furnish such testimonials as will shew the applicant to be fit for the post sought."[74] The first of the two criteria was frequently the more important. A large portion of the correspondence of any secretary of state was devoted to patronage requests by personal or political friends. Northcote sought appointments for "the elder brother of my daughter's fiance,"[75] and for an unemployed fifty-year-old cousin.[76] The Duke of Cambridge was not above putting pressure on Carnarvon to find positions for "rough and ready" soldiers seeking employment.[77] Henry Campbell-Bannerman attempted to obtain a position for a defeated member of Parliament.[78] Lord Rosslyn pressed Granville to find a colonial chaplaincy for his private chaplain, who was in "a sad domestic trouble" and anxious "to move with his children as far from the source of his misfortune as possible."[79] All such requests had to be personally answered by the colonial secretary.

Most requests for patronage, however, were handled by the secretary of state's private secretaries with the assistance of the other members of

72. Kimberley to Gladstone, April 16, 1881, Add. MS 44226, ff. 93–96. "The late Govt thought of nothing but their foolish dream of making Cyprus another Malta, & they filled the island with military officers who with the best will in the world can't carry on civil govt satisfactorily."

73. Heussler, *Yesterday's Rulers*, p. 3.

74. E. Wodehouse's minute of October 4, 1870, on W. E. Smith to Kimberley, October 3, 1870, CO 429/1.

75. Northcote to Carnarvon, April, 1877, PRO 30/6/7, f. 201.

76. Northcote to Carnarvon, April 7, 1874, PRO 30/6/7, f. 16. In 1874 Northcote also requested that Carnarvon secure a position for a nephew who had failed to secure a place in India. Although the candidate was "slow" and suited for work requiring "diligence rather than remarkable ability," Carnarvon found him a £250-a-year clerkship at Hong Kong. Northcote to Carnarvon, August 20, 1874, PRO 30/6/7, ff. 50–51; Carnarvon to Northcote, copy, private, September 26, 1874, PRO 30/6/7, ff. 46–47; Northcote to Carnarvon, September 28, 1874, PRO 30/6/7, ff. 42–43.

77. Duke of Cambridge to Carnarvon, private, April 6, 1874, PRO 30/6/14, ff. 9–10; Duke of Cambridge to Carnarvon, private, October 13, 1874, PRO 30/6/14, ff. 20–21. After considerable pressure, Carnarvon also found a police magistracy in the West Indies for a protégé of the Duke of Cambridge. Duke of Cambridge to Carnarvon, private, July 7, 1875, PRO 30/6/14, ff. 128–129; Duke of Cambridge to Carnarvon, private, May 8, 1876, PRO 30/6/14, ff. 232–233; Carnarvon to Duke of Cambridge, copy, private, March 2, 1877, PRO 30/6/14, f. 292.

78. H. Campbell-Bannerman to Granville, March 3, 1886, PRO 30/29/213.

79. Lord Rosslyn to Granville, April 4, 1886, PRO 30/29/213. The endorsement on this letter read: "Ansd. by Ld G. No doubt as good judge of clergyman as of a horse: but practy no such patronage. Ap. 7."

the Colonial Office. Applications for transfer or promotion were usually sent first to the geographical departments and undersecretaries for their recommendations and then to the private secretaries for consideration in the event of a vacancy.[80] The other departments of the British government often assisted in the selection of men for posts requiring specialized knowledge.[81] In the eighties the Colonial Office also used a special application form for candidates for colonial appointments. This form asked for the candidate's educational and professional qualifications, his experience, and the names of several referees. If he was considered worthy of further examination, the candidate was usually invited to the Colonial Office for an interview with one of the private secretaries. The comments of the private secretaries on these applicants followed a general pattern. "He seems a gentleman: but did not strike me as being particularly bright, though not stupid." "He rowed in the Cambridge eight; and seems to be a strong vigorous man, who would do well on the Gold Coast."[82] What the Colonial Office desired, at least for administrative positions, was not special knowledge or ability in a single area, but a general aptitude for command and the ability to react quickly under pressure. This was essential because frequently an official assigned to one position would be called upon to perform other duties as well. This was especially true in small, poor colonies.[83]

Although there were no major changes in the method of recruitment in the seventies and eighties, the colonial secretaries and permanent

80. The private secretaries played a more important role in the selection of men for the colonial service than has sometimes been recognized. Edward Marsh, *A Number of People: A Book of Reminiscences* (London, 1939), pp. 123–124; Heussler, *Yesterday's Rulers*, pp. 7–9.

81. The Home Office recommended experienced jailers. Home Office to CO, December 6, 1878, CO 144/51. Kew Gardens generally assisted in procuring gardeners and forestry officers. Kew to CO, August 2, 1880, CO 54/530; CO to Kew, February 23, 1886, CO 179/159. Besides assisting with the selection of engineers and technicians, the crown agents also advertised for persons to fill various positions in the colonies, such as matron of the Natal lunatic asylum. CO to Crown Agents, June 26, 1886, CO 179/166. Carnarvon usually conferred with the archbishop of Canterbury on important ecclesiastical appointments and transfers. PRO 30/6/18, *passim*.

82. CO 429/2. These comments were from interviews held in the early eighties.

83. Blake's minute of March 31, 1873, on Bulwer to Kimberley, January 17, 1873, CO 144/40; Minutes on Bulwer to Carnarvon, December 21, 1874, CO 144/43. An extreme case of this occurred in Labuan, which, although it spent three-fourths of its revenue on administrative salaries, was greatly understaffed. A. K. Leys, the brother and private secretary of the acting administrator, served as acting colonial treasurer, surveyor, superintendent of convicts, registrar of shipping, registrar of trade, coroner, postmaster, and harbor master. He was also acting police magistrate, auditor, registrar of the general court, and judge of the general court. He also served as a provisional member of the legislative council and was responsible for the government in the absence of the acting administrator. This information was drawn from Leys's application for permanent colonial appointment enclosed in Treacher to Derby, April 13, 1885, CO 144/59.

officials recognized the importance of securing efficient administrators[84] and they attempted in certain minor ways to recruit abler men. The colonial regulations required that each governor report confidentially at least once a year on the officers under his command,[85] but with few exceptions this instruction was ignored. In 1884 the Colonial Office distributed special forms for officials desiring a transfer or promotion. The governor was also instructed to report, in triplicate, on each candidate. These confidential reports included information on personal qualities (education, social position, and tact), official qualities (industry, energy, loyalty, and self-reliance), special circumstances (intemperate habits, pecuniary liabilities, local ties), and claims to promotion. Two copies of this report were to be sent to the Colonial Office and one was to be retained in the colony. The Colonial Office hoped that these reports would enable it "to compare the claims of officers deserving promotion more accurately than has hitherto been possible and also to judge without delay, when a vacancy occurs, what officers would be willing to accept the appointment."[86] Unfortunately, these reports were not submitted with any regularity.[87]

The Colonial Office also tightened its regulations regarding medical references. Herbert feared that independent medical referees would always certify the health of a candidate if they could. He therefore agreed with Fairfield's suggestion that each applicant for a colonial appointment be certified by a medical officer approved by the Colonial Office. This procedure would prevent the appointment of men "with obvious & serious disorders."[88] Herbert also suggested that all new colonial officials be subjected to a three-year probationary period.[89] Kimberley did not think that an inflexible probationary rule was possible, but he did support a compulsory medical examination.[90]

---

84. Carnarvon to Hicks Beach, copy, private, October 23, 1874, PRO 30/6/9, ff. 99–100; Carnarvon to Duke of Cambridge, copy, April 8, 1874, PRO 30/6/14, ff. 11–12. "It would be unwise and in all ways unsatisfactory to go on with our old system of second rate governors and the accident of the day."
85. *Colonial Office List* (1872), p. 169.
86. Derby's confidential circular dispatch of December 4, 1884, CO 323/359.
87. Heussler, *Yesterday's Rulers*, pp. 9–12.
88. Herbert's minute of December 4, 1880, CO 323/346.
89. Herbert's minute of December 14, 1880, CO 323/346. "A young man entering life should certainly have some secure tenure subject to moderate probation, but in the case of a man (say) over 27 who has either had no profession, or has tried another profession (to put it mildly!) & desires to change, a more complete probation might be useful."
90. Kimberley's minutes of December 6, 1880, and December 15, 1880, CO 323/346. Dr. Gage Brown was the Colonial Office's medical examiner. Adrian's minute of July 24, 1885, on H. Bartlett to Derby, June 1, 1885, CO 429/3.

Despite periodical statements reaffirming the value of exchanges between officials in the colonies and in the Colonial Office,[91] little was done to establish an orderly system of rotation until the secretary-ship of Joseph Chamberlain.[92] Problems with the Treasury arose, how-ever, over questions of pay and pensions, and the exchange program was never really successful. It was not re-established until the 1930's.[93]

The Colonial Office was, however, able to effect major improve-ments in the methods of recruitment to the Ceylon civil service in the seventies and eighties. Prior to 1869 half of the candidates for positions in Ceylon were nominated by the secretary of state and examined in England; the other half were nominated by the governor and ex-amined in Ceylon. Experience showed that the men nominated and examined in London were superior officials,[94] and in 1869, despite protests from the Ceylon officials,[95] the Colonial Office required all candidates to pass the same examination. This examination was held simultaneously in England and Ceylon.[96] In 1877 Robert Meade suggested the introduction of open competition examinations,[97] but Carnarvon refused, and the system of examining nominated candi-dates was continued.[98]

In 1880 Kimberley agreed that future Ceylon cadetships should be filled by open competitive examinations given in England. This new policy was defended on the grounds that it was essential for all candidates to free themselves from their insular narrowness and caste

91. Herbert's minute of July 23, 1870, on CSC to CO, July 9, 1870, CO 323/301; Car-narvon to W. Robinson, copy, private, August 28, 1874, PRO 30/6/41, No. 66; Carnarvon's minute of September 5, 1874, CO 878/5, Vol. 5, No. 97; "Second Report of the Royal (Ridley) Commission," C. 5545, pp. 75–76, *Parl. Paps. 1888*, XXVII.

92. Minutes on Treasury to CO, November 2, 1897, CO 323/417.

93. Kubicek, *The Administration of Imperialism*, pp. 51–53; Burns, *Colonial Civil Servant*, pp. 150–161.

94. H. Robinson to Buckingham, June 26, 1868, CO 54/435. For the early history of the Ceylon civil service see Lennox A. Mills, *Ceylon under British Rule, 1795–1932* (London, 1933), pp. 59–88.

95. Robinson to Granville, July 6, 1869, CO 54/445. To the Colonial Office these protests were the "old story of the claims of the sons of Public Servants to follow in the father's steps." Sandford's minute of August 17, 1869, on Robinson to Granville, July 6, 1869, CO 54/445.

96. Granville to Robinson, September 10, 1869, CO 54/445; CSC to CO, July 20, 1869, CO 54/450.

97. Meade's minute of October 28, 1877, on Gregory to Carnarvon, October 26, 1877, CO 54/511. Herbert hoped that whenever a new system was adopted for Ceylon it could also be applied to "Hong Kong & Straits, and also to Jamaica, Mauritius, & any other Crown Colonies to which the system may advantageously be extended." Herbert's minute of November 12, 1877, on Gregory to Carnarvon, October 26, 1877, CO 54/511.

98. The cadetships of Ceylon, Hong Kong, and the Straits were filled at a common examination in England. Lord Donoughmore's memo of February 2, 1878, CO 54/516. A copy of the new regulations for the eastern cadetships is bound in CO 54/516.

prejudices by spending at least some time studying in England.[99] In addition, it was "next to impossible to get together by private efforts a satisfactory list of nominees."[100] Methods of recruitment for the eastern cadetships changed little in the eighties, but in 1889 G. W. Johnson recommended the holding of joint examinations with the Indian civil service.[101] The Colonial Office was concerned, however, that Ceylon would receive the "leavings" of India.[102] It was not until 1896 that Ceylon examinations were combined with those for the Indian civil service and the first class of the home civil service.[103]

One of the most burdensome and least rewarding parts of the Colonial Office's work was the distribution of honors among the colonists and colonial officials. Although the prime minister allowed the Colonial Office a small number of knighthoods each year and an occasional baronetcy or privy councilorship, the usual mark of colonial distinction was membership in the Order of St. Michael and St. George.[104] Founded in 1818, this order originally conferred the mark of royal favor on Ionians, Maltese, and British officials who had served with distinction in the Mediterranean region. In 1864, however, the Ionian Islands were ceded to Greece, and four years later the order was revamped and enlarged to reward British subjects who rendered important service in or in connection with any of the colonies.[105] In 1879 the order was again expanded to include persons who had performed meritorious service in the area of foreign affairs.[106] The registry of the order remained at the Colonial Office.

When the Colonial Office was reorganized in 1870, Rogers appointed the chief clerk ex officio secretary and registrar of the Order of St. Mi-

99. Longden to Kimberley, confidential, October 15, 1880, CO 54/528; Kimberley to Longden, confidential, December 9, 1880, CO 54/528.
100. Meade's minute of November 30, 1880, on CSC to CO, November 13, 1880, CO 54/530.
101. Johnson's minute of July 20, 1889, on CSC to CO, July 17, 1889, CO 54/585.
102. Minutes on CSC to CO, July 21, 1891, CO 54/598. Fairfield later argued that "it does not matter a pin whether we get the *very best* youths at the crammers, because so much of their future success depends on appearance, temper, and common sense, which are not tested by examinations. As it is we safeguard ourselves against getting fools which is about all that we can hope for." Fairfield's minute of November 8, 1892, on CSC to CO, November 2, 1892, CO 54/605.
103. CO to CSC, December 5, 1895, CO 54/627.
104. Correspondence involving the Order of St. Michael and St. George is bound in the CO 447 series. Other honors correspondence is in the CO 448 series.
105. Sir Ivan De La Bere, *The Queen's Orders of Chivalry* (London, 1961), pp. 130–131; *Colonial Office List* (1870), pp. 218–219.
106. Herbert's minute of January 17, 1879; Herbert to Currie, copy, January 29, 1879; Currie to Cox, May 1, 1879, CO 447/34.

chael and St. George.[107] The registrar handled most of the routine correspondence of the order. Applications for membership and important correspondence were referred to Herbert and the other members of the secretariat for consideration. The secretaries of state, whose interest in the order varied considerably,[108] generally took their advice. Correspondence on the other types of honors passed through the principal clerk of the general department and was disposed of in a similar manner.[109] Because the number of available honors was limited, great care and time were taken in their distribution, the Colonial Office's primary objective being to offend as few colonists as possible.

The distribution of honors, like appointments, was frequently based on considerations other than merit. Carnarvon regarded honors as the worst part of his work because "where it is possible to make one really eminent selection it is necessary to make fifty commonplace ones."[110] Colonial chief justices usually received knighthoods because of their official position.[111] Honors were also given to enhance the dignity of the Order of St. Michael and St. George,[112] to maintain the loyalty of the colonists,[113] to extract a favor in return,[114] or simply to redress a geographical imbalance.[115] Many eminent colonists did of course receive marks of distinction, but in Herbert's opinion "the greatest

107. Rogers' minute of August 3, 1870, CO 878/5, Vol. 4, No. 39.
108. CO 447/18, 33–35, 44, passim. Kimberley, Carnarvon, and Derby saw a great deal of this correspondence; Hicks Beach was less interested.
109. CO 448/1A–5, passim.
110. Carnarvon to Disraeli, copy, private, March 25, 1875, PRO 30/6/11, ff. 61–64.
111. The prime minister, who submitted all knighthoods to the queen for approval, usually attempted to reduce the number of honors granted to colonists. See for example Kimberley to Gladstone, May 4, 1881, Add. MS 44226, ff. 105–106; Gladstone to Kimberley, copy, May 9, 1881, Add. MS 44226, f. 167; Kimberley to Gladstone, May 9, 1881, Add. MS 44226, ff. 107–108. On this occasion Kimberley reduced his demands for knighthoods recalling that "one of the reasons why Queen Elizabeth beheaded Lord Essex was said to be that he made too many knights when Ld Lt of Ireland."
112. Carnarvon hoped that the Duke of Manchester would accept a K.C.M.G. because it would make the future distribution of honors easier. "Each man desires the high rank without reference to others or sometimes his own merits and I own that I think there would be an advantage in having a Duke in the second class of the SM & G." Carnarvon to Disraeli, copy, June 15, 1874, PRO 30/6/11, ff. 17–18.
113. Kimberley to Gladstone, private, August 23, 1871, Add. MS 44224, ff. 197–200. "There is a growing American feeling in the W. India Islands, wh I am sure it is politic to counteract, & the grant of honors is no bad way of doing so."
114. Kimberley to Gladstone, private, June 7, 1871, Add. MS 44224, f. 143. "I think the P. C. would be the best reward for Sir J. Macdonald, but I would certainly give him nothing till we see what course he takes as to the Treaty [of Washington] in Canada. Payment for results is the safest course in this case."
115. In 1882 Gladstone urged Kimberley to give William McArthur a K.C.M.G. for his parliamentary action on Fiji in 1874 and also because "MacArthur is a Northern Irishman by birth: we have missed the Northern Irish in our late batch of Baronets, & this K.C.M.G. would be hailed in Ulster." Gladstone to Kimberley, May 20, 1882, copy, Add. MS 44545, f. 141.

Australian," W. C. Wentworth, died unhonored.[116] Most honors were given for political service. As late as 1884 no colonist had been knighted for academic or scientific achievements, although Herbert felt that "it could hardly be maintained that such services are not as deserving as those of successful & not always over-scrupulous politicians."[117]

The method of distributing colonial honors changed very little during the seventies and eighties. The secretaries of state continually attempted to obtain more knighthoods from prime ministers who desired to use them to reward friends at home.[118] The Colonial Office was also forced to defend its own honors from other departments, especially the War Office and the Admiralty. When Cardwell requested ten C.M.G.'s and K.C.M.G.'s for members of the Red River expedition, Kimberley raised strong objections.[119] He feared that too many military appointments would lower the prestige of the Order of St. Michael and St. George in the eyes of the colonists.[120] Although the procedure for distributing awards did not greatly change, the number of honors distributed increased rapidly. When Herbert retired in 1892, he retained his position as chancellor of the order and continued to offer his advice and assistance on "all such unimportant matters."[121] This enabled Meade, his successor, and the secretaries of state to devote their time to more pressing subjects.

116. Herbert's minute of July 19, 1873, on John Stuart to Kimberley, May 15, 1873, CO 447/18. Another prominent Australian, Dr. J. D. Lang, could not be honored because of the many indiscreet things that he said in public. Kimberley's minute of July 20, 1873, on ibid.
117. Herbert's minute of June 23, 1884, on Lansdowne to Derby, confidential, May 29, 1884, CO 448/2.
118. Herbert's minute of October 31, 1886, CO 447/44; Holland to Salisbury, March 1, 1887, Salisbury Papers.
119. Cardwell to Duke of Cambridge, copy, private, October 21, 1870, PRO 30/48/5/14, f. 206; Kimberley to Cardwell, October 23, 1870, PRO 30/48/5/31, ff. 77-80. "My stomach rises at Surgeon Major Young, who made such excellent preparations for sick & wounded, if there had been any. Surely you will agree to leave him out."
120. Kimberley to Cardwell, private, January 5, 1879, PRO 30/48/5/32, ff. 2-3.
121. Meade to Ripon, September 6, 1894, Add. MS 43557, ff. 202-203; Meade to Ripon, December 22, 1894, Add. MS 43558, ff. 39-41.

CHAPTER VI

The Colonial Office and
the Treasury

IN 1876 THE AUDITOR
general of Natal complained of persecution by his official colleagues. If
he pointed out financial irregularities, the auditor stated that the colonial treasurer became angry. If he confined himself to arithmetic, the
financial committee of the legislative council accused him of neglecting his duties. The auditor naturally felt that his professional
reputation was being compromised by the difficult conditions under
which he worked.[1] Francis Graham, a second-class clerk at the Colonial Office, summed up the auditor's problem as follows:

The position of the Auditor is a most invidious one. He is an officer of the
executive government whose function it is to see that his brother officers
do their duty in money matters. When one considers the smallness of
official society in most Crown Colonies, and the contempt with which most
men look upon accounts, it is easy to conceive that the auditor, if he does
his duty thoroughly is considered a "bore" and a contemptuous fault
finder. Add to this, that practically the Auditor's only appeal in cases of
dispute is to the Governor, who, it is but natural to expect will be inclined
to support those officers who are most frequently associated with him in
the administration of the Government, especially if as must be often the
case, he thinks the details of the "figure palaver" not worth the while to
master. I think therefore that when an occasion offers the auditor deserves
all the support which the Secretary of State can properly give him.[2]

The position of the Treasury officials within the small official community in London was similar to the auditor's position in Natal.
Because of their responsibility for supervising the expenditures of
other departments, the Treasury officials were commonly regarded
as bores or faultfinders by the other government officials who were
less interested in financial questions. Aware of their unpopularity,

1. Enclosures in Bulwer to Carnarvon, November 15, 1876, CO 179/121.
2. Graham's minute of February 17, 1877, *ibid.*

the Treasury officials frequently adopted defense mechanisms which further aggravated their problems with other departments.

The prevalent economic theories of the late nineteenth century stressed the passive role of government in the English economy. The creation of wealth was the responsibility of private individuals and companies and not the government. The Treasury officials concentrated on keeping governmental expenditure at a minimum and not on economic planning. The chancellor of the exchequer was forced to defend every expenditure or increase in taxation before a questioning House of Commons. In the opinion of Gladstone, the champion of frugality in government, the Treasury was admirably designed for "controlling, sifting, & repressing the operations of other Depts."[3] Because of the Treasury's tenacity in defending the public purse, it was rumored in Whitehall that Sir Reginald Welby, the permanent secretary of the Treasury, had a statuette of "the British taxpayer" on his chimney-piece, "before which he performed his obeisance day and night."[4]

The Treasury was organized to enable it to exercise close financial control over the other departments of the civil service. It was divided into a finance division and four "control" divisions which scrutinized the accounts of the other offices. The Colonial Office was grouped with the Foreign Office, the Admiralty, the War Office, and the Office of Woods in the second division.[5] Sir Reginald Welby emphasized that the primary function of the Treasury was to maintain "financial order throughout the service." Unfortunately, problems frequently arose when the Treasury encountered a departmental head who was more interested in efficiency than in frugality.[6] Such a conflict of interests could easily lead to serious disputes.

A powerful Cabinet Minister does not accept readily a decision of the Treasury which overrules something he proposes, and in practice that is a considerable check upon the power of control. . . . When a minister is interested in a question, it very shortly resolves itself into one between him and the Chancellor of the Exchequer, because he goes to the Chancellor of the Exchequer, and then it becomes a question in which the Chancellor

3. Gladstone to Lowe, December 26, 1868, Add. MS 44301, f. 35.
4. West, *Contemporary Portraits*, p. 164. Before going to a conference at the Treasury, Robert Meade assured Welby that the Colonial Office would furnish the coal, "lest an excess should be caused in your vote for fuel and light." *Ibid.*
5. For the allocation of the Treasury's work in the eighties see Sir Thomas L. Heath, *The Treasury* (London, 1927), pp. 97–102.
6. "First Report of the Royal (Ridley) Commission," C. 5226, p. 2, *Parl. Paps. 1887*, XIX.

of the Exchequer very constantly maintains the Treasury view; but over a long period of years, probably that is not always the case.[7]

Welby believed that most departmental heads misunderstood the nature of the Treasury's control. Contrary to popular opinion, the Treasury did not reconsider the policies of other departments; it merely provided a financial check.

It appears to me that the control of the Treasury is really the Control of the Chancellor of the Exchequer, and that it is given to the Chancellor of the Exchequer because it is essential that the public and Parliament should be satisfied that somewhere or other in the Government there is a guarantee for what I call financial order; that there is some authority that will watch the progress of public expenditure, the obligations which the different departments are incurring, and will give timely warning that expenditure or those obligations are either outrunning the revenue provided for the year, or engaging the nation too deeply in future years.[8]

The members of the Ridley Commission had difficulty understanding how the Treasury could come to a financial opinion on a proposal without judging its other merits. Although Welby reiterated that the Treasury exercised a purely financial control, he did admit that "*prima facie* good grounds for incurring the expenditure comes within the business of the Treasury as dealing with financial order."[9] In actual practice the Treasury seldom distinguished between financial order and departmental policy. The Colonial Office officials believed that the Treasury frequently dictated colonial policy. Evelyn Ashley, the parliamentary undersecretary from 1882 to 1885, was especially outspoken on this subject: "The Treasury—whenever South African matters crop up—becomes intolerable. They dictate our despatches for us, condemn our policy & insult those whom we employ—they should be told to stick to their accounts."[10]

Herbert and his colleagues recognized the importance of the Treasury being "the official caretaker of the taxpayers' interests."[11] Although they occasionally regretted the "paralyzing control" of the

7. *Ibid.*, p. 7. Welby believed that you could "never rely on the permanent officers standing firm, if their Chiefs desert them." Welby to Edward Hamilton, very private, December 4, 1884, Hamilton Papers, Add. MS 48624.

8. "Second Report of the Royal (Ridley) Commission," C. 5545, p. 11, *Parl. Paps. 1888*, XXVII.

9. *Ibid.*

10. Ashley's minute of February 21, 1883, on Treasury to CO, February 5, 1883, CO 179/150. De Kiewiet also emphasizes the importance of the Treasury in the creation of colonial policy in South Africa. *The Imperial Factor in South Africa*, pp. 9–10.

11. Meade's minute of December 12, 1878, on Treasury to CO, September 25, 1878, CO 323/337.

Treasury,[12] Meade and Herbert believed in fiscal responsibility, at least in theory, as much as Welby did. They and their political superiors emphasized that social improvements in the colonies depended upon the growth of local revenue.[13] The younger clerks were usually more critical of Treasury control than the members of the secretariat. In 1891 Charles Lucas argued that the Colonial Office should represent the interests of the crown colonies more vigorously. Regarding the military contribution exacted from Ceylon, he remarked,

Of late years, as far as I can judge, the leading people in the colonies have been more & more regarding [the Colonial Office] as their friend, & it is very important to maintain such a feeling. I incline to think less harm would be done in the long run if a larger increase were exacted, after it had been made patent that the Colonial Office had made its stand & been overborne, than if a smaller increase were exacted—the Colonial Office simply acting as the mouthpiece of the imperial Government. The point is this, what is just or unjust, the money is taken by force not agreed to, the resentment felt at this course may be against the Imperial Government as a whole or against the Home part of the Imperial Government. It is not good that these colonies should hold that the whole English Government is against them & that their immediate superiors who ought to be their protectors are no better than the rest.[14]

Herbert, however, did not view the Colonial Office as the colonial lobby; he regarded it as a department of the British government which was required to cooperate with the Treasury. He feared that if the colonists knew "that H. M. Ministers [were] not in accord with one another" there would be other difficulties. The Colonial Office should confine itself to representing the interests of the colonies in the interdepartmental negotiations leading to "the collective decision of H. M. Govt."[15]

Most colonial decisions necessitating the expenditure of large sums of money, such as the annexation of a new colony or the guaranteeing

12. Hemming's minute of November 7, 1888, on Robinson to Knutsford, October 17, 1888, CO 417/23; Carnarvon's minute of March 22, 1876, on Bulwer to Carnarvon, December 31, 1875, CO 179/118.
13. Herbert's minute of August 5, 1875, on Low to Carnarvon, April 26, 1875, CO 144/44. "I am in despair at the state of the [Labuan] prisons—but it is all a question of money." Carnarvon's minute of August 5, 1875, on Low to Carnarvon, April 26, 1875, CO 144/44.
14. Lucas' minute of January 29, 1891, on WO to CO, January 1, 1891, CO 54/598. See also Graham's minute of November 17, 1878, on Treasury to CO, September 25, 1878, CO 323/337. The young clerks also seem to have resented the power and prestige that the Treasury clerks enjoyed in the eyes of the public. See especially Hamilton, *Nineteenth Century and After*, p. 611, and Just's minute of July 28, 1891, on CSC to CO, July 21, 1891, CO 54/598.
15. Herbert's minute of February 3, 1891, on WO to CO, January 1, 1891, CO 54/598.

of a colonial loan, were debated by the cabinet. The Treasury was especially concerned about votes which could cause trouble in Parliament, such votes requiring the support of the entire government.[16] In the cabinet the Treasury was only one, albeit an important, department of the government.[17] Once a decision had been reached by the cabinet, Treasury control was confined to supervising the way in which the money was spent.

The Treasury frequently assisted the Colonial Office in its administration of the colonies and its subdepartments, advising on complex financial or currency questions.[18] The Treasury also furnished the Colonial Office with a "bogey" on which to blame the rejection of inconvenient or unjustifiable colonial requests.[19] The mere existence of this stringent Treasury control deterred the Colonial Office from making or supporting requests for financial assistance except in very strong cases. The Colonial Office was forced to scrutinize closely every colonial project requiring the financial support of the British taxpayer.[20] This everpresent threat of Treasury opposition probably played a greater role in determining Colonial Office policy than formal Treasury intervention.

The problem of Treasury control was complicated when more than one government office was involved in an expenditure. This was especially true when the War Office and the Colonial Office discussed the payment of imperial garrisons stationed in the colonies. The secretariat of the Colonial Office frequently complained that the War Office was more concerned with reducing their own estimates than in providing an adequate defense for the colonies. As Robert Meade, the Colonial Office's military expert, explained to Carnarvon:

In fighting the War Office we have to do with two branches of the establishment. 1. The Horse Guards proper whose chief idea is to find employment for as many officers as possible, and who consequently get to look upon the Colony as a sort of valuable pasture where generals, military secretaries and A.D.C.'s can be turned out to feed at other people's ex-

16. Northcote to Carnarvon, private, June 15, 1877, PRO 30/6/7, f. 205; Northcote to Carnarvon, private, February 10, 1876, PRO 30/6/7, f. 124; Northcote to Carnarvon, private, January 8, 1877, PRO 30/6/7, ff. 185–186.

17. Kimberley to Granville, March 28, 1871, PRO 30/29/55, ff. 223–225; Northcote to Carnarvon, private, June 15, 1877, PRO 30/6/7, f. 205.

18. Meade's minute of October 13, 1878, on Treasury to CO, April 3, 1878, CO 323/337; Minutes on Treasury to CO, December 8, 1873, CO 309/111.

19. Carnarvon to Northcote, copy, February 12, 1876, PRO 30/6/7, ff. 125–126.

20. Minutes on Lees to Derby, July 7, 1884, CO 152/157; Carnarvon's minute of March 22, 1875, on Bulwer to Carnarvon, December 31, 1875, CO 179/118; Hemming's minute of November 7, 1888, on Robinson to Knutsford, October 17, 1888, CO 417/23.

pense—2. the clerks who make it their principal duty to cut down Imperial Estimates by throwing every possible expense upon the Colony—The result is a tangled maze of figures which it can hardly be expected that the Secretary of State for War will go into, but it is of great importance that his attention should be directed to the subject if we are to arrive at a solution acceptable to both parties.[21]

The amount of the Ceylon military contribution proved to be a serious source of controversy between the two departments. Before a settlement could be reached, it was necessary to enlist the assistance of the Treasury.

Ceylon, like India, contributed to the cost of its imperial garrison. Despite Ceylonese objections, however, the amount of the contribution was steadily increased until by 1864 the colony paid the entire cost of the garrison. Ceylon was promised an inquiry into this question in 1874.[22] The result of this War Office inquiry was that the annual contribution was slightly reduced,[23] but not enough to satisfy the auditor general of Ceylon. He continued to object to the large number of engineers and staff officers stationed in Ceylon.[24] Robert Meade opposed forcing Ceylon to pay for an engineering staff costing almost as much as the work that it supervised. After consulting with the India Office, which had similar problems with the War Office, he proposed a compromise contribution. To avoid a "tangled maze of figures," Meade suggested that Ceylon pay a "lump sum" for its garrison of 1,020 men.[25] Carnarvon agreed; he believed that £100 per man was sufficient.[26]

The War Office ignored Meade's rather crude suggestion. The 1875–1876 Army Estimates charged Ceylon the amount recommended by the 1874 War Office committee. In a letter which one clerk feared would "lead to controversy rather than to any practical effect,"[27] the Colonial Office expressed surprise that the War Office had not reconsidered Ceylon's contribution.[28] The War Office replied two months later, arguing that Ceylon's payment represented "the full present cost

21. Meade's minute of November 11, 1874, on J. Douglas to CO, August 23, 1874, CO 54/495.
22. Mills, *Ceylon under British Rule*, pp. 113–117.
23. WO to CO, July 23, 1874, CO 54/495.
24. J. Douglas to CO, August 23, 1874, *ibid*. Douglas also objected to paying the cost of recruiting and training the troops in England.
25. Meade's minute of November 11, 1874, on J. Douglas to CO, August 23, 1874, *ibid*.
26. Carnarvon's minute of December 4, 1874, on J. Douglas to CO, August 23, 1874, *ibid*.
27. Round's minute of March, 1875, on Army Estimates for 1875–1876, CO 54/499.
28. CO to WO, March 12, 1875, *ibid*.

of the force demanded by the Government of the Island."[29] The Colonial Office was just as uncompromising when it replied seven months later. The Colonial Office stated that it could not accept the report of a departmental committee as final. If the War Office did not modify its view, the governor of Ceylon would be instructed "to pay at the rate which His Lordship [Carnarvon] has already stated is the highest which he would feel warranted in authorizing."[30]

Gathorne Hardy, the secretary of state for war, correctly complained to Carnarvon about this Colonial Office communication. "This goes through the ordinary official channels here & produces the same astonishment as your department would probably feel if I was to wish that if I had not my own way I should withdraw the troops."[31] The dispute continued for several months, but finally as a result of private communications between Hardy and Carnarvon,[32] the two departments agreed on a compromise figure. All that was now needed was the approval of the Treasury.[33] The War Office, however, justified the compromise to the Treasury on the grounds that the colony could not afford to pay the entire cost of its garrison.[34] The Treasury consequently refused to sanction the arrangement. If a colony could not pay for its entire defense, the difference had to be submitted to Parliament in the form of a separate vote. "It will then be in the power of Parliament to determine whether on good grounds of Imperial policy it is right that assistance should be given to the Colony."[35] The Colonial Office was naturally upset at this misrepresentation of its reasons for opposing the original Ceylon military contribution. Ceylon was not poor; the cost of its garrison was excessive.[36] Meade complained that the War Office, by repudiating Carnarvon's and Hardy's private agreement, was engaging in "sharp practice." "If business is to be con-

29. WO to CO, July 1, 1875, *ibid.*
30. CO to WO, January 31, 1876, *ibid.*
31. Hardy to Carnarvon, February 2, 1876, PRO 30/6/12. Hardy also feared that any concession granted to Ceylon would have to be extended to India.
32. Hardy to Carnarvon, June 9, 1876; Herbert to Carnarvon, June 9, 1876; Hardy to Carnarvon, July 11, 1876; Carnarvon to Hardy, copy, July 12, 1876; Hardy to Carnarvon, July 14, 1876, PRO 30/6/12.
33. WO to CO, July 21, 1876, CO 54/505.
34. WO to Treasury, December 4, 1876, enclosed in WO to CO, December 22, 1876, *ibid.*
35. Treasury to WO, December 19, 1876, enclosed in WO to CO, December 22, 1876, *ibid.*
36. Round's minute of January 8, 1877; Cox's minute of January 9, 1877; and Meade's minute of April 28, 1877, on WO to CO, December 22, 1876, *ibid*; War Office to CO, September 10, 1877, CO 54/511.

ducted in this fashion it is useless for two cabinet ministers to meet & settle (as they think they have done) the question."[37]

When additional private negotiations between Hardy and Carnarvon failed to produce any agreement,[38] the Colonial Office simply dropped the question. Meade believed that the War Office should continue the correspondence with the Treasury. The War Office, not the Colonial Office, required the approval of the Treasury.[39] When the War Office refused to consult the Treasury, Charles Lucas, a new second-class clerk, argued that the Colonial Office should "make it pretty clear that we must have our terms granted or no contribution at all will be forthcoming."[40] Robert Meade was more moderate, however, and the question was referred to an interdepartmental committee. When no agreement was reached, Hicks Beach, the secretary of state, admitted that he did not see any way for the dispute to be settled.[41]

In 1883 the War Office still complained that Ceylon's contribution did not meet the full cost of its defenses.[42] This did not upset the Colonial Office, however; Herbert and Meade were content to allow the War Office and the Treasury to make the initial move.[43] The Treasury simply recommended that the deficit be met by reducing the size of the garrison.[44] In 1884 another interdepartmental committee finally agreed to a five-year arrangement whereby Ceylon would pay a lump sum of £60,000 a year for its garrison.[45] Charles Lucas, who had conducted most of the negotiations, justifiably hoped that when the

37. Meade to Carnarvon, October 20, 1877, CO 54/511; Carnarvon to Hardy, copy, private, October 22, 1877, PRO 30/6/12. Carnarvon complained privately to Hardy. "My object is to avoid an interdepartmental wrangle; but if we cannot agree to carry out our agreement then I think the only course is for the Colony to accept a reduction in the military force to be maintained so as to bring the expense within the limits which we ought to incur for such objects. This however is I am aware a result which the D. of Cambridge does not desire."

38. Hardy to Carnarvon, private, October 25, 1877; Carnarvon to Hardy, copy, private, October 29, 1877, PRO 30/6/12.

39. Meade's minutes of July 30, 1878, and August 19, 1878, on WO to CO, July 20, 1878, CO 54/516; CO to WO, August 21, 1878, ibid.

40. Lucas' minute of October 28, 1878, on WO to CO, October 25, 1878, ibid.

41. Round's undated minute on WO to CO, October 25, 1878, ibid; Meade's minute of March 14, 1880, and Hicks Beach's minute of March 17, 1880, on WO to CO, January 23, 1880, CO 54/530.

42. WO to CO, November 14, 1883, CO 54/551.

43. Minutes on WO to CO, November 14, 1883, ibid.

44. Treasury to CO, December 13, 1883, CO 54/550. Carnarvon had recommended this in 1877, but the Duke of Cambridge opposed any reduction. Carnarvon to Hardy, copy, private, October 22, 1877, and Carnarvon to Hardy, copy, October 29, 1877, PRO 30/6/12.

45. Treasury to CO, May 27, 1884, and Treasury to CO, June 10, 1884, CO 54/556; Treasury to CO, April 13, 1885, CO 54/562.

five years had expired some other member of the office would be responsible for the question.[46] In 1889 when Ceylon's contribution was reassessed, the dispute was reopened with unabated hostility. This time, however, an agreement was reached in only eighteen months.[47]

Although the Colonial Office officials realized that Treasury control over large colonial expenditures was necessary and desirable, they were highly critical of the way in which the Treasury exercised this control. A common complaint was that the Treasury did not allow the secretary of state sufficient discretion in approving minor expenditures. Carnarvon argued that the "whole explanation of trumpery little details [was] really a waste of time & money." He believed that the colonial secretary should have a small fund of about £150 a year to pay "little miscellaneous charges."[48] No such discretion was permitted, however. In 1886 Kew Gardens offered to prepare a digest of information relating to the vegetable resources of the empire. Herbert believed that the work would certainly be worth the expenditure of £15, and the proposal was sent to the Treasury for approval.[49] The Treasury predictably suggested that the cost of this project be divided among the various colonies. This, in Richard Ebden's opinion, would "create ridicule & excessive cost," and the question was dropped.[50]

In its desire to keep expenditures at a minimum, the Treasury even interfered with the structure of the accounts department of the Colonial Office, an action which was deeply resented by Herbert and Meade. Before 1870 the accountant had been under the supervision of the chief clerk. When the office was reorganized, however, a separate accounts department was established. Rogers did not believe that either the chief clerk or the principal clerk of the general department could exercise an effective control over the accounts work. They did not have the necessary training.[51] J. S. Lewes, who was transferred from the Emigration Office in 1868, was appointed accounting officer. Most of his duties were routine and did not involve questions of policy. He checked the crown agents' accounts, approved the drawing of salaries by colonial officials, computed pensions and passage money, pre-

46. Lucas' minute of April 14, 1885, on Treasury to CO, April 13, 1885, *ibid.*
47. Minutes on WO to CO, October 15, 1890, CO 54/585; Minutes on WO to CO, January 21, 1891, and Knutsford to Havelock, July 23, 1891, CO 54/598.
48. Carnarvon to Northcote, copy, private, August 30, 1876, PRO 30/6/7, ff. 158–159.
49. Herbert's minute of September 10, 1886, on Kew to CO, September 3, 1886, and CO to Treasury, September 16, 1886, CO 323/366.
50. Minutes on Kew to CO, January 20, 1887, CO 323/370.
51. Rogers' and Sandford's minute of April 19, 1869, enclosed in CO to Treasury, June 28, 1869, CO 323/302.

pared the annual Colonial Office estimate, supervised the payment of parliamentary grants, paid stamp taxes, and approved minor expenditures. Herbert and the colonial secretary saw very few of the accounts letters. They allowed Lewes, in whom they had great confidence, and Robert Meade to handle this uninteresting work. Meade countersigned the accounts papers, but he did not pretend to exercise an effective check on Lewes.[52]

In 1872 the Treasury requested that the permanent head of each department take personal responsibility for the financial transactions of his office.[53] Meade and Herbert disliked the proposal, believing that the undersecretaries, because of their other duties, could not do other "than rely upon the care and fidelity of the officer in charge of accounts."

In a "spending department" the principal function of which is to expend large votes of public money, it is clearly the first duty of the chief permanent officers to supervise such expenditure. But in a department like the Foreign Office or Colonial Office which has primarily to do with questions of policy, & with general administrative duties, incidently disbursing only limited sums the disposal of which has been precisely fixed by the Parliamentary votes, and is under the control of the Controller & Auditor General, the case is reversed, and there would seem to be no advantage, but a serious disadvantage, in making the principal permanent Under Secretary, or one of the other permanent Under Secretaries, the "Accounting Officer."[54]

The Treasury refused to admit the force of Herbert's objections, and they appointed Meade the Colonial Office's "accounting officer." Meade complained that he would have to go into all of the intricate details of Lewes' work. This would result in wasted time, and "an illusory check would be substituted for an efficient one."[55] Herbert suggested that the question could be resolved by making Lewes a financial undersecretary.[56] A meeting with the Treasury proved useless, and the question was dropped for nearly a year. In the interval the Colonial Office ignored the Treasury's instructions, and Lewes continued to sign as "accounting officer."[57] When the question was reopened

52. CO 431/23-29, *passim*; Meade's minute of January 7, 1874, on Treasury to CO, December 30, 1873, CO 431/29.
53. Treasury to CO, October 12, 1872, CO 431/27.
54. Herbert's minute of October 16, 1872, on Treasury to CO, October 12, 1872, *ibid.*
55. Meade's minute of January 7, 1874, on Treasury to CO, December 30, 1873, CO 431/29.
56. Herbert's minute of January 8, 1874, on Treasury to CO, December 30, 1873, *ibid.*
57. Meade's minute of November 2, 1874, on Treasury to CO, December 30, 1873, *ibid.*

in late 1874, Herbert showed more sympathy for the Treasury's position. He believed that the Treasury, in trying to establish a better accounting system in the "spending" departments, was forced to place the same regulations on the Colonial Office.[58] Carnarvon agreed with Meade that it would be a dangerous precedent to allow the Treasury to interfere with the internal administration of the Colonial Office, however. He stressed that the colonial secretary was responsible for "the financial as well as the political administration of his department."[59] This dispute had little effect on the routine of the Colonial Office's accounts department. Throughout the seventies and eighties Meade continued to exercise a very loose control over Lewes' work. Herbert and the colonial secretary saw very few of the letters.[60]

The Treasury not only exercised a tight control over small expenditures, but it frequently did so without consulting the Colonial Office. In 1883, for example, the British government printed the report of the oceanographic expedition of the *Challenger* in the mid-seventies. Without consulting the Colonial Office, the Treasury announced that two copies of the report would be given to Canadian universities and one each to the Cape, New South Wales, New Zealand, and Victoria.[61] Meade and Herbert argued that no copies of the report should be distributed unless they were also given to South Australia, Queensland, and Tasmania.[62] Leonard Courtney, who served as parliamentary undersecretary of the Colonial Office in 1881 and 1882, had apparently learned very little about colonial jealousies. He refused Herbert's request, maintaining that "every Australian will allow that Sydney and Melbourne are now the intellectual centers of the continent."[63] Herbert thereupon simply requested the Treasury to distribute the reports and to relieve the Colonial Office of the necessity of explaining the basis of the selection.[64] The question of the *Challenger* report was reopened in 1886 when Sir Charles Tupper, the high commissioner for Canada, requested a copy for the National Library of

58. Herbert's minute of November 4, 1874, on Treasury to CO, December 30, 1873, *ibid.*

59. Carnarvon's minute on Treasury to CO, December 30, 1873, and CO to Treasury, December 14, 1874, *ibid.*

60. CO 431/43, 76, *passim.*

61. Treasury to CO, January 2, 1884, CO 323/358.

62. Meade's minute of January 15, 1884, and Herbert's minute of January 17, 1884, on Treasury to CO, January 2, 1884; CO to Treasury, January 22, 1884; and Herbert to Courtney, copy, private, March, 1884, *ibid.*

63. Courtney to Herbert, private, March 14, 1884, *ibid.*

64. Herbert to Courtney, copy, private, March 20, 1884, *ibid.*

Canada. Herbert feared that the Colonial Office would be accused of negligence if it failed to obtain a copy. Granville agreed, and he promised to mention the question personally to Sir William Harcourt, the chancellor of the exchequer, and if necessary to the cabinet.[65] Tupper's request was granted, but the neglected Australian colonies did not receive copies until 1895.[66]

The Colonial Office also objected to the fact that the Treasury was bound so tightly in red tape that it could not consider the personal and political aspects of a question. In 1873 Governor Keate died after serving only two weeks on the west coast of Africa. The Colonial Office suggested that since he had received so little pay from the appointment the £175 stamp duty on his commission be refunded to his widow, who was in desperate financial circumstances. The Treasury very properly pointed out that such generosity was contrary to the regulations.[67] Herbert saw nothing to do, but Knatchbull-Hugessen and Kimberley pressed the issue. "It is this niggardly, parsimonious treatment of public servants—not always accompanied by the courtesy of language to soften the blow—which discredits the department which controls the finances of the country."[68] When the Treasury refused to change its position, the question was reluctantly dropped.

The Treasury's insistence on upholding the letter of the law naturally gave its officials a reputation for being hardhearted and indifferent to human feelings. Some Treasury officials actually appear to have cultivated this reputation. In refusing to approve a small vote for maintaining military cemeteries in South Africa, the Treasury argued that "if British Subjects in South Africa do not care to maintain them, the graves must be allowed to sink into decay & ultimate effacement like those of the vast majority of persons buried in this country."[69] The Colonial Office's reaction was predictable. This reply was "one of those astounding statements which [only] a Treasury Clerk could produce."[70] Other departments had similar problems with the Treasury,

65. Minutes on Tupper to Herbert, March 13, 1886, CO 323/364.
66. Treasury to CO, April 20, 1886, CO 323/365; circular dispatch of September 24, 1895, CO 323/401.
67. Treasury to CO, June 12, 1873, CO 323/314.
68. Knatchbull-Hugessen's minute of June 18, 1873, on *ibid*. Herbert wished that the Treasury "would more frequently vouchsafe a reasoned and considerate reply to applications which they are not prepared to accede to." Herbert's minute of December 10, 1873, on Treasury to CO, December 8, 1873, CO 309/111.
69. Treasury to CO, May 18, 1888, CO 417/25.
70. Hemming's minute of May 23, 1888, on Treasury to CO, May 18, 1888, *ibid*. "National honour, patriotism, respect for brave men who died doing their duty to their

and the question of military cemeteries was referred to an interdepartmental committee. This committee gave the various departments an opportunity to trade stories about the Treasury's heartlessness. Fairfield reported to the Colonial Office that when the Admiralty had requested some money for a graveyard, the Treasury had replied that "the bodies should be dug up and thrown into the sea."[71]

The Treasury was also frequently criticized for being dilatory and careless in its work. Kimberley was particularly displeased with the delays caused by the Treasury.[72] As an example of the "disorganization of the Treasury," he cited the 1873 contract for the Cape mails. This contract had been granted without any consultation with the Colonial Office, and it had needlessly provoked the colonists and had aroused the opposition in Parliament.[73] Kimberley's attitude was not unique among cabinet members.[74] The natural resentment of the Treasury's authority was heightened by the brusque manner in which it frequently conducted its work.[75] T. H. Farrer, the permanent undersecretary of the Board of Trade, vigorously condemned the way in which Treasury control was exercised.

But I think you [Sir Ralph Lingen] deceive yourself about the Treasury. Undoubtedly they have assumed more and more power; and their language is less and less civil and more and more dictatorial. And on the other hand the business is so far as I can judge less well done than it used to be. There is no public office where there are (so far as our experience goes) such delays and such blunders. It gives one the impression that young men without knowledge and experience have got into places too high for them. And there is undoubtedly an impression in the service that the Treasury clerks take uncommonly good care of themselves, whilst they snub other departments.

You will find that these impressions—or similar impressions—prevail amongst the best men at this office, the Colonial Office, the Privy Council Office, the Admiralty, the Post Office, etc., etc., to an extent as it seems to

country—all such ideas are of course mere foolish sentiment, & to be utterly discarded if there is any possibility by doing so of saving a few pounds!" See also Webb's minute of May 23, 1888, and Herbert's minute of May 24, 1888, on Treasury to CO, May 18, 323/349.

71. Fairfield's minute of January 20, 1890, on Treasury to CO, January 8, 1890, CO 417/49.

72. Kimberley's minute of June 19, 1873, on Treasury to CO, June 14, 1873, CO 323/314; Kimberley's minute of May 3, 1881, on Treasury to CO, April 28, 1881, CO 323/349.

73. Kimberley, *Journal*, June 28, 1873, p. 39.

74. Minutes on Granville to Clarendon, Bruce, and Cardwell, private, January 12, 1870, PRO 30/29/68, ff. 37–39.

75. Robert Lowe was not "the least disposed to contend that the letters of the Treasury [were] models either of style or courtesy." Lowe to Granville, November 5, 1872, PRO 30/29/66.

me I have never known before. And I do not agree that this is a good thing.[76]

It was commonly believed within the Colonial Office that the Treasury regarded colonial questions as unworthy of consideration by the chancellor of the exchequer. Problems receiving the colonial secretary's fullest consideration were frequently disposed of by minor Treasury officials.[77] W.A.B. Hamilton complained that many carefully worked out Colonial Office plans received only a curt reply "not infrequently capable of being 'spotted' as the handiwork of a comparatively minor official."[78] A rapid reply by the usually dilatory Treasury was regarded as proof that the question had not received full consideration.[79] If the secretary of state felt that a subject deserved the personal attention of the chancellor of the exchequer, he usually wrote a private note to accompany the official letter.[80]

In defense of the Treasury it should be noted that whenever a government office sought approval for a new expenditure it invariably attempted to find a precedent in another department. It was also a common practice to enlist the support of other departments in seeking new appropriations.[81] The Treasury naturally resented this ganging up, helping to explain "My Lords'" devotion to the regulations. Unless the Treasury was very strict, Northcote feared that whatever was done by one department would lead to demands in others.[82] It was also essential, from the perspective of the Treasury, that every expenditure be "put in a shape in which it can be brought before Parliament."[83] The result was that the Treasury's decisions were frequently "in accordance with law though not with equity."[84] Welby

76. Farrer to Lingen, 1872, in Sir John Woods, "Treasury Control," *Political Quarterly*, XXV (October–December, 1954), 375.

77. Graham's minute of November 17, 1878, on Treasury to CO, September 25, 1878, CO 323/337.

78. Hamilton, *Nineteenth Century and After*, p. 611.

79. Ebden's minute of October 9, 1875, on Treasury to CO, August 27, 1875, CO 323/323. "The last two letters read more like a routine refusal than the result of any real consideration of the case. They are neither of them signed by the Secretary. One is dated only 5 days and the other only 7 days later than the letters to which they replied to. Suspiciously rapid for the Treasury."

80. Carnarvon to Northcote, copy, private, June 11, 1874, PRO 30/6/7, f. 21; Carnarvon to Northcote, copy, private, August 16, 1877, PRO 30/6/7, f. 225.

81. Kew to CO, August 5, 1881, CO 323/350; Local Government Board to CO, May 17, 1880, CO 323/346; Minutes on FO to CO, August 3, 1876, CO 323/328.

82. Northcote to Carnarvon, June 12, 1874, PRO 30/6/7, f. 22.

83. Northcote to Carnarvon, confidential, December 11, 1876, PRO 30/6/7, f. 177.

84. Herbert's minute of January 11, 1882, on Treasury to CO, December 8, 1881, CO 323/349. See also Treasury to CO, March 23, 1880, CO 323/344; Memo on Mr. Woods' Case, CO 323/350; Kimberley to Gladstone, October 18, 1880, Add. MS 44225, ff. 225–226.

summarized the Treasury's position very well, arguing that in "a day of sentimental statesmen who are ready to do wonders with other people's money," it was the Treasury's duty to uphold "the truth of economical Government." He believed that the most important ingredient in a good secretary of the Treasury was "sturdiness & carelessness of unpopularity in defense of the Public Purse."[85] Treasury officials would undoubtedly have felt that they were neglecting their duty if they had been too popular with other departments.

The Colonial Office was not, of course, blameless in its relations with the Treasury. Herbert and his colleagues seldom approved major expenditures without obtaining the approval of the Treasury,[86] but they were not so careful in minor matters. Edward Fairfield feared that there was considerable justification for the Treasury's "old standing grievance" that the Colonial Office circumvented their financial authority by committing them to minor expenditures without an opportunity for criticism. He believed that the Colonial Office should be more careful in obtaining the Treasury's approval of new appointments.

To write them in regard to an ordinary administrative appointment in a Colony where they are supposed to exercise full control, and to tell them that the appointment was already made, thereby implying that criticism would be too late, would stir the embers of their wrath into a flame, and provoke an angry and probably insolent unmannerly reply.[87]

Insubordinate or incompetent officials in the colonies also created trouble between the Colonial Office and the Treasury. An especially bitter controversy resulted from Theophilus Shepstone's mission to the Transvaal in 1877. Since he was not trained in bookkeeping, his accounts were very poorly kept, and in 1883 the Colonial Office and the Treasury were still arguing over how the money had actually been spent.[88]

85. Welby to Hamilton, very private, November 28, 1884, Add. MS 48624.
86. In 1890 Sir Henry Loch, the high commissioner for South Africa, requested permission to visit Bechuanaland to negotiate with the native chiefs. Although the Colonial Office feared that Loch contemplated "an imposing display in the Indian Style," permission was immediately granted. Goschen, the chancellor of the exchequer, was on the continent, and no time could be lost. "Our reply to the Treasury remonstrance will be that the expenditure was to my mind of such importance that I could not take upon myself to stop it and postponement would have had the same effect." Herbert's minute of September 17, 1890, and Knutsford's minute of September 18, 1890, on Loch to Knutsford (tel.), September 15, 1890, CO 417/46.
87. Fairfield's minute of August 11, 1886, on Treasury to CO, July 31, 1886, CO 417/12.
88. Minutes on Bulwer to Kimberley, April 22, 1882, CO 179/140; Treasury to CO, March 11, 1882, CO 291/16; Herbert's minute of December 6, 1882, on Bulwer to Kimberley, April 22, 1882, CO 179/140.

Despite criticisms of the Treasury's close scrutiny of colonial expenditures, in 1870 the officials at the Treasury voluntarily relaxed their control over the finances of the crown colonies. Rogers regarded this "small departmental good deed" as one of Granville's most important achievements during his first term at the Colonial Office.[89] Before 1870 the Colonial Office and the Treasury exercised a joint control over the expenditures of certain crown colonies. The annual estimates of these colonies had to be approved by both departments. In April, 1868, however, Sir Frederic Rogers proposed that the Treasury relinquish its responsibility for this work.[90] He insisted that there was no rational reason why certain colonies were forced to submit to financial control by the Treasury and others were not. "The distinction [was] not grounded on any views of fitness or expediency, but on historical accident." Rogers pointed out that the supervision of the Treasury did not always secure good financial management, and its absence did not invariably result in bankruptcy. An efficient colonial administration did not require Treasury assistance, and an inept one was not aided by it. In addition, the submission of colonial estimates to the Treasury, which was "of necessity uninformed on those matters of fact which really regulate the expediency of expenditure," caused inconvenient delays and expenses. Because of these inconveniences, some colonies frequently disregarded the regulations. Ceylon, for example, usually spent its revenue before the Treasury sanctioned the annual appropriation ordinance. Rogers also complained that rigid Treasury control resulted in considerable unnecessary correspondence between the two offices. If the Treasury confined itself to supervising expenditures affecting "Imperial interests" or "the monetary conditions of the Empire," at least five hundred letters a year would be saved.[91]

Although the permanent secretary of the Treasury, G.A. Hamilton, believed that Treasury control had been "sound and useful,"[92] the Treasury agreed to most of Rogers' recommendations. The Treasury very properly insisted, however, that it must continue to exercise control over the expenditure of colonies receiving imperial grants in aid. All colonial acts affecting currency or the security of colonial loans

---

89. Blachford to Granville, February 2, 1886, PRO 30/29/213.
90. Treasury to CO, September 25, 1878, CO 323/337.
91. CO to Treasury, June 28, 1869, CO 323/302.
92. Tyler, "Sir Frederic Rogers," p. 81.

were to be submitted to the Treasury for approval.[93] This arrangement resulted in fewer delays and disputes with the Treasury in the seventies. This was partly, however, a result of the Colonial Office's negligence in submitting the required estimates.

In 1878 the Colonial Office received "a violent philippic . . . couched in an unusually virulent tone."[94] The Treasury complained that, excepting the Falkland Islands, the Colonial Office had not regularly submitted the estimates of colonies receiving grants in aid. The Treasury threatened to instruct the comptroller and auditor general to reject the accounts of any colony receiving a grant in aid.[95] Herbert and Meade frankly admitted that they had been remiss in carrying out the earlier agreement, but the tone of the Treasury's letter made them anxious to prove that the Colonial Office's carelessness had been exaggerated. In any event, the Treasury was partly responsible for the misunderstanding because it had not written sooner.[96] The Colonial Office replied that the estimates of colonies receiving grants for specific purposes had not been forwarded because such grants in aid did not indicate a failure in a colony's finances.[97] In personal communications with the Treasury officials, Meade suggested that only the estimates of crown colonies receiving grants in aid for their general expenditures should be approved by the Treasury. The financial returns of colonies receiving grants for specific purposes would be sent to the Treasury for its information only.[98] The two offices eventually settled the dispute along these lines,[99] and during the eighties the Colonial Office was much more conscientious about sending the required returns to the Treasury.

The only significant change in the relations between the Treasury and the Colonial Office in the seventies and eighties was this freeing of solvent crown colonies from the direct financial control of the Treasury. The remaining controls exercised by the Treasury throughout this period, however, made it impossible for the Colonial Office to initiate any major programs of social and economic development of the

93. Treasury to CO, April 28, 1870; CO to Treasury, June 3, 1870; Treasury to CO, July 8, 1870, CO 323/301.
94. Meade to Welby, copy, May 6, 1879, CO 323/340.
95. Treasury to CO, September 25, 1878, CO 323/337.
96. Graham's minute of November 17, 1878, and Herbert's minute of December 28, 1878, on Treasury to CO, September 25, 1878, CO 323/337.
97. CO to Treasury, January 1, 1879, *ibid.*
98. Meade's minute of February 25, 1879, on Treasury to CO, September 25, 1878, CO to Treasury, February 26, 1879, *ibid.*
99. Memorandum of July 11, 1879, enclosed in Treasury to CO, July 17, 1879, CO 323/340.

crown colonies. The chancellor of the exchequer had to defend all expenditures of imperial funds before a questioning parliament, and he was not eager to support new demands from other departments. Even Joseph Chamberlain, whose personal and political influence was much greater than that of his predecessors, found it very difficult to obtain money for his schemes of colonial development.[100] The complaints leveled by Herbert and Meade against the manner in which the Treasury exercised its control continued well into the twentieth century. The comments of Sir Alan Burns, who served in both the Colonial Office and several crown colonies, show how little Treasury control changed in the half-century after Herbert's retirement.

The control of the Treasury over expenditure led to vexatious delays and a parsimony in administration at a time when the conditions of [British Honduras] made it more than ever necessary that speedy and generous expenditure should be authorised. . . . If a Governor cannot be trusted to use his discretion in the appointment on an additional junior clerk without reference to a Treasury official in Whitehall, then, in my view, that Governor should not have been appointed to the post he holds. And if the Governor and his senior officials and the members of the Legislative Council have examined the annual estimates of expenditure in detail, as they have to do, then it seems quite unnecessary that approval of these estimates should be delayed for months while comparatively junior Treasury officials check the details over again in London. . . . No doubt also the Treasury officials themselves were overworked and were not to blame; but the system was a disastrous one and I hope it will be ended.[101]

As long as the watchword of British colonial administration continued to be economy, little change in the Treasury's approach to financial control could be expected.

100. Kubicek, *The Administration of Imperialism*, chap. iv.
101. Burns, *Colonial Civil Servant*, p. 129.

CHAPTER VII

The Colonial Office and the Civil Service, 1876-1892

THE FORMAL STRUCTURE of the Colonial Office changed little in the period after 1872. The reorganization of the office in that year introduced prestigiously high salaries and a rigid division of labor, making the Colonial Office what might be regarded as a satiated establishment. The civil service reformers of the seventies had nothing to offer the Colonial Office's secretariat and upper-division clerks except lower salaries. Herbert and Meade therefore showed little interest in the larger questions of civil service reform. The organization and routine of the Colonial Office was naturally modified, but the changes were minor and designed to meet specific problems, such as the rapid increase in the volume and complexity of work, the improvements in communications, and its changing relations with the colonies. Between 1874 and 1876, Carnarvon added a third assistant undersecretary, appointed two resident clerks, and strengthened the upper division of the office. These changes did not, however, affect the basic principles on which the office had been reorganized in 1872—unrestricted open competition and a strict division of labor. The personnel of the office also changed little. Following Edward Wingfield's appointment as assistant undersecretary in 1878, the secretariat remained unchanged until 1892, when Herbert retired and Fairfield was promoted from the ranks. No new upper-division clerks were appointed to the Colonial Office between 1882 and 1889.

The reaction of the secretariat to the recommendations of the Playfair Commission was indicative of the Colonial Office's general attitude toward civil service reform during the seventies and eighties. This commission, chaired by Lyon Playfair, was appointed in 1874 to consider the condition of the civil service. Like Northcote and Trevelyan twenty years earlier, Playfair and his colleagues stressed the importance of maintaining a sharp distinction between mechanical and intellectual work. They recommended the establishment of two classes of clerks common to the entire civil service. A relatively small number of administrative or upper-division clerks would receive salaries beginning at £100 and rising to £400 a year. The lower-division clerks would perform most mechanical tasks, and they would receive lower salaries. The Playfair Commission recommended that promotion within each class be based entirely on merit. In the interest of maintaining a strict division of labor, however, it urged that promotion of lower-division clerks into the upper division be made very difficult.[1] The commission also anticipated that the establishment of two service-wide clerical classes would unify the British civil service.

The Playfair Commission's report was condemned by Herbert and his colleagues. They did not oppose the creation of a new class of lower-division clerks, but they argued that the salaries recommended for the upper-division clerks were not sufficient to induce good men to compete for positions in the civil service.[2] In a letter drafted by Robert Meade,[3] the Colonial Office insisted that the complexity of its work required clerks possessing "a somewhat exceptional degree of general intelligence."

It would be easy, if it were necessary, to give many illustrations of the magnitude and still more of the variety and complication of the interests concerned. They cannot be measured in Lord Carnarvon's opinion by any statements of the revenue, population or trade of those Colonies under the direct administration of this Office, considerable as these now are; but it will be readily understood that the questions wh. arise in this class of Colonies are of so difficult and delicate a nature as to require the exercise of the highest ability that can be commanded.

Meade also criticized the Playfair Commission for its failure to consult with the more important departments such as the Home Office, the Foreign Office, the Colonial Office, and the Treasury.[4]

Sir Stafford Northcote, the new Conservative chancellor of the exchequer, did not support civil service reform as vigorously as Robert Lowe had done.[5] The Order in Council of February 12, 1876, omitted many of the commission's recommendations. A new class of lower-

1. A copy of the commission's first report was sent to the Colonial Office for comment in Treasury to CO, February 18, 1875, CO 323/323.
2. Herbert's minute of March 28, 1875, on *ibid.* The initial salary of the junior clerks in the Colonial Office had been raised from £100 to £250 a year in 1872.
3. Meade's minute of March 27, 1875, on *ibid.* "I think I have shewn sufficient reasons why the Commissioners' scheme is impracticable so far as we are concerned."
4. CO to Treasury, April 14, 1875, *ibid.*
5. Cohen, *Growth of the British Civil Service*, p. 134.

division clerks was established to replace the old supplementary clerks and copyists. They received an annual salary of £80 rising by triennial increments of £15 to £200.[6] The Order in Council did not, however, mention the establishment of a service-wide class of upper-division clerks except in connection with promotion. Able and conscientious lower-division clerks could be promoted into the upper division after they had served at least ten years.[7]

The Colonial Office did not oppose this new class of lower-division clerks, although it was careful to protect the interests of the supplementary clerks already in the office.[8] Herbert and his colleagues anticipated that the supplementary clerks, copyists, and civil service writers would eventually be replaced by the Playfair clerks.[9] Herbert was careful, however, to prevent the new lower-division clerks from rising above their station. None of them were promoted into the upper division of the Colonial Office between 1876 and 1888.[10] Incentive for these new clerks was provided for by "staff appointments" which had been originally designed for the supplementary clerks.[11] During the seventies and eighties, the Treasury urged the other government departments voluntarily to adopt the recommendations of the Playfair Commission regarding the upper-division class.[12] These recommendations were not embodied in the Order in Council of February 12, 1876, however, and the Colonial Office retained the higher salaries which had been granted in 1872. Fortunately for Herbert the constitutions of the Colonial Office and the Treasury were very similar, and the Treasury could not attack Herbert's decision without creating doubts concerning the efficiency of its own office establishment. Both departments were equally threatened by the demands for civil service reform which developed in the eighties.

6. These salaries were for a six-hour day. In offices which worked seven hours a day the pay began at £90 and rose to £250. Duty pay not exceeding £100 a year could also be given to the lower-division clerks. Order in Council of February 12, 1876, enclosed in Treasury to CO, February 14, 1876, CO 323/328.
7. Ibid.
8. Minutes on Treasury to CO, February 14, 1876, ibid.
9. CO to Treasury, July 14, 1876, ibid.
10. "Second Report of the Royal (Ridley) Commission," C. 5545, p. 77, Parl. Paps. 1888, XXVII. They were, however, permitted to compete for the higher positions in the civil service at the regular examinations. W. Tarn to Blake, January 20, 1881, CO 323/334; Ebden's minute of September 25, 1885, on Lower Division Clerks to Meade, July 29, 1885, CO 323/362.
11. Treasury to CO, January 26, 1877, CO 323/332. These positions included the librarian, superintendent of the registry, and superintendent of copying.
12. "Second Report of the Royal (Ridley) Commission," C. 5545, p. 2, Parl. Paps. 1888, XXVII.

Herbert's and Meade's lack of interest in civil service reform was shared by the political heads of the Colonial Office. The colonial secretaries following Carnarvon (1874–1878) showed little desire to change the routine and organization of the office. Unlike Kimberley and Carnarvon, they seldom interfered with the day-to-day operation of the office, allowing Herbert and Meade to suggest the necessary reforms. Sir Michael Hicks Beach became colonial secretary in 1878 when Carnarvon resigned in protest over Disraeli's eastern policy. His short term at the Colonial Office was dominated by events in the Transvaal and Zululand.[13] There are no overt signs of friction between Hicks Beach and his permanent staff, but "Black Michael" earned a reputation as being "an over-bearing and forcibly-spoken man."[14] After his resignation as colonial secretary in 1880, he showed little interest in colonial topics. Kimberley's second (1880–1882) secretaryship was disturbed by the war in the Transvaal,[15] and he welcomed a transfer to the India Office in December, 1882.[16]

Lord Derby, Kimberley's successor, had resigned with Carnarvon from Disraeli's Conservative government in 1878. During the first two years of his second administration, Gladstone tried to recruit Derby for his own cabinet.[17] Derby finally accepted the Colonial Office.[18] Although Derby was a very able and lucid person,[19] he had considerable difficulty in making decisions. Unlike Kimberley or Carnarvon, he rarely wrote long minutes, preferring instead to discuss every important question personally with Herbert. The Colonial Office staff eventually became convinced that Derby was incapable of forcing the cabinet to make a decision. Robert Meade was especially

13. For Hicks Beach's term at the Colonial Office see Lady Victoria Hicks Beach, *Life of Sir Michael Hicks Beach* (2 vols.; London, 1932), I, 63–179. Shortly after his appointment, Disraeli offered him promotion to the India Office, but he refused it. *Ibid.*, I, 84–85. In later life he served as president of the Board of Trade and as chancellor of the exchequer.

14. Olivier, ed., *Sydney Olivier*, p. 33; Arthur Ponsonby, *Henry Ponsonby: His Life from His Letters* (London, 1942), pp. 186, 279; Escott, *Pillars of the Empire*, pp. 122–127; *Times* (London), May 1, 1916, p. 6b; An appreciation by Lord George Hamilton in *Hicks Beach*, II, 377–378.

15. Kimberley to Ripon, private, September 3, 1881, Add. MS 43522, ff. 269–274.

16. Kimberley to Ripon, private and confidential, January 14, 1883, Add. MS 43523, ff. 1–3. Kimberley had been offered the Indian viceroyalty in 1880.

17. Gladstone to Granville, secret, November 15, 1881; Granville to Gladstone, private, November 25, 1881; Granville to Gladstone, May 17, 1882, in Ramm, ed., *Political Correspondence, 1876–1886*, I, 310, 314, 371.

18. Derby to Gladstone, December 25, 1882, Add. MS 44141, ff. 63–64. Derby stated that he preferred the Colonial Office to any other government office.

19. George Hamilton, *Reminiscences*, p. 135; Edward Hamilton, *Diary*, October 21, 1881, Add. MS 48631, f. 76.

disturbed; he complained to Edward Hamilton, Gladstone's private secretary, that Derby acted as though he was ashamed to disclose disagreeable truths to his colleagues.[20] Evelyn Ashley, Derby's parliamentary undersecretary, frequently complained that his chief's indecision made it very difficult to defend the government in the House of Commons.[21] By the time he left the Colonial Office in 1885, Derby was known by the "not very reverent nick name" of "Dawdling Derby."[22]

The next three colonial secretaries, Col. F. A. Stanley (June, 1885–February, 1886), Lord Granville (February–August, 1886), and Edward Stanhope (August, 1886–January, 1887), did not remain at the Colonial Office long enough to have an impact on its organization or routine. In addition, Stanley and Granville were not effective administrators. Meade remarked that having Stanley appointed as Derby's successor was "jumping from the frying pan into the fire!!"[23] Granville's effectiveness in office had declined rapidly during his last years at the Foreign Office (1880–1885). He received the Colonial Office in 1886 because Queen Victoria objected to sending him back to the important Foreign Office.[24] Granville was ill during much of his second term at the Colonial Office,[25] and Kimberley did much of his work. Edward Stanhope, Granville's Conservative successor, quickly won the respect of the Colonial Office staff.[26] His greatest achievement was the calling of the first Colonial Conference for 1887. Before

20. Hamilton, *Diary*, September 30, 1884, Add. MS 48637, f. 100. "Meade who came over this afternoon was open-mouthed about the difficulty of transacting business with Lord Derby. Lord D., according to Meade, never can be got to make up his mind, is for letting everything drift, is always trying to evade responsibility; and whenever he does give a decision it is merely an endorsement of what is put before him by the Colonial Office authorities." Hamilton, *Diary*, September 1, 1884, Add. MS 48634, f. 62.

21. For example, see Ashley's minute of July 18, 1884, on Bulwer to Derby (tel.), July 16, 1884, CO 179/153.

22. Hamilton, *Diary*, January 10, 1885, Add. MS 48638, f. 124. Derby's colleagues apparently did not think highly of his abilities either. Hamilton, *Diary*, June 20, 1885, Add. MS 48640, f. 128; Dilke, *Diary*, August 30, 1881, Add. MS 43924, f. 59; Alfred E. Gathorne-Hardy, *Gathorne Hardy: First Earl of Cranbrook* (2 vols.; London, 1910), II, 50.

23. Hamilton, *Diary*, August 30, 1885, Add. MS 48641, f. 58. Stanley was Derby's younger brother. Lord Spencer Hartington joked that they had a family arrangement whereby they divided the pay of the Colonial Office. Elizabeth Longford, *Victoria R. I.* (London, 1964), p. 476. See also Stanley to Carnarvon, July 1, 1885, PRO 30/6/55, No. 2.

24. George E. Buckle, ed., *The Letters of Queen Victoria* (3rd series; 3 vols.; London, 1930), I, 25, 29, 35. Edward Hamilton believed that Granville should have sought "a dignified refuge," such as the presidency of the council. "To go from one administrative post to another is to accentuate his failure at the office which he relinquished." Hamilton, *Diary*, February 1, 1886, Add. MS 48642, f. 123.

25. Granville to Pope Hennessy, copy, July 19, 1886, PRO 30/29/213.

26. Hamilton, *Nineteenth Century and After*, p. 606. Unlike some of his predecessors, Stanhope was very interested in his work, being a strong supporter of the Imperial Federation League. Stanhope to Salisbury, June 18, 1885, Salisbury Papers.

the conference met, however, Stanhope's administrative ability had earned him promotion to the War Office.

Sir Henry Holland, Stanhope's successor, had served as legal adviser and assistant undersecretary at the Colonial Office from 1867 to 1874. He resigned in 1874 to enter Parliament but retained a close association with his old office. The Colonial Office continued to consult him on certain types of legal work, especially questions dealing with copyright laws.[27] He also served on several parliamentary commissions inquiring into colonial subjects.[28] Holland received his first political office in 1885 when he was appointed financial secretary to the Treasury.[29] In 1887 he was appointed colonial secretary in Salisbury's second ministry,[30] retaining that position until 1892, a longer time than any secretary of state for the colonies since Lord Bathurst (1812–1827).

Although Holland was intimately acquainted with the Colonial Office's work, he was not an effective secretary of state. Admittedly a very poor debater and speaker,[31] he disliked the pressure of facing a questioning House of Commons. When his health deteriorated in late 1887, he was grateful for the opportunity to escape to the House of Lords as Baron Knutsford.[32] Holland was a very junior cabinet minister, and he was unwilling to press his views strongly upon his colleagues. His son later observed that

he was a singularly modest man with too little trust in himself, and that is why he made no great impression in his political life. He succeeded in all the posts he held, but his success lay in getting the work done well and smoothly, in keeping peace when quarrels seemed inevitable, and in sinking his own personality—a lovable trait but not one which makes a man shine out in the history of his country. As one of the officials said of him when he was Secretary of State for the Colonies: "Lord Knutsford is always right. He leaves the office for a Cabinet Meeting determined to press for

27. Bramston to Holland, December 7, 1880, CO 323/347.
28. Holland to Carnarvon, August 11, 1879, PRO 30/6/52, ff. 18–19; Dilke to Gladstone, December 28, 1881, Add. MS 44149, ff. 61–62.
29. Holland to Salisbury, private, June 17, 1885, Salisbury Papers.
30. Holland was not Salisbury's first choice for the position. He first considered Lord Lansdowne, Lord Cranbrook, and Lord Iddesleigh, withdrawing the latter's name when it became apparent that the colonies would object to his "apparent feebleness." Salisbury to the Queen, copy, January 3, 1887; Salisbury to Hicks Beach, copy, private, January 7, 1887; Salisbury to Cranbrook, copy, private, January 8, 1887; and Salisbury to the Queen, copy, January 10, 1887, Salisbury Papers.
31. Holland to Gladstone, private, June 21, 1879, Add. MS 44460, ff. 167–168; Holland to Salisbury, private, June 17, 1885, Salisbury Papers. His son emphasized how much he disliked to speak in public. Holland, *In Black and White*, p. 71.
32. Salisbury to Holland, copy, October 12, 1887; Holland to Salisbury, February 14, 1888, Salisbury Papers.

this or that, but he comes back without it." His successor, Mr. Joseph Chamberlain, was the exact opposite in this.[33]

Although Holland and Salisbury were congenial colleagues, their relationship was an unequal one. Holland was too willing to accept Salisbury's opinion, even on the most minor questions.[34] He did little to raise the prestige of the Colonial Office in the eyes of the public. Joseph Chamberlain (1895–1902) was much more successful in obtaining for the Colonial Office influence commensurate with its responsibilities.

Holland's relations with the permanent staff of the office were naturally excellent. He respected the opinions of Herbert and Meade, his former colleagues, and there is no indication of any conflict between them. If anything, Holland was too interested in the details of the Colonial Office's work. He wrote extensive minutes on a great variety of subjects, especially legal topics, not recognizing the difference in the functions of the permanent and parliamentary officials. He failed to encourage the further delegation of responsibility to the principal clerks and the secretariat, being afraid that decisions would be made without his knowledge.[35] Basically, Holland was pleased with the Colonial Office's development after the reorganization of 1872, and he was not willing to make any fundamental changes in its constitution. In this he agreed with Herbert and Meade.

The parliamentary undersecretaries during this period took almost no interest in the organization and routine of the office.[36] This had not always been the situation, because in the early nineteenth century no sharp distinction between the permanent and political undersecretaries existed. The office's work was divided between them on a geographical and topical basis, and the political undersecretary did not necessarily leave office with the colonial secretary.[37] Increasingly, however, the political undersecretary was forced to devote his time to

33. Holland, *In Black and White*, pp. 211–212. Sir Charles Dilke regarded Holland as a perfect example of a man with "early Christian" or "Apostolic" manners. Gwynn and Tuckwell, *Life of Dilke*, II, 564.

34. Holland felt compelled to obtain Salisbury's permission simply to attend dinners given by colonial agents general. Holland to Salisbury, private, November 19, 1887; Knutsford to Salisbury, January 25, 1889, Salisbury Papers.

35. Knutsford's minute of November 1, 1889, CO 323/374.

36. Knatchbull-Hugessen was not even consulted on the 1872 reorganization. Knatchbull-Hugessen to Kimberley, June 19, 1872, CO 537/22.

37. Murray, *West Indies and the Development of Colonial Government*, pp. 120–126. R. J. Horton served as parliamentary undersecretary under three consecutive colonial secretaries. *Ibid.*, pp. 146–147.

parliamentary work. Under Sir James Stephen, the permanent under-secretary became the secretary of state's chief administrative adviser, but the distinction between the two undersecretaries was not entirely clear as late as 1870. Lord Granville, who had served at the Foreign Office,[38] was unsure of the relative power of each officer. "I have always considered that there was absolute equality between Political & Permanent UnderSecretaries. So far as my experience goes, it wd never enter into the mind of a Political U. S. to attempt, of his own authority, to overrule or set aside the decision of the permanent U. S."[39] Lord Clarendon and Gladstone agreed.

Despite Granville's confusion, the functions of the Colonial Office's parliamentary undersecretary were fairly well defined by the seventies. He supervised certain types of Colonial Office work, such as suspension cases and military and emigration questions.[40] The amount of time devoted by a parliamentary undersecretary to this general work depended on his ambition and interest. His primary responsibility was, however, to keep the Colonial Office "safe" in Parliament. Since most of the colonial secretaries sat in the House of Lords, this meant facing an increasingly inquisitive House of Commons.[41] All important telegrams and dispatches were sent to him, enabling him to answer any unannounced questions.[42] Notices of announced questions were registered by the private secretaries or members of the registry.[43] Herbert usually drafted the replies to these questions, having them approved by the colonial secretary. In these cases, the parliamentary undersecretary was simply the mouthpiece of the Colonial Office.[44] The position

---

38. As late as 1876, the permanent and political undersecretaries at the Foreign Office divided the superintendence of the office's work on a geographical basis. For the development of the permanent undersecretaryship of the Foreign Office see Mary Adeline Anderson, "Edmond Hammond, Permanent Under Secretary of State for Foreign Affairs, 1854–1873" (doctoral thesis, University of London, 1956), *passim*.

39. Granville's note of January 15, 1870, PRO 30/29/68, ff. 31–33.

40. Herbert's minute of March 11, 1878, CO 878/6, Vol. 6, No. 40; Grant Duff, *Diary, 1873–1881*, II, 223–224.

41. C. S. Fortescue was regarded as a model undersecretary because he had the ability to make people think "that he has given the fullest explanation that is possible, and yet, when he has concluded, nobody knows exactly what he has said, or what there is to rejoin to." Oshert Wyndham Hewett, *Strawberry Fair: A Biography of Francis Countess Waldegrave, 1821–1879* (London, 1956), pp. 181–182.

42. Ebden's minute of January 22, 1879, CO 878/6, Vol. 6, No. 51; Herbert's minute of May 18, 1880, CO 878/6, Vol. 6, No. 73.

43. Herbert's minute of January 24, 1871, and Rogers' minute of January, 1871, CO 878/5, Vol. 4, No. 61; Herbert's minute of May 14, 1871, CO 878/5, Vol. 5, No. 85.

44. During the parliamentary session, the political undersecretary attended the office very irregularly. For this reason he was given a private secretary to keep him abreast of the office's work. Holland's minute of March 11, 1871; Knatchbull-Hugessen to Kimberley, June 19, 1872, CO 537/22.

of the parliamentary undersecretary was frequently very difficult. As Sydney Buxton (1892–1895) remarked,

The position of an Under-Secretary of State in a great Department—even where specific and prescribed duties are allotted to him—is somewhat difficult and anomalous. He feels not unfrequently that he is neither flesh nor fowl nor good red herring. His use and wont, his authority and responsibilities, his enjoyment of and interest in his post, depend in a very large degree on his Chief.45

Certainly, the parliamentary undersecretaryship of the Colonial Office was not regarded as an important position. The ability of the individuals who filled this position was frequently not very high. Most of them served only a short time, averaging less than two years during the seventies and eighties. Their appointments were invariably politically motivated, depending less on a candidate's ability and interest in the colonies than on his political claims or his ability to cause trouble if excluded from office.

Edward Knatchbull-Hugessen (1871–1874) was transferred to the Colonial Office because "his shoulders [were] not quite broad enough for the present very heavy work of the [Home Office]."46 James Lowther (1874–1878), a "typical Yorkshireman, as he may be seen on the Doncaster race-course,"47 was recognized as one of the free lances of the Conservative party. Lowther received his appointment in 1874 because Disraeli wanted "in the minor and working places, to include every 'representative' man, that is to say everyone who might be troublesome."48 Lowther made little impression at the Colonial Office. His character and temperament, as Charles Lucas later explained, "always appeared to greater advantage in the freedom of opposition than under the restraint of office."49

Leonard Courtney (1881–1882) and Evelyn Ashley (1882–1885) were probably the most able parliamentary undersecretaries of this

45. Lucien Wolf, *Life of the First Marquess of Ripon* (2 vols.; London, 1921), II, 323. See also James, *Rosebery*, p. 152.
46. Gladstone to Kimberley, copy, private, December 28, 1870, Add. MS 44539, f. 118; Knatchbull-Hugessen to Gladstone, private and confidential, January 2, 1871, Add. MS 44111, ff. 42–43. When Gladstone formed his second ministry in 1880, Knatchbull-Hugessen did not receive a position. Hamilton, *Diary*, May 9, 1880, Add. MS 48630, f. 11. For a more favorable view of Knatchbull-Hugessen's ability and influence see W. David McIntyre, *The Imperial Frontier in the Tropics, 1865–75: A Study of British Colonial Policy in West Africa, Malaya and the South Pacific in the Age of Gladstone and Disraeli* (London, 1967), pp. 59–65.
47. Escott, *Pillars of the Empire*, pp. 126–127.
48. Disraeli to Lady Bradford, February 27, 1874, in Buckle, *Disraeli*, II, 636.
49. *DNB*, XXII, 483.

period. Courtney, a strong opponent of Kimberley's Transvaal policy,[50] was appointed to the Colonial Office in August, 1881, in spite of Kimberley's objections.[51] Courtney was an extremely competent official, however, and Kimberley eventually came to have a high regard for his ability, especially in financial affairs.[52] Evelyn Ashley, Courtney's successor, was one of the most respected junior ministers of his day.[53] Gladstone was especially pleased with the way Ashley performed in the House of Commons.[54] His relations with the vacillating Derby were not smooth, however; he desired clear and forthright policies to defend, something which Derby was unable to provide.[55]

Earl Dunraven (June, 1885–February, 1886, and August, 1886–January, 1887), G. Osborne Morgan (February, 1886–August, 1886), and Earl Onslow (January, 1887–February, 1888) did not serve long enough to make any great impression on the Colonial Office. Baron Henry de Worms' appointment in February, 1888, was "an inevitable incident" of Holland's peerage. Salisbury argued that the Colonial Office would be a safe place for de Worms, who was "exceedingly clever—with all the tenacity of his race—and a knowledge of the value of advertisement Mrs. Gladstone herself has never surpassed." Salisbury did not trust de Worms with secret communications, and all confidential matters were kept from him.[56] Like most of his predecessors, de Worms had very little real power.

The permanent and political heads of the Colonial Office hesitated at making major changes in the organization of the office's upper division after 1872, but they did promote certain reforms in the lower division, which handled the mechanical work. This was necessary because the lower division of the Colonial Office's establishment had

50. Courtney accepted the undersecretaryship of the Home Office in 1880 on the understanding that he could abstain on all Transvaal divisions. G. P. Gooch, *Life of Lord Courtney* (London, 1920), pp. 159–165. Like Lowther, Courtney was "capable of being very useful in office and very much the reverse out of office." A. G. Gardiner, *The Life of Sir William Harcourt* (2 vols.; London, 1923), I, 393.
51. Kimberly to Gladstone, June 28, 1881, Add. MS 44226, ff. 160–161.
52. Kimberley to Gladstone, May 3, 1883, Add. MS 44228, f. 70; Hall, *Colonial Office*, p. 51.
53. Kimberley had requested Ashley instead of Courtney in 1881. Kimberley to Gladstone, June 28, 1881, Add. MS 44226, ff. 160–161. See also Chamberlain's minute on Kimberley to Gladstone, May 10, 1882, Add. MS 44227, f. 157; and Dilke to Granville, August 17, 1881, Add. MS 43879, f. 142.
54. Hamilton, *Diary*, August 6, 1883, Add. MS 48634, f. 40; Ashley to Hamilton, March 14, 1883, Add. MS 48623.
55. Ashley's minute of July 18, 1884, on Bulwer to Derby (tel.), July 16, 1884, CO 179/153.
56. Salisbury to Knutsford, private, February 13, 1888; Salisbury to Knutsford, April 17, 1891, Salisbury Papers.

been largely neglected in the earlier inquiries and reforms. The introduction of the new class of lower-division clerks in 1876, the new technological developments, and the completion of a spacious new Colonial Office building made it desirable to reorganize the office's lower division. Civil service reformers and the lower-division clerks themselves, however, provided most of the impetus for change.

A new block of office buildings for the Foreign Office, the India Office, and the Colonial Office had been planned in 1856. Sir Gilbert Scott, the architect, submitted a design for a gothic building, but Palmerston rejected it, preferring instead an Italian design.[57] The Foreign and India offices were completed in 1868, but it was not until 1876 that the Colonial Office finally occupied its new quarters.[58] The basement housed the crown agents' department. There were also several rooms, including a kitchen, for the messengers, porters, and the housekeeper and his wife. The ground floor was entirely taken up by the crown agents, the remnants of the Colonial Land and Emigration Commission, and the accounts department of the Colonial Office. The choice first floor of the new building contained the plush offices of the secretary of state and the members of the secretariat. There were also waiting rooms for the use of colonial visitors.[59] The second and third floors were occupied by the clerks assigned to the geographical departments. There was also a large library on the second floor.[60] Rooms for the two resident clerks were on the third floor.[61]

The increased size of the new Colonial Office necessitated the hiring

57. Jeffries, *Colonial Office*, pp. 113–115; Hertslet, *Recollections of the Old Foreign Office*, p. 14.

58. Carnarvon and Herbert momentarily feared that the overcrowded War Office would appropriate part of the new building. Carnarvon to Hardy, copy, private, May 14, 1874; Hardy to Carnarvon, May 15, 1874, PRO 30/6/12; CO to Treasury, April 23, 1875, CO 323/324.

59. Carnarvon's office was so large that he stated that "it requires time to see who is walking across it." Hardinge, *Carnarvon*, II, 63–64. The size of the new office building enabled the Colonial Office to become something of a museum as well. The permanent undersecretary's room contained portraits of all the colonial secretaries since the Earl of Hillsborough (1768). The Bank of South Australia placed a bust of Wakefield outside Herbert's room, where all of the colonists visiting the office would be certain to see it. When Herbert died, his bust was placed in the front hall. Jeffries, *Colonial Office*, pp. 13–14; Meade's minute of July 10, 1876, on Bank of South Australia to CO, July 5, 1876, CO 323/329; *Times* (London), March 28, 1906, p. 8d.

60. Hall, *Colonial Office*, p. 49. In 1873 the Colonial Office library contained approximately seven thousand volumes, exclusive of parliamentary papers and colonial acts. Treasury to Board of Trade, January 29, 1873, enclosed in Treasury to CO, January 29, 1873, CO 323/314. The Colonial Office permitted visitors to work in the library.

61. The information on the distribution of rooms was drawn from the tables enclosed in CO to Office of Works, June 20, 1874, CO 323/320. Naturally, the rooms were frequently reassigned as new departments were created and old ones were abolished. Demolition of the old Colonial Office was begun in 1878.

of a larger cleaning and maintenance staff. The Colonial Office received permission to add four new charwomen to the original staff of six at wages of fourteen shillings a week.[62] A laborer was employed to operate the new and unreliable lift. He also attended to the gas and heating apparatus of the office.[63] J. Burridge was the head office keeper during most of the seventies and eighties. In addition to supervising the work of the charwomen, messengers, porters, and laborers, he provided refreshments for the clerks.[64] He also received the incoming mails and kept a record of the mailbags sent out of the office.[65] Finally, there was Stokes the "odd man," who was dismissed in 1878 when he went "on the drink again."[66]

The Colonial Office also employed numerous porters, doorkeepers, and messengers. These positions were filled primarily by men who had previously served one of the colonial secretary's friends or by pensioners from the army or navy. The porters attended the Colonial Office's two doors, and they informed visitors whether or not the person they desired to see was present at the office. Unfortunately Frederic Bridges, in charge of the prestigious Downing Street door, was extremely garrulous and troublesome,[67] and he was discharged in 1885. In soliciting a new doorkeeper, the Colonial Office requested that he be young, active, and intelligent, able to assist guests and to give directions quickly.[68] The messengers, who were reorganized into three distinct classes in 1880,[69] were employed on both indoor and outdoor service. The outdoor messengers carried boxes and pouches of dispatches and letters between the Colonial Office and the homes of the colonial secretary and the undersecretaries when they were not present in London. Occasionally they took dispatches to Windsor or Balmoral. They also

62. CO to Treasury, December 9, 1875, and Treasury to CO, December 20, 1875, CO 323/323. Two more charwomen were added in 1876. Burridge to Cox, March 8, 1876, CO 323/329. The housekeeper supervised the work of the cleaners.
63. Treasury to CO, January 8, 1876, CO 323/328.
64. In 1886 a meal of meat, vegetables, and bread could be obtained for one shilling. A pint of ale was four pence, and a large bottle of stout cost six pence. CO 878/6, Vol. 7, No. 80.
65. Rogers' minute of October 1, 1869, CO 878/5, Vol. 4, No. 16A; Gairdner's minute of February 23, 1869, CO 537/22.
66. Cox's minute of October 12, 1878, CO 878/6, Vol. 5, No. 45.
67. Ebden's minute of June 13, 1885, on Bridges to Derby, March 17, 1884, CO 323/359. There were frequent complaints that Bridges could give no information to visitors and that they were left to wander around the office. FO Adrian's minute of October 27, 1885, CO 323/362.
68. CO to CSC, October 28, 1885, CO 323/362. John Bramston directed that the doorkeeper summon guides for visitors by whistling up the lift. Bramston's minute of October 27, 1885, *ibid*.
69. CO to Treasury, February 28, 1880, and Treasury to CO, April 26, 1880, CO 323/340. The maximum pay of a first-class messenger was £150 a year.

delivered official letters, notes, and personal messages which could not be intrusted to the regular post. The indoor messengers received and guided visitors to the Colonial Office and transported papers from room to room.[70] There was also a library messenger who indexed the printed papers and newspapers.[71]

The Colonial Office's lower division in the seventies was composed of a bewildering variety of clerical classes—supplementary clerks, copyists, and civil service writers. Within each of these classes there were also several rates of pay; the copyists, for example, could work either by the piece or by the hour.[72] The supplementary clerks and copyists were placed under the supervision of the principal clerk of the general department, and there was little personal contact between these clerks and the upper-division staff. Their duties consisted almost entirely of copying, indexing, and the registering of dispatches, tasks which were looked down upon by the university-trained clerks. When the new Colonial Office was occupied in 1876, the supplementary clerks and copyists were assigned to their own separate workrooms.[73]

The creation of the Playfair class of lower-division clerks in 1876 was designed to promote greater uniformity in the lower division of the British civil service. The Treasury anticipated that these clerks, who would do copying as well as the other mechanical tasks, would in time replace the old supplementary clerks, copyists, and civil service writers. To provide incentive for these new clerks, the Colonial Office in 1880 reorganized its general department into five subdepartments: correspondence, parliamentary printing, copying, the registry, and the library. The superintendent of each of these subdepartments received duty pay, an incentive for all of the lower-division clerks.[74] Most of the lower-division clerks were not content with this concession, however, and the civil service reform of the eighties was largely a result of their agitation.

The increasing number of Playfair lower-division clerks in the Colonial Office was accompanied by a reduction in the number of copyists and writers. This development was accelerated by a decision

70. Gairdner's minute of February 23, 1869, CO 537/22.
71. CO to Treasury, July 14, 1876, CO 323/328.
72. W. Robinson's minute of October 7, 1870, CO 537/22.
73. Herbert's minute of December 1, 1875, CO 878/6, Vol. 6, No. 12.
74. CO to Treasury, April 19, 1880, and enclosures, CO 323/346. It was only after considerable private negotiation that the Treasury agreed to the creation of these five supervisory positions. Treasury to CO, June 18, 1880, CO 323/344.

in 1872 to discontinue making copies of all outgoing letters and dispatches, the rough draft being retained as a record of the dispatch.[75] Some copyists sought employment in other departments, and some were eventually promoted into the new class of lower-division clerks.[76] Although the old class of copyists had disappeared by the eighties, the Colonial Office continued to employ a few civil service writers who were paid by the piece.[77] The jobs of these men, however, were threatened by a new technological advance—the typewriter. The Treasury recommended the adoption of the typewriter as early as 1878,[78] but it was not used extensively at the Colonial Office until the early nineties.[79] By 1909 the Colonial Office had a staff of twenty-four "lady typewriters." No one except the superintendent of copying and his assistant were permitted to enter the room where these women worked.[80] In addition, some clerks began to type their minutes, a practice which was discouraged as being too noisy and leading to verbosity.[81]

The number of new Playfair clerks in the civil service increased very rapidly, especially in offices such as the Post Office requiring a large proportion of mechanical laborers. In 1888 there were approximately three thousand of these clerks.[82] Adopting some of the new trade union ideas, the lower-division clerks formed an association through which to present their grievances and to muster parliamentary support. It was the agitation of this group that led to the appointment of the Ridley Commission in 1886 to inquire into the state of the civil service.

The first real attempt by the Playfair clerks to improve their position

75. Herbert's minute of March 5, 1872, CO 878/5, Vol. 5, No. 28. As early as 1870 many Colonial Office copyists sat idle for several hours each day. Robinson's minute of October 21, 1870, on Jennings to Robinson, October 21, 1870, CO 878/5, Vol. 4, No. 49.
76. Treasury to CO, October 21, 1876, CO 323/328.
77. "Second Report of the Royal (Ridley) Commission," C. 5545, p. 90, Parl. Paps. 1888, XXVII. In 1891 the Colonial Office employed eight such writers. CO to Treasury, September 23, 1891, CO 323/386.
78. Treasury to CO, March 25, 1878, CO 323/337.
79. Minutes on Margaret Boys-Smith to W. A. B. Hamilton, December 21, 1891, CO 323/387. The "lady typewriters" began at fourteen shillings and rose to twenty-four shillings a week. It was found from experience that one typist could do the work of two male copyists. Treasury to CO, March 23, 1892, CO 323/389.
80. Sir Cosmo Parkinson, The Colonial Office from Within, 1909–1945 (London, 1947), pp. 27–28.
81. Kubicek, The Administration of Imperialism, p. 33.
82. Cohen, Growth of the British Civil Service, p. 141. The Colonial Office had only thirteen lower-division clerks at the time of the Ridley Commission's inquiry. "Second Report of the Royal (Ridley) Commission," C. 5545, p. 86, Parl. Paps. 1888, XXVII.

was the unsuccessful presentation of a petition to the Treasury in 1881.[83] Another effort was made two years later, when 1,500 lower-division clerks signed a memorial stating their grievances. This memorial was sent to the Treasury by the clerks in the Colonial Office, who appear to have taken a lead in the agitation. The lower-division clerks complained that their work was more demanding than had been intended when their salary scale had been established in 1876. In some offices, they argued, Playfair clerks performed the same duties as the more highly paid upper-division clerks. Most of their complaints, however, were directed against the sharp division of labor in each office and the difficulties in securing a promotion from the lower division into the upper division. The memorial maintained that the division of labor was entirely artificial and designed to promote discontent. A "workable and general system of promotion" was essential if the Playfair clerks were not to be deprived of all incentive.[84]

The Treasury's detailed reply was uncompromising toward the lower-division clerks. The Treasury was greatly disturbed by the manner in which the memorial had been presented; complaints of civil servants should be forwarded through departmental heads.[85] The Treasury reiterated its belief in the necessity of maintaining a rigid division of labor within each office. The Treasury also insisted that the pay of the lower-division clerks was commensurate with their duties. The lords of the Treasury did, however, give the lower-division clerks hope for promotion, at least in some departments.

Although the number of Lower Division Clerks promoted to the Higher Division must always bear a small proportion to the number not so promoted, it is not necessary that they should be an insignificant proportion of the Upper Division. On the contrary, My Lords look forward to that Division's being largely replenished, in certain Departments, from the best members of the Lower Division.[86]

The upper-division clerks and the secretariat of the Colonial Office showed little sympathy with the demands of their lower-division col-

83. Treasury to CO, July 8, 1881, CO 323/349. The Treasury replied at length to this memorial, which was primarily concerned with the question of salaries, but it refused to make any concessions.
84. Lower Division Clerks to Treasury, October, 1883, enclosed in CO to Treasury, October 13, 1883, CO 323/356.
85. Richard Ebden remarked that unfortunately the lower-division clerks had two loyalties, "one to the office they are assigned to & one to the class they belong to." Ebden's minute of September 25, 1885, on Lower Division Clerks to Meade, July 29, 1885, CO 323/362.
86. Treasury to CO, June 19, 1884, CO 323/358.

leagues.[87] Richard Ebden, who supervised the work of the Colonial Office's lower division, was uncertain about the nature of their complaints. If the Playfair clerks received the same pay and advantages as the university-trained clerks, the latter would then be in a position to object. Ebden did admit, however, that some of the lower-division clerks were developing skills which would enable them to be promoted; some incentive for ability should be found.[88] No one in the Colonial Office seriously considered promoting Playfair clerks into their own upper division.

The agitation of the lower-division clerks resulted in a new Treasury inquiry into the problems facing the civil service. It also prompted the Colonial Office officials to review the constitution of their own office. If nothing else, the petitions of the Playfair clerks showed how little uniformity in regulations existed among the various departments of state. The Treasury immediately attempted to establish a uniform seven-hour day for civil servants,[89] to regulate the political and commercial activities of civil servants,[90] and to promote uniformity on questions of leave, office hours, and pay. In addition, a royal commission was appointed in 1886 to inquire into these questions as well as the complaints of the lower-division clerks. Each department was requested to furnish the commission with a detailed description of its staff and establishment.[91]

The Colonial Office suggested no major reforms to the commission.[92] Meade and Herbert were afraid, however, that the Colonial Office, with its highly paid upper-division clerks, would be altered as a result of the commission's inquiry. It was no secret that the Treasury regarded the Colonial Office establishment as top-heavy.[93] Within the office, some of the new second-class clerks and principal clerks com-

87. Minutes on Lower Division Clerks to Meade, October 6, 1883, CO 323/356; Minutes on Treasury to CO, June 19, 1884, CO 323/358.
88. Ebden's minute of September 25, 1885, on Lower Division Clerks to Meade, July 29, 1885, CO 323/362.
89. The lower-division clerks in the Colonial Office began to work a seven-hour day in 1884, but the upper division still worked only six hours. Treasury to CO, December 8, 1884, CO 323/358.
90. In 1884 the Treasury ruled that any civil servant seeking a seat in Parliament had to resign his position. Herbert regarded this decision as a feeble attempt to deal with a much larger question. Herbert's minute of January 12, 1885, on Treasury to CO, November 19, 1884, ibid. In 1888 the Treasury placed restrictions on civil servants accepting directorships in public companies. Treasury to CO, December 12, 1888, CO 323/373.
91. Sec. of Royal Commission to CO, November, 1886, CO 323/366.
92. CO to Sec. of Royal Commission, December 23, 1886, ibid.
93. Herbert stated that the Treasury believed that there were "too many Generals and Colonels in our small army." Herbert's minute of July 29, 1880, CO 323/346.

plained that they were not given sufficient responsibility and author-ity.[94] In an attempt to forestall the commission and to accommodate the upper-division clerks, Meade requested that Ebden and two second-class clerks, R. L. Antrobus and W. H. Mercer, devise a plan to relieve the upper-division clerks of all mechanical work. Following prolonged and careful consideration, Antrobus submitted three long memos on this subject in early 1888. These memos together with the com-ments of the other clerks constitute the only thorough analysis of the structure of the office between 1872 and Joseph Chamberlain's secretaryship.

Antrobus' principal complaint was that the second-class clerks still did too much mechanical work. Despite the reforms of 1872, the sec-ond-class clerks decoded telegrams, filled in printed forms, searched for previous papers, and wrote short, unimportant drafts. Antrobus estimated that the upper-division clerks spent at least sixteen man-hours each day on these menial tasks. He suggested that, as vacancies occurred, three upper-division clerks be replaced by four Playfair clerks.[95] Antrobus also recommended that some Playfair clerks be assigned to the geographical departments, which would then each consist of three upper-division and two lower-division clerks. The lat-ter would register the dispatches departmentally and search for the previous papers on the subject. The dispatches would then be handled by the upper-division clerks in the order of their urgency, each clerk dealing with a subject or group of colonies with which he had become thoroughly familiar. A principal clerk would continue to supervise the work of the entire geographical department. Antrobus believed that closer contact between the two clerical classes would enable the Colonial Office to function more smoothly.[96] He also proposed to en-large the general department, giving it responsibility for such topics as prisons, education, bankruptcy, postal affairs, audits, and defense. A topical division of labor would help to reduce "the divergent action on the part of different depts, which so often haggles outsiders."[97] In the twentieth century, this recommendation was adopted.

94. Hemming to Herbert, May 3, 1880, *ibid.* Hemming urged that the principal clerks be given the power to dispose of more papers without consulting the secretariat.
95. Antrobus' memo of April 21, 1888, CO 323/374. He also proposed that the central registry be abolished. If the dispatches were registered in the geographical departments, the time occupied in the transit of papers would be saved. Antrobus' memo of April, 1888, CO 323/374.
96. Antrobus' memo of April 21, 1888, CO 323/374.
97. *Ibid.*

Antrobus was also critical of the practice of submitting most papers to the assistant undersecretaries for their approval; the highly paid principal clerks should be given more authority.

The mass of work is so great that the assnt und. secretaries are compelled to take the work of the clerks to a very great extent on trust. In this case wouldn't it be better to place the responsibility on the right shoulders? Work done under a sense of responsibility is always better done, and there is no real danger of the clerks taking too much responsibility on themselves. The advantage would be that the under secretaries would then have more time to give to the larger matters, involving questions of principle or policy; and the less important work would be far more promptly done.

Antrobus believed that one of the assistant undersecretaryships should be abolished as soon as a vacancy occurred. He was especially critical of the Colonial Office's policy of employing two legal assistant undersecretaries. Like the Treasury, he did not believe that the amount of legal work justified the cost; the law officers could be consulted if a second opinion was required.

It is impossible for the existing system to be continued much longer: for the three asst. undersecretaries cannot deal with the great mass of routine work as promptly and efficiently as it ought to be dealt with. There must be more persons invested with the kind of discretion specified [by the Treasury]. This can be satisfactorily done, without any additional expense, by simply employing the clerks upon the duties on account of which their present salaries are paid to them. Two Under Secretaries would then be better able to keep up with the more important work than four are now: the legal adviser would be a better lawyer: and the clerks wd. feel that they were responsible for the business entrusted to them and would be encouraged to put their whole strength into their work.[98]

Antrobus' criticisms of the organization and routine of the Colonial Office were almost identical with the later comments of the Ridley Commission.

The reaction of the members of the office to Antrobus' suggestions revealed a considerable difference of opinion between the new second-class clerks and the "old stagers," who had entered the office by limited competition between 1856 and 1870.[99] Antrobus' proposals received

98. Antrobus' memo of 1888, CO 323/374. This memo was sent to Meade on May 5, 1888.

99. Olivier regarded the new clerks as "a younger, more distinctly intelligent class of men" than the survivors of the old "patronage system of Civil Service recruiting." Most of the older principal and first-class clerks were, in his opinion, "too sleepy" to add much to the work of a qualified junior. Olivier, ed., Sydney Olivier, p. 31.

solid support from outspoken new clerks like Sydney Olivier and Sidney Webb. Olivier strongly objected to the amount of mechanical work the second-class clerks were expected to perform.[100] The primary spokesman for the status quo was Richard Ebden, the principal clerk of the general department. He was vigorously seconded by A. W. L. Hemming, the principal clerk of the African department. Ebden emphatically denied that the second-class clerks spent too much time on routine work; a certain amount of mechanical work was unavoidable. He also opposed the abolition of the central registry and the absorption of the lower-division Playfair clerks into the geographical departments. He feared that this would undermine the principle of a division of labor within the Colonial Office.[101]

The disagreement between the older and younger members of the office was partially a result of the theoretical basis of the reorganization of 1872. Although men such as Ebden, Hemming, and Edward Fairfield had been pleased with their substantial raises, they were fully aware that the new pay scale adopted in 1872 was designed to attract an abler class of clerks than themselves.[102] The fact that no new upper-division clerks entered the office between 1870 and 1877 also created an age difference between the two groups. In their desire to become statesmen immediately upon entering the office, the new second-class clerks undoubtedly annoyed the older men. In later life, Sir Augustus Hemming concluded that allowing the second-class clerks to minute dispatches was a mistake.

I was brought up officially at the feet of men like Herman Merivale, Lord Blachford, and Sir Henry Taylor, among the ablest of civil servants, and the idea of a youngster fresh from a public school or university, or even from a Board School, presuming to spoil official paper and waste official time by the expression of his crude and undigested "views" and "suggestions" is enough to make those eminent men turn uneasily in their graves. . . . Let the junior clerks learn their business by making themselves thoroughly acquainted with the practice and routine of the Office, and by studying the minutes and drafts of their superiors, and then, in due course

100. Marginal comments on Antrobus' memos, CO 323/374.
101. *Ibid.* Earlier in the year, both Ebden and Meade maintained before the Ridley Commission that a sharp division of work was essential to the Colonial Office. "Second Report of the Royal (Ridley) Commission," C. 5545, pp. 77, 86–87, *Parl. Paps. 1888,* XXVII.
102. Herbert admitted this in 1874 when he assured the Treasury that the number of principal clerks would be reduced in the future if open competition did secure "a superior brand of clerks." CO to Treasury, July 9, 1874, CO 323/319.

of time, they will be qualified to offer suggestions which may be valuable and practical, and of real assistance to the higher officials.

I am strongly of opinion that the present system is productive of many evils, not the least of which is the fact that it fosters and encourages an intellectual arrogance among the junior clerks leading them to despise and shirk the more humble, but none the less useful, part of their duties. The "cocksureness" of the rising race of civil servants (I speak within my own experience) is remarkable. They seem never to have heard of the saying, that "we are none of us infallible, not even the youngest."[103]

Meade, Herbert, and Knutsford admitted the force of some of Antrobus' criticisms, but in general they supported Ebden, Hemming, and the status quo. Meade argued that the rapidly increasing volume of work made it impossible to reduce the number of upper-division clerks. A smaller number would make it very difficult to operate the office efficiently during periods when clerks were ill or on leave. It was also desirable to be able to send upper-division clerks on special missions to the colonies, a practice which should be encouraged and not restricted. Meade did, however, suggest that in the future additional work could be handled by employing more Playfair clerks.[104]

Herbert was extremely critical of Antrobus' proposals for allowing the upper-division clerks to assume greater responsibility for the work of the office. He believed that the Colonial Office already did too much minuting, the work being "excessively laboured." He argued that the office would be more efficient if it operated like a commercial house. If the papers were seen first by the undersecretaries, a great deal of needless minuting could be saved. Frequently the second-class clerks wrote long and able minutes, but because they did not know the views of the secretary of state on the subject, the minutes were "in the wrong direction." Nevertheless, Herbert did not propose any major changes in the method of circulating papers. He feared that such change would not be acceptable to the second-class clerks, and "their feelings & views" had to be the primary consideration in any departmental reform. Like Meade, Herbert did not believe that the number of upper-division clerks could be reduced.[105] Knutsford said little on the question of office routine, being convinced that the Colonial Office's work had

103. Sir A. W. L. Hemming, "The Colonial Office and the Crown Colonies," *Empire Review*, II (1906), 502–503.
104. Meade's marginal comments on Antrobus' memos of 1888; Meade's minute of May 10, 1888, CO 323/374.
105. Herbert's minute of May 11, 1888, *ibid.*

"never been better done." He, too, strongly opposed any reduction in the number of upper-division clerks or undersecretaries.[106]

The only major change resulting from Antrobus' inquiry was an increase in the principal clerks' powers to dispose of certain papers without reference to the assistant undersecretaries. To Robert Meade, this had been "an integral part of the scheme on which the office [had] been reorganized."[107] He proposed to give the principal clerks "wide powers" while still maintaining a firm control over the office's work. The principal clerks of each department, or in his absence the first-class clerk, was empowered to dispose of all requests for leave, ordinary requisitions to the crown agents, reports of wrecks, reports of executions, periodical returns, ordinary inquiries, simple acknowledgments, and in general all routine papers where there was no doubt concerning the correct answer. They were also permitted to sign certain letters in the absence of an assistant undersecretary.[108] Although Knutsford approved this change, he urged that "nothing of importance, or unusual in character" be withheld from the secretariat.[109]

In an attempt to balance the work of the office, there was also a redistribution of the responsibilities of the four geographical departments. The major change was the division of the old African department. South African work was combined with the work of Ceylon, Hong Kong, the Straits, and Cyprus. West Africa, Mauritius, and Malta became another department. Edward Fairfield was picked to head the new South African department because of his "intimate knowledge" of the area. His promotion was based on merit, there being two first-class clerks senior to him at the time. Meade also suggested that the titles of the geographical departments, which were largely meaningless, be dropped, and the departments were referred to by number.[110]

The secretariat's fear that the Ridley Commission would propose major changes in the structure of the Colonial Office proved to be unfounded. In their testimony before the commission in January, 1888, Meade and Ebden reiterated that a sharp division between intellectual and mechanical clerks must be maintained. The Colonial Office's work was simply too complex and important to be handled by lower-

---

106. Knutsford's minute of May 14, 1888, *ibid.*
107. Meade's minute of May 10, 1888, *ibid.*
108. Meade's minute of October 28, 1889, *ibid.*
109. Knutsford's minute of November 11, 1889, *ibid.*
110. Meade's minute of January 2, 1889; Knutsford's minute of January 3, 1889; Herbert's minute of January 10, 1889, CO 323/378.

division clerks; a large number of university-trained men was essential to the smooth operation of the Colonial Office.[111] The representatives from the Treasury, the Home Office, and the Board of Trade presented similar arguments.[112] Only officials representing the less prestigious departments supported the arguments of the lower-division clerks. Sir Algernon West from the Inland Revenue Office believed that the entire division of labor between the two clerical classes was unworkable. With the possible exception of the Treasury, he insisted that experienced lower-division clerks could perform most of the duties of the upper-division clerks.[113]

The Ridley Commission's second report supported the division of labor within each office. By supporting Meade's position, the report was a reaffirmation of the Northcote-Trevelyan Report and the recommendations of the Playfair Commission. The commissioners did agree, however, that the dividing line between intellectual and mechanical work had been placed too low; some members of the upper division could easily be replaced by Playfair lower-division clerks. The commissioners also recognized that in some offices, such as the Treasury, the Foreign Office, and the Colonial Office, it was necessary to recruit a higher proportion of "men of more liberal education . . . [and] a wider and more cultivated view of public affairs than can, as a rule, be expected from youths entering by lower examination."[114] With regard to the vexed question of promotion from the lower division into the upper division, the Ridley Commission had nothing original to suggest. It realized that some incentive must be provided for men of extraordinary ability, but the lower-division clerks did not have a "right" to promotion. Finally, the commission recommended that the upper division of the civil service be standardized in the same way that the lower division had been in 1876.[115]

The Treasury accepted, with slight modifications, the Ridley Commission's recommendations concerning the lower-division clerks.[116] By an Order in Council of March 21, 1890, the Treasury established

111. "Second Report of the Royal (Ridley) Commission," C. 5545, pp. 75–76, 86–87, *Parl. Paps. 1888*, XXVII.
112. *Ibid.*, pp. 5–6, 24, 379.
113. *Ibid.*, pp. 249–250. "I venture to say that when the competition took place for the upper divisions in the Treasury and the Colonial Office I could have given men from my office, redundant clerks, who would have been admirably fitted for those places, but that may be my opinion only."
114. *Ibid.*, pp. xi, xvii:
115. *Ibid.*, pp. xiv–xvii.
116. Treasury minute of August 10, 1889, enclosed in Treasury to CO, August 28, 1889, CO 323/376.

rigid and uniform regulations covering hours of labor, leave, and pay of these clerks. Promotion into the upper division was also made slightly less difficult.[117] The Treasury did little, however, to reduce the number of upper-division clerks in the civil service and to standardize this class. It was only in the twentieth century that the Treasury issued uniform regulations for the upper-division clerks.[118]

Herbert and Meade were greatly relieved at the manner in which the Treasury had implemented the recommendations of the Ridley Commission.[119] As a compromise gesture, the Colonial Office made a few voluntary concessions to the commission. When a vacancy occurred in the office's upper division in 1888, Meade and Herbert accepted a clerk from another office instead of selecting one by open competition. The Ridley Commission had argued that transfers of clerks would promote the creation of a unified civil service.[120] The Colonial Office also attempted to employ a greater percentage of lower-division clerks. When Sidney Webb resigned in 1891, Meade proposed that two lower-division clerks be appointed instead of a new second-class clerk. He had, however, no intention of allowing lower-division clerks to enter the upper division; they were to be employed solely on clerical work.[121] Finally, the Ridley Commission and the Treasury had both recommended that the initial pay of the new second-class clerks be reduced from £250 to £200 a year. When another vacancy in this class occurred in 1892, the Colonial Office adopted this revised salary scale.[122] These concessions did not result in any fundamental changes in the constitution of the Colonial Office. The strict division of labor was maintained, and the office's prestige resulting from its high salaries and interesting work was not damaged.

Although the secretariat was pleased at the outcome of the Ridley

117. "Order in Council (Dated the 21st of March 1890) Relating to the Second Division of the Civil Service," C. 5997, pp. 4–5, *Parl. Paps. 1890*, LVIII.

118. Cohen, *Growth of the British Civil Service*, pp. 150–151.

119. Questions regarding the large number of upper-division clerks in the Colonial Office were being raised in Parliament at this time. 3 *Hansard*, CCCXXI (December 11, 1888), 1757.

120. After personally interviewing several candidates, Knutsford selected H. J. Read, an upper-division clerk from the War Office. Read had entered the civil service with distinction, and the War Office was very unhappy when Knutsford recruited one of their ablest men. CO to Treasury, May 15, 1888; minutes on Read to Meade, October 11, 1888; CO to WO, December 19, 1888, CO 323/374.

121. Minutes on Webb to Ebden, August 20, 1891, and minutes on Westbrook to Meade, September 1, 1891, CO 323/387. This experiment was not regarded as binding the Colonial Office to employing more lower-division clerks in the future.

122. Ebden's minute of October, 1889, on Treasury to CO, September 6, 1889, CO 323/376; CO to Treasury, December 23, 1891, CO 323/387; CO to CSC, December 30, 1891, CO 323/384.

Commission's inquiries, the lower-division clerks, who had expected some improvement in their position, were keenly disappointed. By 1891 they were again petitioning the Treasury and the Colonial Office for better pay and greater promotional opportunities.[123] Herbert, Meade, and Knutsford regarded their demands as "unreasonable" and refused to make any concessions. The Colonial Office's secretariat had agreed to employ more lower-division clerks in order to relieve the second-class clerks of all clerical work, but it again refused to permit these men to aspire to positions in the upper division.[124] The Treasury supported this position, arguing that the pay and working conditions of the lower division-clerks afforded an adequate remuneration for the work they performed.[125] The principles upon which the Colonial Office was based—open competition and a sharp division of labor—were simply confirmed by the investigations held in the eighties. There was not another major inquiry into the question of civil service reform until the MacDonnell Commission of 1912. In the absence of any outside pressures, the permanent officials of the Colonial Office made very few changes in the organization and routine of the office.

Herbert resigned from the Colonial Office in 1892 on the advice of his doctor,[126] his place being taken by Sir Robert Meade, the senior assistant undersecretary.[127] Lord Knutsford pressed Salisbury to grant Herbert a peerage upon his retirement. Herbert was a bachelor, and his title would lapse upon his death. Until then he would be "a great acquisition" to the Conservatives in the House of Lords.[128] Salisbury preferred, however, to "pay in as small coin" as possible, and Herbert received only the G.C.B.[129] After his retirement, Herbert continued to take an active interest in colonial questions. The Colonial Office

123. Westbrook to Meade, September 1, 1891, and CO to Treasury, December 1, 1891, CO 323/387; Treasury to CO, October 12, 1893, CO 323/393.
124. Minutes on Westbrook to Meade, September 1, 1891, CO 323/387. See also Meade to Ripon, October 6, 1894, Add. MS 43558, ff. 4–5.
125. Treasury to CO, October 12, 1893, CO 323/393. Between 1890 and 1894 only twelve men out of a total of 3,500 lower-division clerks were promoted into the upper division. The main incentive for these clerks continued to be the various staff appointments in each office. Cohen, *Growth of the British Civil Service*, pp. 148–149.
126. Knutsford to Salisbury, December 2, 1891, Salisbury Papers.
127. Meade's replacement was Edward Fairfield, whose appointment was based solely on merit. Richard Ebden, whose services had been "long & good," was given a C.B. as a consolation prize. Salisbury agreed to the C.B. despite the fact that such honors were scarce. "C.B.'s won't die. I think of advertising the order as a prophylactic against Influenza." Knutsford to Salisbury, December 2, 1891; Salisbury to Knutsford, copy, December 4, 1891, Salisbury Papers.
128. Knutsford to Salisbury, confidential, December 9, 1891, Salisbury Papers.
129. Salisbury to Knutsford, copy, private, May 22, 1892; Herbert to Salisbury, July 25, 1892, Salisbury Papers.

offered him a governorship, but he preferred to stay at home. He continued to give the Colonial Office advice on appointments and honors, and he even returned to the office as permanent undersecretary for a brief period in 1899–1900.[130] Outside the office Herbert took an interest in the development of the colonies. He was a member of the British Empire League[131] and a vice president of the Royal Colonial Institute, presiding at several of their annual meetings.[132] He also served as the agent general for Tasmania. At the time of his death in 1905 he was serving on a commission appointed by Joseph Chamberlain to inquire into the question of tariff reform.[133]

Herbert's successors as permanent undersecretary, Robert Meade (1892–1897) and Edward Wingfield (1897–1900), showed little desire to change the structure of the office. The size of the Colonial Office grew rapidly in the nineties, but the functions of the various clerical classes and the organization and routine of the office were not radically changed.[134] The senior officials of the Colonial Office, such as Meade and Wingfield, had received their administrative educations under Herbert, and they were satisfied with the evolution of the office in the seventies and eighties. By seizing the opportunities offered as a result of the introduction of open competition in 1870, Herbert had reorganized his office in a manner designed to recruit the ablest men from the competitive market and to raise the prestige of the Colonial Office. His immediate successors had no desire to jeopardize these gains. Joseph Chamberlain was interested in such reforms as a further delegation of responsibility, the establishment of an orderly system of exchange between the Colonial Office and the colonies, and a greater use of new technological innovations, but his permanent staff showed little interest in them.[135] The modern Colonial Office, with its propensity for advisory boards, such as the Tropical Diseases Bureau

130. CO to Treasury, December 27, 1899, CO 323/449.
131. Sydney H. Zebel, "Joseph Chamberlain and the Genesis of Tariff Reform," Journal of British Studies, VII (November, 1967), 138.
132. Royal Colonial Institute, Proceedings, XXV (1893–1894), 358.
133. W. A. S. Hewins, The Apologia of an Imperialist: Forty Years of Empire Policy (2 vols.; London, 1929), I, 77.
134. Two additional upper-division clerks were appointed in 1896. CO to Treasury, May 22, 1896, CO 323/407. In 1898 a fourth assistant undersecretary and one principal, four first-class, and two second-class clerks were added to the establishment. Treasury to CO, September 7, 1898, CO 323/431. For a detailed discussion of administrative changes during the Chamberlain period see Kubicek, The Administration of Imperialism, chap. ii.
135. Kubicek, The Administration of Imperialism. chap. ii.

and the Imperial Bureau of Entomology,[136] and its emphasis on the economic and social development of the crown colonies, was primarily a product of the twentieth century. Sir Ralph Furse, who entered the office in 1910, believed that World War I marked the real end to the "old Colonial Office." After 1919 the "virus of departmentalism" infected the office "swiftly and pervasively."[137]

136. For a list of the various advisory boards in 1945 see Parkinson, *The Colonial Office from Within*, pp. 56–62.

137. Furse, *Aucuparius*, pp. 43–44. The best descriptions of the Colonial Office in the twentieth century are Parkinson, *The Colonial Office from Within*, *passim*, and Kenneth Robinson, *The Dilemmas of Trusteeship: Aspects of British Colonial Policy between the Wars* (London, 1965), pp. 29–60.

Selected Bibliography

A NOTE ON SOURCES

This study was based primarily on the correspondence of the general department of the Colonial Office preserved in the Public Record Office in London. This C.O. 323 series, consisting of approximately one hundred volumes for the period 1868–1892, contains correspondence on questions of interest to more than one colony, such as foreign treaties, defense, trade, and imperial federation. The general correspondence with the Treasury, which had to approve all major alterations in the structure of the Colonial Office, was invaluable for studying the internal organization of the office. Purely departmental changes were described in the office minutes (C.O. 878 series). In addition to the general correspondence, the files of at least one colony in each of the four geographical departments were consulted to determine how the clerks conducted their work.

The private papers used have all been mined by other historians in recent years, although not from the standpoint of administrative history. The Granville and Carnarvon Papers deposited at the Public Record Office were especially valuable for the background to the reorganization of 1870 and for the administrative changes during the period from 1874 to 1878. Carnarvon's papers were also useful in studying the relations between the colonial secretary and his colleagues in the cabinet—especially Sir Stafford Northcote, the chancellor of the exchequer. The Gladstone Papers, deposited at the British Museum, were important in studying the secretaryships of Kimberley and Derby. The Salisbury Papers at Christ Church, Oxford, contained considerable material of interest on the Colonial Office in the late eighties.

There was no systematic attempt to record the services of the members of the Colonial Office and the overseas colonial service. The personal sketches in the *Colonial Office List* help to fill this gap, however. Other information was gathered from biographies, memoirs, newspapers, civil service reports, and minutes in the Colonial Office files. The *Parliamentary Papers* were of special importance for the parliamentary enquiries held on the question of civil service reform in 1875 and 1887–1888. The testimony given before these commissions was helpful in comparing the structure of the Colonial Office to that of the other departments.

PART I: PRIMARY SOURCES
A. *Private Manuscript Collections*

Cardwell Papers (Public Record Office)
PRO 30/48/5/28–33, primarily correspondence with Granville (1868–1870) and Kimberley (1870–1874).

Carnarvon Papers (Public Record Office)
PRO 30/6/1–8, 10–18, 20, 25–27, 42–45, 52–53, 146, primarily correspondence with the Queen, government colleagues, and colonial governors, 1874–1878.

Cross Papers (British Museum)
BM Add. MS 51268, correspondence between Cross and Carnarvon, 1874–1878.

Dilke Papers (British Museum)
BM Add. MS 43880–43881, 43891, 43924–43926, primarily correspondence with Granville and Kimberley (1880–1885) and confidential diaries, 1880–1884.

Gladstone Papers (British Museum)
BM Add. MS 44107, 44111, 44119–44120, 44141–44142, 44224–44229, 44287, 44301, 44392, 44420, 44460, 44517, 44539–44548, 44638–44647 including correspondence with Kimberley, Derby, and Lowe and cabinet minutes, 1868–1885.

Granville Papers (Public Record Office)
PRO 30/29/52, 55, 66, 68, 73–75, 120, 135, 213, including correspondence with Lowe (1868–1870), Kimberley (1870–1882), and Derby (1882–1885).

Hamilton Papers (British Museum)
BM Add. MS 48623, 48630–48658, primarily diaries, 1880–1892.

Musgrave Papers (Duke University Library)
Correspondence with Carnarvon and Knutsford.

Ripon Papers (British Museum)
BM Add. MS 43515, 43522–43527, 43553—43554, 43556–43558, including correspondence with Kimberley, Gladstone, Sydney Buxton, Robert Meade, and Edward Fairfield, 1892–1895.

Salisbury Papers (Christ Church, Oxford)
Knutsford correspondence, 1885–1892; Stanley correspondence, 1886; Stanhope correspondence, 1885–1886; correspondence with the Queen, 1886–1887; unbound in boxes.

Shaw Papers (British Museum)
BM Add. MS 50553, correspondence with Sidney Webb and Sydney Olivier, 1883–1899.

B. *Public Documents, Manuscript (PRO)*

CO 48	Cape	1872–1890
CO 54	Ceylon	1870–1890
CO 96	Gold Coast	1870–1874
CO 144	Labuan	1870–1892
CO 152	Leeward Islands	1874–1884
CO 179	Natal	1870–1892
CO 234	Queensland	1860–1866, 1870–1892
CO 291	Transvaal	1878–1880
CO 309	Victoria	1870–1892
CO 323	Colonies, General	1866–1899
CO 384	Emigration	1870–1877, 1880, 1884
CO 386	Land and Emigration Commission	1870–1877
CO 417	South Africa	1884–1892
CO 429	Patronage	1870–1885
CO 431	Accounts	1870–1885
CO 447	Order of St. Michael and St. George	1870–1885
CO 448	Honors	1870–1885
CO 449	Governors' Pensions	1869–1910
CO 537	Supplementary	1868–1880
CO 878	Office Minutes	1867–1895
CO 879	Confidential Print (Africa)	1870–1890
FO 366	Office Minutes	1870–1878

C. *Government Publications*

Colonial Office List. London.
Great Britain. *Hansard's Parliamentary Debates.*
————. *Parliamentary Papers.*

D. *Published Private Papers, Speeches, and Memoirs*

Abbot, Evelyn, and Lewis Campbell. *The Life and Letters of Benjamin Jowett.* 2 vols. London, 1897.
Amery, L. S. *My Political Life.* 3 vols. London, 1953.
Bowen, Sir George. *Thirty Years of Colonial Government.* Edited by Stanley Lane-Poole. 2 vols. London, 1889.
Buckle, George E., ed. *The Letters of Queen Victoria.* 3rd series. 3 vols. London, 1930.
Burns, Sir Alan. *Colonial Civil Servant.* London, 1949.
Carnarvon, Earl of. *Essays, Addresses and Translations.* Edited by Sir Robert Herbert. 3 vols. London, 1896.

————. *Speeches on Canadian Affairs.* Edited by Sir Robert Herbert. London, 1902.

De Kiewiet, C. W., and F. H. Underhill, eds. *Dufferin-Carnarvon Correspondence, 1874–8.* Toronto, 1955.

Dowden, Edward, ed. *Correspondence of Henry Taylor.* London, 1888.

Earle, Sir Lionel. *Turn Over the Page.* London, 1935.

Furse, Sir Ralph. *Aucuparius: Recollections of a Recruiting Officer.* London, 1962.

Godley, Arthur (Lord Kilbracken). *Reminiscences of Lord Kilbracken.* London, 1931.

Grant Duff, Sir Mountstuart E. *Notes from a Diary, 1873–1881.* 2 vols. London, 1898.

Hamilton, Lord George. *Parliamentary Reminiscences and Reflections, 1886–1906.* London, 1922.

Hertslet, Sir Edward. *Recollections of the Old Foreign Office.* London, 1901.

Hewins, W. A. S. *The Apologia of an Imperialist: Forty Years of Empire Policy.* 2 vols. London, 1929.

Holland, Sidney. *In Black and White.* London, 1926.

Hutchinson, Horace G., ed. *Private Diaries of the Rt. Hon. Sir Algernon West.* London, 1922.

Johnson, G. W. *The Evolution of Woman, from Subjugation to Comradship, with a Memoir.* London, 1926.

Kimberley, John, First Earl of. *A Journal of Events during the Gladstone Ministry, 1868–1874.* Edited by Ethel Drus. London, 1958.

Marindin, George Eden, ed. *Letters of Frederic Lord Blachford, Under-Secretary of State for the Colonies, 1860–1871.* London, 1896.

Marsh, Edward. *A Number of People: A Book of Reminiscences.* London, 1939.

Morley, John. *Recollections.* 2 vols. New York, 1917.

Müller, Georgina Max, ed. *The Life and Letters of the Right Honourable Friedrich Max Müller.* 2 vols. London, 1902.

Olivier, Margaret, ed. *Sydney Olivier: Letters and Selected Writings.* London, 1948.

Parkes, Sir Henry. *Fifty Years in the Making of Australian History.* 2 vols. London, 1892.

Parkinson, Sir Cosmo. *The Colonial Office from Within, 1909–1945.* London, 1947.

Ponsonby, Arthur. *Henry Ponsonby: His Life from His Letters,* London, 1942.

Ramm, Agatha, ed. *The Political Correspondence of Mr. Gladstone and Lord Granville, 1868–1876.* 2 vols. London, 1952.

————. *The Political Correspondence of Mr. Gladstone and Lord Granville, 1876–1886.* 2 vols. Oxford, 1962.

Rodd, Sir James Rennell. *Social and Diplomatic Memories, 1884–1893.* London, 1922.

Royal Colonial Institute. *Proceedings.*
Taylor, Sir Henry. *Autobiography, 1800–1875.* 2 vols. London, 1885.
West, Sir Algernon. *Contemporary Portraits: Men of My Day in Public Life.* London, 1920.
———. *Recollections, 1832 to 1886.* 2 vols. London, 1899.
Zetland, Marquis of, ed. *The Letters of Disraeli to Lady Bradford and Lady Chesterfield.* 2 vols. London, 1929.

E. *Newspapers*

Spectator. London.
Times. London.

F. *Contemporary Articles*

Bramston, Sir John. "The Colonial Office from Within," *Empire Review,* I (April, 1901), 279–287.
Hamilton, Sir William Baille. "Forty-four Years at the Colonial Office," *Nineteenth Century and After,* LXV (April, 1909), 599–613.
Hemming, Sir A. W. L. "The Colonial Office and the Crown Colonies," *Empire Review,* II (1906), 501–511.

PART II: SECONDARY

A. *Books*

Abbott, A. W. *A Short History of the Crown Agents and Their Office.* London, 1959.
Anonymous. *Saville Club: 1868–1923.* London, 1923.
Benians, E. A., *et al.,* eds. *The Cambridge History of the British Empire.* 9 vols. in 8. Cambridge, 1929–1959.
Bernays, Charles Arrowsmith. *Queensland Politics during Sixty (1859–1919) Years.* Brisbane, 1919.
Bertram, A. *The Colonial Service.* London, 1930.
Boase, Frederic, ed. *Modern English Biography.* 6 vols. Truro, 1892–1921.
Bolton, G. C. *A Thousand Miles Away: A History of North Queensland to 1920.* Brisbane, 1963.
Briggs, Asa. *Victorian People: A Reassessment of Persons and Themes, 1851–67.* Chicago, 1955.
Carrothers, W. A. *Emigration from the British Isles.* London, 1929.
Cell, John W. *British Colonial Administration in the Mid-Nineteenth Century: The Policy-Making Process.* New Haven, 1970.
Chapman, J. K. *The Career of Arthur Hamilton Gordon, First Lord Stanmore, 1829–1912.* Toronto, 1964.
Childe–Pemberton, William S. *Life of C. B. Adderley, 1st Lord Norton, 1814–1905.* London, 1909.
Clapham, J. H. *An Economic History of Modern Britain.* 3 vols. Cambridge, 1926–1938.

Cohen, Emmeline W. *The Growth of the British Civil Service, 1780–1939*. London, 1941.

Cole, Margaret, ed. *The Webbs and Their Work*. London, 1949.

Coombs, Douglas. *The Gold Coast, Britain and the Netherlands, 1850–1874*. London, 1963.

Cowan, C. D. *Nineteenth-Century Malaya: The Origins of British Control*. London, 1961.

Craig, Sir John. *A History of Red Tape*. London, 1955.

Dale, H. E. *The Higher Civil Service of Great Britain*. London, 1941.

De La Bere, Sir Ivan. *The Queen's Orders of Chivalry*. London, 1961.

De Kiewiet, Cornelius W. *British Colonial Policy and the South African Republics, 1848–1872*. London, 1929.

———. *The Imperial Factor in South Africa: A Study in Politics and Economics*. Cambridge, 1937.

Elliott, Sir Ivo, ed. *The Balliol College Register, 1833–1933*. 2nd ed. Oxford, 1934.

Ensor, R. C. K. *England, 1870–1914*. Oxford, 1936.

Escott, T. H. S. *King Edward and His Court*. London, 1908.

———. *Pillars of the Empire: Sketches of Living Indian and Colonial Statesmen, Celebrities, and Officials*. London, 1879.

Farr, David M. L. *The Colonial Office and Canada, 1867–1887*. Toronto, 1955.

Fiddes, Sir George V. *The Dominions and Colonial Offices*. London, 1926.

Fitzmaurice, Lord Edmond. *The Life of Granville George Leveson Gower, Second Earl Granville, 1815–1891*. 2nd ed. 2 vols. London, 1905.

Foster, Joseph, ed. *Alumni Oxonienses, 1715–1886*. 4 vols. London, 1887–1888.

Gardner, A. G. *The Life of Sir William Harcourt*. 2 vols. London, 1923.

Gathorne-Hardy, Alfred E. *Gathorne Hardy: First Earl of Cranbrook*. 2 vols. London, 1910.

Gooch, G. P. *Life of Lord Courtney*. London, 1920.

Grillion's Club. *Grillion's Club: A Chronicle, 1812–1913*. Oxford, 1914.

Gwynn, Stephen, and Gertrude M. Tuckwell. *The Life of the Rt. Hon. Sir Charles W. Dilke*. 2 vols. London, 1918.

Hall, Henry L. *The Colonial Office: A History*. London, 1937.

Hamilton, Bruce. *Barbados and the Confederation Question, 1871–1885*. London, 1956.

Hamilton, W. A. B. *Mr. Montenello: A Romance of the Civil Service*. 3 vols. London, 1885.

Hamilton, William B., ed. *The Transfer of Institutions*. Durham. N. C., 1964.

Hardinge, Sir Arthur Henry. *The Life of Henry Howard Molyneux Herbert, Fourth Earl of Carnarvon, 1831–1890*. 3 vols. London, 1925.

Heath, Sir Thomas L. *The Treasury*. London, 1927.

Heussler, Robert. *Yesterday's Rulers: The Making of the British Colonial Service*. Syracuse, N.Y., 1963.

Hewett, Oshert Wyndham. *Strawberry Fair: A Biography of Francis Countess Waldegrave, 1821–1879.* London, 1956.

Hicks Beach, Lady Victoria. *Life of Sir Michael Hicks Beach.* 2 vols. London, 1932.

Hitchens, F. H. *The Colonial Land and Emigration Commission.* Philadelphia, 1931.

James, Robert Rhodes. *Rosebery: A Biography of Archibald Philip, Fifth Earl of Rosebery.* London, 1963.

Jeffries, Charles. *The Colonial Empire and Its Civil Service.* Cambridge, 1938.

———. *The Colonial Office.* London, 1956.

Johnson, Alice. *George William Johnson: Civil Servant and Social Worker.* Cambridge, 1927.

Johnson, George, ed. *The All Red Line: The Annals and Aims of the Pacific Cable Project.* Ottawa, 1903.

Jones, Dorothy. *Cardwell Shire Story.* Brisbane, 1961.

Just, Sir H. W. *Verses.* Cambridge, 1930.

Kelsall, R. K. *Higher Civil Servants in Britain from 1870 to the Present Day.* London, 1955.

Kerr, D. G. G. *Sir Edmund Head, A Scholarly Governor.* Toronto, 1954.

Kubicek, Robert V. *The Administration of Imperialism: Joseph Chamberlain at the Colonial Office.* Durham, N.C., 1969.

Lee, Sidney. *King Edward VII: A Biography.* 2 vols. New York, 1925.

Legge, J. D. *Britain in Fiji, 1858–1880.* London, 1958.

Legh, T. W. *Lord Lansdowne: A Biography.* London, 1929.

Longford, Elizabeth, *Victoria R. I.* London, 1964.

McIntyre, W. David. *The Imperial Frontier in the Tropics, 1865–1875: A Study of British Colonial Policy in West Africa, Malaya and the South Pacific in the Age of Gladstone and Disraeli.* London, 1967.

Mallet, Bernard. *Sir Louis Mallet: A Record of Public Service and Political Ideals.* London, 1905.

Martindale, Hilda. *Women Servants of the State, 1870–1938.* London, 1938.

Mills, Lennox A. *Ceylon under British Rule, 1795–1932.* London, 1933.

Monypenny, W. F., and G. E. Buckle. *The Life of Benjamin Disraeli, Earl of Beaconsfield.* Rev. ed. 6 vols. in 2. London, 1929.

Morley, John. *Life and Letters of W. E. Gladstone.* 3 vols. London, 1903.

Mowat, R. B. *The Life of Lord Pauncefote.* London, 1929.

Murray, D. J. *The West Indies and the Development of Colonial Government, 1801–1834.* Oxford, 1965.

Parnaby, O. W. *Britain and the Labour Trade in the Southwest Pacific.* Durham, N.C., 1964.

Pope-Hennessey, James. *Verandah: Some Episodes in the Crown Colonies, 1867–1889.* New York, 1964.

Public Record Office. *List of Colonial Office Confidential Print to 1916.* London, 1965.

Pugh, R. B. *The Records of the Colonial and Dominions Offices*. London, 1964.

Robinson, Howard. *Carrying British Mails Overseas*. New York, 1964.

Robinson, Kenneth. *The Dilemmas of Trusteeship: Aspects of British Colonial Policy between the Wars*. London, 1965.

Simnett, W. E. *The British Colonial Empire*. London, 1949.

Smith, Richard Mayo. *Emigration and Immigration: A Study in Social Science*. New York, 1890.

Southgate, Donald. *The Passing of the Whigs, 1832–1886*. London, 1962.

Spector, Margaret Marion. *The American Department of the British Government, 1768–1782*. New York, 1940.

Stacey, C. P. *Canada and the British Army, 1846–1871: A Study in the Practice of Responsible Government*. Rev. ed. Toronto, 1963.

Stephen, Sir Leslie, and Sir Sidney Lee, eds. *Dictionary of National Biography*. 25 vols. Oxford, 1917–1927.

Trevelyan, George O. *The Life and Letters of Lord Macaulay*. Rev. ed. 2 vols. New York, 1909.

Venn, J. A., ed. *Alumni Cantabrigienes*, Part II: *From 1752 to 1900*. 6 vols. Cambridge, 1940–1954.

Welby, R., ed. *Annals of the Club, 1764–1914*. London, 1914.

White, Arnold. *Efficiency and Empire*. London, 1901.

Wolf, Lucien. *Life of the First Marquess of Ripon*. 2 vols. London, 1921.

Wright, Maurice. *Treasury Control of the Civil Service, 1854–1874*. Oxford, 1969.

Young D. M. *The Colonial Office in the Early Nineteenth Century*. London, 1961.

B. *Articles*

Barron, T., and Cable, K. J. "The Diary of James Stephen, 1846," *Historical Studies*, XIII (April, 1969), 503–519.

Cell, John W. "The Colonial Office in the 1850's" *Historical Studies Australia and New Zealand*, XII (October, 1965), 43–56.

Drus, Ethel. "The Colonial Office and the Annexation of Fiji," *Transactions of the Royal Historical Society*, 4th series, XXXII (1950), 87–109.

Hughes, Edward. "Sir Charles Trevelyan and Civil Service Reform, 1853–1855," *English Historical Review*, LXIV (January, April, 1949), 53–88, 206–234.

————. "Sir James Stephen and the Anonymity of the Civil Servant," *Public Administration*, XXXVI (1958), 29–36.

Joyce, R. B. "Sir William MacGregor: A Colonial Governor," *Historical Studies Australia and New Zealand*, XI (November, 1963), 18–31.

Knox, B. A. "The Provision of Legal Advice, and the Colonial Office Reorganization, 1866–7," *Bulletin of the Institute of Historical Research*, XXXV (November, 1962), 178–197.

Penson, Lillian M. "The Origins of the Crown Agency Office," *English Historical Review*, XL (April, 1925), 196–206.

Taylor, G. P. "Business and Politics in Queensland 1859–1895," *New Zealand Journal of History*, I (April, 1967), 75–92.

Williams, E. Trevor. "The Colonial Office in the Thirties," *Historical Studies Australia and New Zealand*, II (April, 1942), 141–160.

Woods, Sir John. "Treasury Control," *Political Quarterly*, XXV (October–December, 1954), 370–381.

Zebel, Sydney H. "Joseph Chamberlain and the Genesis of Tariff Reform," *Journal of British Studies*, VII (November, 1967), 131–157.

C. *Unpublished Material*

Anderson, Mary Adeline. "Edmond Hammond, Permanent Under Secretary of State for Foreign Affairs, 1854–1873." Doctoral thesis, University of London, 1956.

Cross, J. A. "The Dominions Department of the Colonial Office: Origins and Early Years, 1905–14." Doctoral thesis, University of London, 1965.

Graham, Neil Illingworth. "Sir George Bowen's Governorship of Queensland: 1859–1867." Master's thesis, University of London, 1962.

Joyce, R. B. "Political Portraits: Bowen and Herbert." Unpublished Manuscript.

Tyler. W. P. N. "Sir Frederic Rogers, Permanent Under-Secretary at the Colonial Office, 1860–1871." Doctoral dissertation, Duke University, 1962.

Index

Index